PRIVATE INTERNATIONAL LAW IN EAST ASIA

This open access book examines the conflict of law rules in East Asian states. With a focus on the laws in Mainland China, Japan and South Korea, the book also looks at the rules of Hong Kong and Taiwan.

Beyond a description of the substance of the current law, the book highlights the evolution these jurisdictions have undergone since being adopters of rules developed in European and North American legal systems. As evidenced by recent modernisations in their private law regimes, these East Asian states are now innovators, creating rules that are more suited to the local concerns. Significantly, the new approaches to private international law taken by China and Japan are themselves being adopted by other jurisdictions, shifting the locus of influence in this important area of law.

The chapters in part one give a contextual overview of the legal regimes of Mainland China, Japan, South Korea and Taiwan. This part is intended to foster a deeper understanding of how the systems are changing to better fit the particular national approaches to law. A more in-depth view of the rules on private international law follows in part two, where the rules of Hong Kong and Taiwan are set forth in addition to those of the rest of China and Japan and South Korea. Part three provides a detailed look at the conflict rules relevant to commercial law, specifically as regards international jurisdiction of courts, while part four examines the rules applying to family law and succession law.

Written in an easily accessible style, the book is a valuable resource for scholars as well as practitioners of East Asian law, private international law, and comparative law.

Volume 9 in the series Studies in Private International Law – Asia

Studies in Private International Law – Asia

Editors: Anselmo Reyes, Wilson Lui and Kazuaki Nishioka
Advisory Editor: Paul Beaumont

Much has been written about private international law in the EU and the US. Less is known about the conflict of laws in Asia. Thus, little attention has been paid so far to the modernisation of private international law codes and rules that has been taking place over the last decade all over Asia. That trend continues. Now is the time to take stock of those reforms that have already taken place and suggest further improvements for the future.

Published under the celebrated series *Studies in Private International Law*, this monograph sub-series provides a forum for discussion and analysis of private international law in Asia. The series is not solely a survey of jurisdictions for practitioners. Comprising in-depth thematic and country-specific studies, each volume considers the private international law of Asian countries from a variety of perspectives. An underlying assumption is that private international law in different jurisdictions follow broad discernible patterns. Each volume in this sub-series highlights those patterns and discusses how rules in different Asian jurisdictions are either converging with, or diverging from, the patterns identified. Such an analytical framework will assist academics, judges, lawyers and legislators to envisage ways in which laws affecting cross-border relationships can be harmonised across jurisdictions and be made more responsive to the needs of citizens in Asia and elsewhere.

Volume 1: Recognition and Enforcement of Judgments in Civil and Commercial Matters
Edited by Anselmo Reyes

Volume 2: Indonesian Private International Law
Afifah Kusumadara

Volume 3: Chinese Private International Law
Edited by Xiaohong Liu and Zhengyi Zhang

Volume 4: Direct Jurisdiction: Asian Perspectives
Edited by Anselmo Reyes and Wilson Lui

Volume 5: Japanese Private International Law
Kazuaki Nishioka and Yuko Nishitani

Volume 6: Indian Private International Law
Stellina Jolly and Saloni Khanderia

Volume 7: Treatment of Foreign Law in Asia
Edited by Kazuaki Nishioka

Volume 8: Choice of Law and Recognition in Asian Family Law
Edited by Anselmo Reyes, Wilson Lui and Kasuaki Nishioka

Volume 9: Private International Law in East Asia: From Imitation to Innovation and Exportation
Edited by Olivier Gaillard and Krista Nadakavukaren Schefer

Private International Law in East Asia

From Imitation to Innovation and Exportation

Edited by
Olivier Gaillard
and
Krista Nadakavukaren Schefer

•HART•
OXFORD • LONDON • NEW YORK • NEW DELHI • SYDNEY

HART PUBLISHING

Bloomsbury Publishing Plc

Kemp House, Chawley Park, Cumnor Hill, Oxford, OX2 9PH, UK

1385 Broadway, New York, NY 10018, USA

29 Earlsfort Terrace, Dublin 2, Ireland

HART PUBLISHING, the Hart/Stag logo, BLOOMSBURY and the Diana logo are trademarks of Bloomsbury Publishing Plc

First published in Great Britain 2024

Open Access was funded by the European Commission.

A catalogue record for this book is available from the British Library.

A catalogue record for this book is available from the Library of Congress.

Library of Congress Control Number: 2023948340

ISBN: HB: 978-1-50997-010-0
ePDF: 978-1-50997-012-4
ePub: 978-1-50997-011-7

Typeset by Compuscript Ltd, Shannon

ACKNOWLEDGEMENTS

The editors would like to acknowledge the generous financial support provided by the Swiss Institute of Comparative Law and the Swiss Confederation that permits us to offer this work as an Open Access publication. We also thank the Institute's management for giving us the time and resources to engage with the authors and produce such a volume.

The views reflected in the chapters are all solely those of the authors in their personal capacity. None of the views are attributable to the Swiss Confederation.

TABLE OF CONTENTS

PART 3
RELATIONS OF COURTS

PART 4
FAMILY AND SUCCESSION LAW

NOTES ON CONTRIBUTORS

Weizuo Chen is Tenured Professor at Tsinghua University, Beijing, China. He currently holds the position of Director of the International Arbitration and Dispute Settlement (IADS) Program and Director of the Research Centre for Private International Law and Comparative Law at Tsinghua University School of Law. He is also an arbitrator at the China International Economics and Trade Arbitration Commission (CIETAC), the Beijing Arbitration Commission/Beijing International Arbitration Center and the Weihai Arbitration Commission, China.

Olivier Gaillard is legal advisor for Swiss law at the Swiss Institute of Comparative Law. He is also a judge at the Tribunal neutre in Lausanne and a lecturer at the University of Geneva (Switzerland) and at the University Savoie-Mont-Blanc (France). He wrote his PhD thesis on the choice of law (*professio iuris*) in international succession matters and has a MA in Japanese Studies.

Samuel Guex is Associate Professor in the Department of East Asian Studies at the University of Geneva, Switzerland. His research interests broadly cover modern Chinese–Japanese–Korean relations. His current research focuses on Japanese–Korean relations and contentious issues related to their colonial past.

Jin Huang is Professor of Law at the China University of Political Science and Law, Beijing, China and is a member of the International Commercial Expert Committee of the Supreme People's Court of China. He holds numerous positions in scholarly organisations in China, including being President of the Chinese Society of International Law as well as of the China Society of Private International Law, and is also active internationally as a scholar and an arbitrator, including serving (since 2017) as a Member of the Permanent Court of Arbitration.

Béatrice Jaluzot is Director of Lyon's Institute for East Asian Studies (Institut d'Asie Orientale, joint research center supported by the CNRS – French National Research Centre) and a tenured associate professor in private law at Lyon's Institute for Political Studies (Sciences-po Lyon). She has been a visiting professor at many Japanese universities, including the University of Tokyo. Her field of research is Japanese law and comparative private law.

Marie Seong-Hak Kim is a historian and jurist based in Minneapolis, US. Her works include *Law and Custom in Korea: Comparative Legal History* (2012), *Constitutional Transition and the Travail of Judges: The Courts of South Korea* (2019) and *Custom, Law, and Monarchy: A Legal History of Early Modern France* (2021). She is currently a Fellow of Käte Hamburger Kolleg 'Einheit und Vielfalt im Recht' in Münster, Germany.

Jong Hyeok Lee is Assistant Professor of Private International Law and Transnational Commercial Law at Seoul National University (SNU) School of Law, South Korea. He currently holds the position of Head of Southeast Asian Law Division at the SNU's Asia-Pacific Law Institute. Before joining the SNU, he taught at Hanyang University and gained practical experience at Lee & Ko, one of Korea's largest law firms.

Wilson Lui is Pre-Doctoral Fellow and Lecturer at the Faculty of Law of the University of Hong Kong. He holds an MPhil from the University of Oxford and an LLM from the University of Cambridge. He is a Chartered Linguist, a Fellow of the Chartered Institute of Arbitrators, a Fellow of the Hong Kong Institute of Arbitrators and a Fellow of Advance HE. He has published three books and more than 15 book chapters and journal articles.

Krista Nadakavukaren Schefer is Vice-Director of the Swiss Institute of Comparative Law. She is also adjunct professor at several law faculties in Switzerland. Her research and publications are mainly in the area of international economic law.

Mari Nagata is a professor at Osaka University, Japan, where she teaches private international law and international civil procedure at the Graduate School of Law and Politics.

Yuko Nishitani is Professor of Private International Law at Kyoto University in Japan and Vice-President of the Hague Academy of International Law. She did research in Europe and the US and was a Senior Legal Officer on Secondment at the Hague Conference on Private International Law (HCCH). She has been a visiting professor at various foreign universities, including the New York University. She has served on legislative committees and represented the Japanese government in several HCCH projects.

Ying-Hsin Tsai is Professor of Commercial Law at National Taiwan University. She received her Doctor of Laws from University of Tokyo. She has practiced as a lawyer with commercial law as expertise. Her research focuses on corporate law, maritime law, payment systems, international business law and the regulation of financial institutions.

Harro von Senger studied law in Zürich, Taipeh and Tokyo and philosophy in Beijing and Freiburg, Germany. He is life-long Professor of Sinology at the Faculty of Philosophy in Freiburg, Germany, and a collaborator at the Swiss Institute of Comparative Law.

Dai Yokomizo is Professor of Private International Law at Nagoya University, Japan. His main research and teaching interests include conflict of laws (private international law), comparative law and private law theory. He is a Supervising Associate Editor of the *Japanese Yearbook of International Law*.

Jun Zheng is co-founder and Managing Director of MEI & HAO SARL and an adjunct faculty of University of Fribourg, Switzerland, teaching Asian business law. He studied law in both China and Switzerland, receiving his PhD in law from the University of Fribourg. He worked as legal counsel in an international law firm in Shanghai and Zurich before working at the Swiss Institute of Comparative Law and setting up his own company.

1

Introduction

KRISTA NADAKAVUKAREN SCHEFER AND JUN ZHENG

Imitation and innovation are concepts well known in multiple areas of scholarship and business practice. Organisational management and technology publications are full of commentary on how new ideas are generated, how their adoption by stakeholders can be promoted, how ideas can be modified to suit different purposes and how the innovations themselves can be ultimately adopted by others as the cycle begins anew. Law-making, too, has been looked at as a process of using, adjusting and applying rules through time and across societies. Judge Benjamin N Cardozo's 1921 classic *The Nature of the Judicial Process* describes the judge's role in the development of the common law as one of finding an applicable rule, comparing the case before him with that rule, adapting the rule with either additional rules or by changing it and then applying the newly formed rule to the case – resulting, in turn, in the new rule being examined and adapted by the next judge.[1]

This 'process of retesting and reformulating'[2] is not limited, of course, to the common law and it is clearly what happens across jurisdictions as well as within them. Indeed, the 'seething melting pot of the law'[3] has allowed for the emergence not only of increasingly unified understandings of legal issues, but also (possibly counterintuitively) to greater adaptability of the law to the particular social circumstances in which it is to be applied.

Exportation of the law has a more fraught connotation. Sometimes referred to as 'legal transplantation',[4] the imposition of a conqueror's rules on a subjugated people or of a powerful state on a less powerful partner – even when done with the intention of assisting – has all too often resulted in an ill-suited layering of a foreign set of rules over the practices of a local society.

Yet exportation can also be driven by demand. As with goods or services, interest in legal instruments designed for one community might emerge in another community facing similar problems. Or innovations can generate calls to make similar adaptations. Exportation in this sense nears imitation – and so the cycle continues.

[1] BD Cardozo, *The Nature of the Legal Process* (Yale University Press, 1921).

[2] ibid 24.

[3] IM Wormser, 'The Development of the Law' (1923) 23 *Columbia Law Review* 701, 715.

[4] See K Yoshida, 'Some Critical Analysis of the Japanese "Legal Transplant" Concept: From the Legal Geography Perspective' (2020) 17 *US-China Law Review* 113; J Ogbonnaya and C Iteshi, 'The Jurisprudential Issues Arising from Legal Transplant: An Appraisal' (2016) 50 *Journal of Law, Policy and Globalization* 1, 2, 12.

I. This Volume

It is from this perspective on the recent changes in private international law in East Asian jurisdictions that we brought together the authors of this volume. The authors are from across Asia and Europe and are familiar with the laws and legal discussions of multiple legal systems. They are thus able to see within them not only the similarities and differences, but also the mutual influences. The editors urged the authors to focus on these influences in describing the developments that have been so rapidly taking place in East Asian jurisdictions.

II. Legal Development Processes

While the laws of Germany, France, the UK and (though newer) the US are deeply rooted in their particular social and political culture,[5] they have nevertheless spread to the rest of the world as model law for other countries by virtue of their international discursive power – Germany's power emerging from the renown of its scholars' thorough analyses of 'legal science', France and the UK's influence stemming largely from having imposed their own rules on their colonial territories, and the laws of the US being exported together with its political ideas during the post-Second World War American-led push towards an international 'development' agenda that included 'rule of law' projects around the globe.

The laws in most other states have gone through different evolutionary processes: either one that moves from subjection to acceptance and adaptation or one that looked to imitate foreign laws.[6] Most East Asian jurisdictions,[7] particularly Mainland China (hereinafter 'China') and Japan, are examples of these two alternative processes.[8] However, the process of legal development did not stop with the adoption of rules. Adaptation to national culture was an important aspect even in terms of the original implementation of Western-based rules. Long years of experience with the Western rules led to increasingly culture-specific systems and a growth in the confidence of national legal communities of the value of rules suited to national cultural norms. The resulting innovations, accompanied by a rise in the international discursive power of China and Japan in particular, makes the next step one of becoming exporters of legal developments to others. Looking to smaller East Asian states is therefore important, too. Korea, in particular, may be a laboratory for legal developments coming from its larger neighbours. Will it, too, begin to adapt and innovate? Is it perhaps already an exporter itself?

[5] T Frankel and T Braun, 'Law and Culture' (2021) 101 *Boston University Law Review Online* 157.

[6] The reasons for the movement of laws has been the topic of numerous comparative analyses, with 'legal circle analysis', 'legal geography analysis' and critical race perspectives, just a few that highlight the exploitative aspects of some of the intra-Asian legal movements. See Yoshida (n 4) 114.

[7] W Chen and G Goldstein, 'The Asian Principles of Private International Law: Objectives, Contents, Structure and Selected Topics on Choice of Law' (2017) 13 *Journal of Private International Law* 411, 412. Note that East Asian jurisdictions do not all follow the same legal traditions: some of them follow the civil law tradition (for instance, Mainland China, Japan, the Republic of Korea, Taiwan, Vietnam, the Philippines and Thailand) and some adhere to the common law tradition (for instance, Hong Kong and Singapore).

[8] C Antons and R Tomasic, *Law and Society in East Asia* (Ashgate, 2013).

III. Private International Law

This volume looks particularly at the legal developments in private international law (PIL), or conflict of laws. This is an area that aims to resolve the jurisdiction, applicable law and recognition and enforcement of foreign judgments in an international/inter-state context.[9] As such, it is an area particularly suited for the adoption of rules from other jurisdictions to ensure compatibility. Given that much of the subject matter of PIL is oriented towards business relations or family matters, the area is also driven towards the adaptation and innovation of rules in order to ensure society's acceptance of the resulting decisions.

A. Imitation

There is consensus among Western scholars that PIL originated in the twelfth century in northern Italy, where the 'interstate' conflict of laws was generated among the city-states due to an increase in trade.[10] The long historical and ample experience in cross-border commercial activities made the European examples the most advanced in the world.[11] However, although PIL provisions appeared very early in some ancient East Asian jurisdictions,[12] the closed social and economic context prevalent in many East Asian jurisdictions – and particularly so in China and Japan – meant that the countries of the region developed their PIL legislation at a very late stage. Beginning well after the rules of the dominant Western powers were already in wide use, China and Japan started by imitating the PIL of European nations, adapting and innovating only when necessary.

China borrowed experiences from Germany, France, Switzerland, Japan, the UK, the US and the Soviet Union.[13] The starting point of borrowing from foreign PIL experience was 1864, when the first international law book, *Elements of International Law*, written by the American author Henry Wheaton, was translated into Chinese. Subsequently, during the latter years of the Qing Dynasty,[14] several books were translated from English into Chinese. It is fair to say that China's imitation of PIL was based mainly on American, English and Japanese textbooks in the later nineteenth and early twentieth centuries.[15] Following the foundation of the People's Republic of China (PRC), especially after the implementation

[9] P Sooksripaisarnkit and S Garimella (eds), *China's One Belt One Road Initiative and Private International Law* (Taylor & Francis, 2018); 'PIL' and 'conflict of laws' are the two most commonly used terms. While there are slight differences between the two terms, they are quite often considered as the same or similar subject. See G van Calster, *European Private International Law*, 2nd edn (Hart Publishing, 2016) 1, 4.

[10] S Symeonides, 'Early Choice-of Law Doctrine and the Traditional System' in S Symeonides (ed), Choice of Law, (Oxford University Press, 2016) 45, 47.

[11] See van Calster (n 9) 2.

[12] For instance, in the seventh century, ancient China had provisions on PIL in the Act of Yong Hui in the Tang dynasty. In the 'Chapter of General Provisions of the Act of Yong Hui', it was speculated that: 'Disputes between people of other cultural origin shall be settled in accordance with their national law; for disputes between people of different ethnic origins, this law shall be applied.' Q He, 'China's Private International Law (1978–2008)' (2010) 5 *Frontiers of Law in China* 188, 197; R-P Liu, 'China's Practice of Private International Law' (2001) 34 *Comparative and International Law Journal of Southern Africa* 1, 4.

[13] Y Zhao and M Ng, 'The Law, China and the World: An Introduction', in *Chinese Legal Reform and the Global Legal Order* (Cambridge University Press, 2017) 1.

[14] The Qing Dynasty was China's last imperial dynasty, lasting nearly 300 years from 1636 to 1912 AD.

[15] He (n 12) 197.

of the 'opening-up' policy in 1978, China developed its PIL rapidly, based on the most advanced PIL provisions in other jurisdictions, such as Germany, Switzerland and Japan as well as the EU and the Hague Conference on PIL.[16]

Japan has a similar experience to Chinese legislation in relation to PIL. The first Japanese legislation in PIL (Old 'Horei'), which never entered into force, was modelled on the conflict-of-law provisions of the Italian Civil Code of 1865. The existing Japanese PIL Act, which was enacted on 1898 and revised in 1990, referred to the legislation and writings of many foreign jurisdictions, such as France, Belgium, Italy and Switzerland, and especially the German Civil Code Enforcement Law.[17] In addition to China and Japan, the specific rules of the PIL in most East Asian jurisdictions have been influenced by the PIL provisions of continental European countries, such as the Introductory Act to the German Civil Code.[18]

B. Innovation

Starting from imitation, modern PIL in China and Japan has evolved and innovated over the past century. The deepest innovations began in earnest when the PIL codes were revised in the late 2010s. Although both countries learned from European continental jurisdictions such as Germany and Switzerland, their evolution presents different characteristics in key aspects.

In China, anti-foreign sentiments and lack of foreign contacts in the early years of the PRC meant that the rules of PIL and the study on the subject were absent (even forbidden) for several years. Judicial authorities were also reluctant to apply foreign law when they dealt with cases with foreign-related elements.[19] The starting point for the development of PIL was the opening-up policy in 1978, when China began actively participating in international civil and commercial exchanges. As a result, conflicts between domestic and foreign legal systems became inevitable. Following the return of Hong Kong and Macao to Mainland China in 1997 and 1999 respectively, conflicts arose not only due to the differences between the domestic and foreign legal systems, but also from the different jurisdictions within China (the so-called inter-regional conflicts among Mainland China, Hong Kong and Macao).[20] This led to China's gradual realisation of the significance of the application of foreign law.[21]

PIL has evolved rapidly over the last 40 years. Since the 1980s, conflict-of-law rules have emerged scattered throughout diversified single acts, such as the General Principles of Civil Law of the PRC, the Succession Law of the PRC, the Foreign-Related Contract Law of the PRC, the Maritime Law of the PRC, the Copyright Law of the PRC, the Patent Law of the PRC, the Trademark Law of the PRC and several judicial interpretations.[22] With the

[16] ibid 198.

[17] H Egawa, 'Progress or Revision of the Private International Law of Japan' (1962) 6 *Japanese Annual of International Law* 1, 2.

[18] Chen and Goldstein (n 7) 413.

[19] T Chen, 'Private International Law of the People's Republic of China: An Overview' (1987) 35 *American Journal of Comparative Law* 445, 445.

[20] J Huang and A Qian, '"One Country, Two Systems", Three Law Families, and Four Legal Regions: The Emerging Inter-Regional Conflicts of Law in China' (1995) 5 *Duke Journal of Comparative & International Law* 289.

[21] Chen (n 19) 446.

[22] Liu (n 12) 6, 7; X Fan and Q Li, 'Comparative Study on Selected Aspects of the Latest Private International Law Legislation across the Taiwan Straits' (2015) 10 *Frontiers of Law in China* 316, 324.

2011 Law of the People's Republic of China on Choice of Law for Foreign-Related Civil Relationships (the 2011 Choice-of-Law Act), China enacted its first separate PIL statute. Having introduced several innovations, such as the most significant relationship doctrine (Article 6), party autonomy (Chapter VI) and habitual residence as the connecting factor for determining *lex personalis*, the Act was considered a great innovation in Chinese PIL legislation.[23] Nonetheless, like all the East Asian jurisdictions,[24] there is no separate statute which codified all the three PIL matters mentioned above in China.

In Japan, since the first PIL statute (Horei) was enacted in 1898, the Horei has been amended in 1989 and 2006. The 1989 amendment focused on the choice-of-law rules relating to marriage, the relationship between parent and child and some general provisions, which mainly sought equality between men and women.[25] In family law matters, contrary to PIL legislation in China, which incorporates habitual residence or domicile doctrine, the 1989 amendment followed the principle of nationality, like many other East Asian jurisdictions such as the Republic of Korea, Taiwan, Vietnam, Indonesia, the Philippines and Thailand,[26] as this principle is considered to reflect the individual's cultural background.[27] Since 2001, Japan has undertaken a judicial reform which also touches upon PIL. In 2006, Japan promulgated the Act on General Rules for Application of Laws,[28] in which it has shifted its focus to seek internal consistency with its existing practice and doctrine. The 2006 Act keeps the traditional application of the principle of nationality in family law matters. As to the international jurisdiction in civil and commercial matters as well as in status and family matters, new rules were adopted in 2011 and 2018 separately, which were largely based on previous case law. In certain respects, Japan's jurisdiction rules deviate from the European continental tradition and adopt their own unique structure.[29]

C. Exportation

Globalisation provides the driving forces for legal norms to circulate globally and has fundamentally altered the position of East Asian states relative to their Western counterparts since the turn of the millennium.

Not surprisingly, in the past few years Chinese PIL has evolved in many respects. Due to the dramatic increase in international civil and commercial cases before Chinese courts, China set up an International Commercial Court (CICC) in 2018 which specifically aims to deal with foreign-related commercial cases. In addition, China proposed a guiding principle of foreign-related rule by law in 2020 and since then Chinese PIL scholars have been working on the construction of legal system so as to foster this.[30]

[23] Fan and Li (n 20) 326; Q Xu, 'The Codification of Conflicts Law in China: A Long Way to Go' (2017) 65 *American Journal of Comparative Law* 919.
[24] Chen and Goldstein (n 7) 414.
[25] J Torii, 'Revision of Private International Law in Japan' (1990) 33 *Japanese Annual of International Law* 54, 56; Nishitani, ch 7 in this volume.
[26] Chen and Goldstein (n 7) 414.
[27] Nishitani, ch 7 in this volume.
[28] Act No 78 of 2006.
[29] Nishitani, ch 7 in this volume.
[30] J Huang, 'On Strengthening the Legal System on the Construction of Foreign-Related Rule by Law (论加强涉外法治体系建设)', 2022, https://fzyjs.chinalaw.org.cn/portal/article/index/id/1178.html.

Japan has historically been an active exporter of its laws. Having taken inspiration from European legal thought, Japan actively implemented those rules on its colonial territories, in particular Taiwan and Korea. Today, it is reconceiving its European-based rules, moving forward with innovations that make PIL more suited to its cultural norms. With the internationalisation of rules also apparent, Japan's adjustments of the rules will be watched with interest by the region's legal communities. These new rules, grounded in the values of the domestic culture, are now ripe to be exported, intentionally or unintentionally, and their experiences shared by other countries.

With states borrowing legal norms, procedures and institutions from different jurisdictions, a so-called mixture of different species is occurring in the legal world,[31] and China's, Japan's and Korea's PIL provisions are a part of this mixing. China's 2011 Choice-of-Law Act has, to a certain extent, responded to impulses from, among others, Japanese PIL. Korea's 2022 revision of its PIL looked beyond Germany and Japan to ensure the fullest range of impulses. The influences of Swiss and US rules are also important.

Taiwan and Hong Kong are also innovators. Having been heavily influenced by both Chinese and Japanese laws, Taiwan always maintained its customs in family law matters and today is showing itself more able to adapt quickly to changing social norms than some of its neighbours. Its innovations are therefore potentially powerful models for imitation by those who were formerly rule exporters. Hong Kong's common law heritage makes it also a jurisdiction open to innovations, particularly when paired with its positive approach to soft law instruments. As its rules and dispute settlement procedures develop within the jurisdiction's very particular context, it is likely to be the source of significant novel ideas for managing cross-border conflicts.

Meanwhile, as the member states of the Hague Conference on PIL, both China and Japan have actively participated in the negotiations on the drafting of international conventions in PIL issues, which strengthen the influence of their PIL at the international level. Regionally, too, great efforts have been made to harmonise (rather than unify) PIL in East Asian jurisdictions. One of the important achievements of these efforts is the drafting of Asian Principles of PIL (APPIL).[32] Despite the limited participants to this project so far,[33] it is anticipated that the project would strengthen the influence of the PIL in the East Asian jurisdictions to the rest of world.

D. Background to the Volume

This volume is the result of a symposium organised by the Swiss Institute of Comparative Law (SICL) on the topic of 'New Developments in East Asian Law', which took place on 4 and 7 May 2021. Originally organised for the spring of 2020, the Symposium was postponed for one year due to the COVID-19 pandemic and was then held – in light of the

[31] Antons and Tomasic (n 8) 376.

[32] Chen and Goldstein (n 7).

[33] So far, there are 10 participating East and Southeast Asian countries and regions, including Japan, the Republic of Korea, Mainland China, the Hong Kong Special Administrative Region, Taiwan, Vietnam, Indonesia, the Philippines, Thailand and Singapore. The initiative was mainly advocated by academics in these jurisdictions and there are no official participants in the project. See Chen and Goldstein (n 7) 416.

continuing health crisis – completely online. Nevertheless, the speakers made the most of their opportunity to exchange with each other and the global audience to address the latest changes to PIL in the East Asian region.

In putting together this volume, the editors expanded their search for authors beyond the conference participants to ensure a broader view of the region. The result is a collection of insights from a mix of some of the most well-known and established scholars in the world with younger scholars and practitioners touching on both general and specific aspects of PIL in China, Japan, South Korea, Hong Kong and Taiwan.

Part I provides an overview of the legal systems of China, Japan and South Korea in order to introduce the reader unfamiliar with the law of this geographical region to the basic systems in which PIL sit. Harro von Senger's insights into the legal system of China in Chapter 2 are invaluable, given his long-standing experiences with China and Chinese legal scholars. He points to the critical role of the ruling Communist Party ideologies in the legal system, something that continues to have a tremendous influence on how China receives and adjusts to foreign influences, as well as the impulses the country sends out into the neighbouring region. Béatrice Jaluzot's explanations of the development of Japanese law in Chapter 3 is equally enlightening. She leads the reader through the three 'waves' of modern Japan's legal developments before describing not just Japanese law-making and dispute resolution mechanisms, but also pointing out how the legal education of prospective Japanese lawyers shapes the view of law in that country. Marie Kim's discussion in Chapter 4 of South Korea's legal system rounds out Part I. Kim describes Korea's legal transitions from its neo-Confucianist roots, through its colonial past to its postcolonial present, emphasising how the Japanese influence on Korea was itself influenced by Japan's adoption of British practices of judge-made law and its courts' adherence to local customs. She then takes the specific example of the succession law on compulsory share to illustrate how Korean law takes, responds to and adapts legal ideas to suit its social needs. The relationship of Taiwan's legal system with that of Japan's laws is described by Ying-Hsin Tsai in Chapter 5. Tsai notes the influence of Japan's colonial power over today's Taiwanese legal system, bringing in a double foreign influence because of Japan's own adaptations of German law. However, she also underlines that Taiwan's law was always influenced by Chinese law, which itself was influenced by European law and US law, even while maintaining traditional Taiwanese customary law.

Part II then examines more closely the PIL systems themselves. In Chapter 6, Jin Huang examines the innovations of China's 2011 Conflict-of-Law Act and its judicial interpretation. He reveals that the 2011 Act is a milestone for Chinese PIL, as it is the first-ever separate and unified law on the applicable law for foreign-related civil relationships. He concludes that the Act demonstrates China's increased openness through the newly established people-oriented, people-friendly, confident and open-minded legislation. In Chapter 7, Yuko Nishitani then delineates Japan's PIL developments from a nationalisation, regionalisation and internationalisation perspective. She realises that it remains a challenge how to build bridges for a regional and international cooperation in East Asia, in part because the multiple systems within the geographical area are so different. Added to this is the fact that there are a number of non-recognised states whose citizens nevertheless have transboundary legal disputes with others, meaning that courts need to assess how to deal with 'conflicts of laws' in a manner that is politically sensitive as well as legally sound. In Chapter 8, Wilson Lui examines the special case of Hong Kong's PIL. Despite being a part of a state, Hong Kong's legal system is separate from that of China and so it has to manage relations with both non-Chinese and the Mainland Chinese legal systems. The common law approach that Hong Kong uses, especially in combination with its 'borrowing' of foreign judges, has made it particularly adaptable as well as very receptive to adoption of rules. Its flexibility may also lead to its greater role as an exporter of approaches. Finally, in Chapter 9, Jong Hyeok Lee looks at the newest rules of South Korean PIL, giving a broad overview of questions of international adjudicatory jurisdiction as adjusted by the New Korean Private International Law Act of 2022, and recognition and enforcement of foreign judgments. He illustrates the South Korean Supreme Court's approach to the rules through a discussion of numerous recent judgments. The South Korean approach to PIL, though long based heavily on Japanese and European principles, is nevertheless quite distinct. It, too, is becoming an innovator of law and a source of inspiration on its own.

Part III takes a look at one set of specific issues in PIL: those related to the relation of courts. The first broad topic is that of jurisdiction and courts. In Chapter 10, Dai Yokomizo looks at choice-of-courts agreements in Japan. In Chapter 11, Samuel Guex dives into a particularly fraught matter to look at how the courts of Japan and South Korea have approached the interpretation of an international treaty differently in response to the tensions over the matter of reparation of forced workers. Guex shows how courts in the two jurisdictions may use different interpretive methods to decide the same legal question in parallel, and in the end come to opposite conclusions. This highlights a need to consider carefully any assumptions about a smooth path towards increasingly harmonious decision-making across jurisdictions.

Laws relating to family matters are the second broad topic in PIL the book takes up. Part IV starts with Chapter 12 by Weizu Chen, addressing China's modernization of how its courts treat international family law matters. He explores family-related PIL from the perspective of jurisdiction, applicable law, and recognition and enforcement of judgments, and comes to the conclusion that China still needs to further modernise its PIL. In Chapter 13, Mari Nagata analyses a number of issues of international family law in Japan. Her analysis mainly focuses on surrogate motherhood, same-sex marriage and international child abduction. The case studies she presents allow the reader to grasp the extent of the challenges facing the Japanese courts in areas such as these, where social norms are themselves evolving daily.

In Chapter 14, Olivier Gaillard addresses the rules applicable to international successions in China, Japan and South Korea. He looks at the different approaches and the underlying objectives of such laws in each jurisdiction. The Japanese approach has remained tied to the unitary factor of nationality since the end of the nineteenth century, while China's approach is similar to that of the common law systems. South Korean law has innovated, using the influence of both Japanese law and Swiss law to implement a mechanism for allowing the deceased to choose the applicable law. This innovation, Gaillard proposes, could become a model for export.

We hope that the publication of this volume allows readers with little knowledge of East Asian legal systems to gain an understanding of the approaches to those systems, while permitting readers who are familiar with those laws to understand more fully the mechanisms by which these systems reflect, respond to and strive to influence each other and the international legal systems of which we are all a part.

PART 1

General Overview of Legal Regimes

2

Introduction to the Law of the People's Republic of China

HARRO VON SENGER

This is the first sentence of the Constitution of the People's Republic of China (PRC) of 11 March 2018: 'China is one of the countries with the longest history in the world.'[1] In contrast to all other ancient legal cultures, the Chinese legal culture was not broken off in the distant past like the Egyptian culture was as a result of the Arab-Islamic conquest.[2] What was said at the end of the nineteenth century still applies in the twenty-first century: 'With Chinese law we are carried back to a position where we can survey, so to speak, a living past and converse with fossile men.'[3]Indeed, even without official interference, Chinese legal heritage exerts an underground influence on today's law of the PRC. According to the polarity norm of the Chinese Communist Party (CCP) – 'Make the past serve the present [古为今用]'[4] – China's legal heritage is considered by the CCP to be a treasure chest, providing valuable suggestions for solving the problems of the present and offering manifold illustrative material for the consequences of incorrect governance.

In view of this, a look at Chinese legal history is essential for a non-superficial introduction to the law of the PRC. Accordingly, we first turn to the past to see the historical influences on Chinese legal thought that will allow us to converse with the modern Chinese lawyer. This is followed by a brief explanation of the Chinese legal systems as they are today, with a focus on the law of the mainland of the PRC. We then turn to the norms and concepts that guide modern Chinese legal thought.

[1] For an English translation of the Constitution of the PRC, see www.npc.gov.cn/englishnpc/constitution2019/201911/1f65146fb6104dd3a2793875d19b5b29.shtml.

[2] R Heuser, 'Frühzeitliche Rechtsordnungen in China (10.-1§. Jahrhundert vor Christus)' (2008) *Zeitschrift für Chinesisches Recht* 283.

[3] E Harper Parker, 'Comparative Chinese Family Law' in NB Dennys et al (eds), *The China Review or Notes and Queries on the Far East, Vol VIII, July, 1879, to June, 1880* (Guojia Tushuguan Chubanshe) 69, https://babel.hathitrust.org/cgi/pt?id=uc1.31175033574644&view=1up&seq=2.

[4] H von Senger, 'Recent Developments in the Relations between State and Party Norms in the PRC' in SR Schram (ed), *The Scope of State Power in China* (School of Oriental and African Studies, 1985) 171–207.

I. The Historical Legacy

China developed its own legal culture over thousands of years.[5] In contrast to Europe and the many European and Anglo-inspired legal systems around the world, this country has:

- no ancient Hellenic heritage;
- no ancient Roman heritage;
- no Judeo-Christian heritage;
- no Germanic heritage;
- no 'Enlightenment'-like movement in the sense of emancipation from a dominant monotheistic religion;
- no colonial heritage (with the exceptions of Hong Kong and Macao).

China's heritage is therefore truly its own. It takes its inspiration from a number of Chinese schools of thought, including the following:

- Confucianism with the 'Analects'[6] of Confucius (551–479 BC)[7] and the work *Mengzi*[8] of Mencius (371 BC–289 BC)[9] as main sources;
- Legalism with the book *Han Fei Zi*[10] by the most important representative of Legalism, Master Han Fei (c 280–233 BC),[11] as the main source;
- philosophical Taoism with the *Daodejing*[12] as the main source and Lao Zi[13] (flourished sixth century BC) as the presumed author;
- military theory, with the work *Sun Zi Bingfa* (*Sun Zi. The Art of War*)[14] as the main source and Sun Zi (which flourished in the fifth century BC) as the presumed author.

[5] JA Cohen, R Randle Edwards and Fu-Mei Chang Chen (eds), *Essays on China's Legal Tradition* (Princeton University Press, 1981); H von Senger, 'Aspekte des Rechts im traditionellen China' *Neue Zürcher Zeitung*, 16 July 1970, 17; H von Senger, 'Einflüsse traditionellen Rechtsdenkens in der Volksrepublik China' in P Trappe (ed), *Contemporary Conceptions of Law, IVR World Congress (Basel 27/8–1/91979), ARSP Archiv für Rechts- und Sozialphilosophie* (Franz Steiner Verlag, 1982) 93; H von Senger, 'Vom schweren Atem mehrtausendjähriger Geschichte', *Neue Zürcher Zeitung*, 9 January 1987, 38.

[6] 'The Analects – Chinese Text Project' English translation by James Legge, https://ctext.org/analects.

[7] Chinese philosopher, https://www.britannica.com/biography/Confucius.

[8] 孟子 '*Mengzi* – Chinese Text Project', English translation by James Legge, https://ctext.org/mengzi.

[9] Chinese philosopher, https://www.britannica.com/biography/Mencius-Chinese-philosopher.

[10] *The Complete Works of Han Fei Zi, A Classic of Chinese Legalism*, translated with Introduction, Notes, Glossary and Index by K Liao (Arthur Probsthain, 1939), https://phi.project.sinica.edu.tw/%E5%BB%96%E6%96%87%E5%A5%8E/1939The%20Complete%20Works%20of%20Han%20Fei%20Tzu%20A%20Classic%20of%20Chinese%20Political%20Science%20(scan).pdf.

[11] Chinese philosopher, https://www.britannica.com/biography/Han-Feizi.

[12] *THE TAO TEH KING*, by Lao-Tse, translation by James Legge, https://gutenberg.org/files/216/216-h/216-h.htm.

[13] RT Ames and M Kaltenmark, 'Laozi: Chinese Daoist Philosopher', https://www.britannica.com/biography/Laozi.

[14] H von Senger (translation and commentaries). *Sun Zi. Die Kunst des Krieges* (Reclam Verlag, 2021).

A. Confucianism

Confucianism, which was not interested in transcendental questions, paved the way for atheistic Marxism. Marxism, which also plays a dominant role in Chinese law, could therefore more easily become an authoritative ideology for China than Christianity could.

B. Legalism

Under Legalist thought, the ruler would not be subject to the law. As the maker of the law,[15] he stood above the law. However, in the exercise of his rule he should abide by the laws he has enacted, uninfluenced by personal relationships and subjective moods. According to Legalist thought, the law should be used as a tool to promote agriculture and to foster a strong army.

Legalist theories were influential during the period of the Warring States (475–221 BC). During these years, China was split into many smaller and larger states, and the ultimate goal of most rulers was to gain supremacy over the whole country. As Legalist thought would suggest, the law was seen as an instrument to attain the supreme political goal, namely the unification of China. This goal was attained in 221 BC, when the ruler of the Qin state succeeded in bringing all of the states together into a single empire. As a legalist, Shang Yang had initiated significant reforms of the administration and in the economy that supported Qin's military conquests and ensured a centralisation of power.

One controversy between representatives of Confucianism and Legalism has lost none of its relevance in the PRC to this day, namely the pros and cons of 'rule of persons' (人治 *renzhi*) and 'rule by law' (法治 *fazhi*).[16] Confucians believed that morally flawless men should rule, as then the people will behave well without laws. Legalists objected that charismatic and morally exemplary rulers were extremely rare and that one cannot assume that anyone will measure up to such a standard. The relevant question was how men of average calibre could successfully rule. This should be possible based on law (penal and administrative law, not private law).

In the Constitution of the RPC, the expression 法治 (*fazhi*) is used. The literal translation 'law rule' is ambiguous. 'Law rule' can be understood as 'rule of law' or 'rule by law'. In the English version of the Constitution, it is mostly translated as 'Rule of Law'.[17] But 法治 is practised in the PRC in the legist tradition as rule *by* law.

[15] Y Honglie, *Zhongguo Falu Sixiang Shi* [*History of Chinese Legal Thought*] (Shangwu Yinshuguan, 1964), vol 1, 56.

[16] Mao Zedong's reign was an example of 'rule of a person', whereas the leaders of the CCP after Mao, including Xi Jinping, have chosen the way of 'rule by law'. See T Zhang, 'Xi's Law-and-Order Strategy: The CCP's Quest for a Fresh Source of Legitimacy' *Foreign Affairs*, 27 February 2023.

[17] Article 5.1: ' The People's Republic of China shall practice law-based governance and build a socialist state under the rule of law.'

C. Taoism and Military Doctrine

Taoism and ancient military doctrine emphasised stratagems, which have influenced China's handling of law since ancient times.[18] To this day in China, the stratagems are means of outwitting the authoritarian structures and their systems of norms. In the novel *Shuo Tang* (*Tales from the Tang Dynasty*), Emperor Tai Zong's (626–49) campaign against Koguryo on the Korean peninsula is reported. Faced with the boundless sea to be crossed, the Emperor's courage fails. General Xue Rengui, who, along with the other commanders, does not approve of the abandonment of the campaign, devises a stratagem. The next day, the commanders invite the Emperor to visit a rich farmer who lives directly by the sea. The farmer, they say, wants to deliver the provisions for the crossing and to speak to the Emperor. The Emperor unsuspectingly goes to the farmer's house. While they talk, the ground begins to shake. Only now does the Emperor realise that he has been lured onto a ship and that the entire fleet has already set sail. The fait accompli enlivens the Emperor's resolve and he daringly presses eastwards. The General has succeeded.

In this story, written about 500 years ago, a ruse technique is used. Placed in a treatise with over 35 stratagems, this stratagem comes first. 'Crossing the sea by deceiving the Emperor' indicates the perceived importance of using cunning techniques to challenge an authoritarian. It is true that pre-modern China was an authoritarian state, but this does not mean that the ruler's subordinates were merely passive recipients of orders. By means of cunning, they were often able to go their own way. In the PRC too, authority is repeatedly circumvented by stratagems such as 'steganography' (hiding a secret message in an apparently harmless message).[19] The insubordination of subordinates is reflected in the idiom '上有政策，下有对策 [for every measure from above, there will be a countermeasure from below]',[20] for which I found 47,600,000 hits on Baidu, the Chinese counterpart to Google, on 19 February 2023.

The use of cunning also helped individuals – both then and now – to enjoy individual fulfilment in their lives. In pre-modern China there was no 'fight for the law',[21] as Rudolf Jhering, the nineteenth-century scholar of sociological legal thought, put it. But in China, like nowhere else in the world, the 'art of cunning' has been perfected to circumvent authoritarian law.

D. The Influence of Ancient Schools on Modern China

The ancient Chinese schools of thought influence the legal culture of the PRC because none of these schools of thought put forward liberal-democratic concepts. Democracy never

[18] See H von Senger, *36 Strategeme für Juristen* (Stämpfli Verlag, 2020).

[19] One example of this was a student's attack on the Premier Li Peng (who many believed to be responsible for the deadly scenes of violence in Beijing on 4 June 1989) in a seemingly harmless poem. On 20 March 1991, barely two years after the violent suppression of the 4 June 1989 riots in Beijing, the overseas edition of the *People's Daily*, the mouthpiece of the CPC Central Committee, published a poem by the student (who was in the US) on p 2. The editors of the *People's Daily* apparently failed to notice that the poem contained a criticism of Premier Li Peng which is revealed when, starting with the first line of the poem, one puts the characters together diagonally from top right to bottom left, and then crowns the resulting statement with the entire last line.

[20] English translation available at https://www.linguee.com/chinese-english/translation/%E4%B8%8A%E6%9C%89%E6%94%BF%E7%AD%96%EF%BC%8C%E4%B8%8B%E6%9C%89%E5%B0%8D%E7%AD%96.html.

[21] R von Ihering, *Der Kampf um's Recht*, https://www.projekt-gutenberg.org/jhering/kampfrec/chap001.html.

existed in pre-modern China. Over the millennia, China was an authoritarian country and after 221 BC, a centralised empire, which, however, often disintegrated into various states, each of which was governed by a monarchy.

In 1911 AD the Republic of China was established on the Chinese mainland. It was only after this that liberal democratic ideas gained influence in China. However, due to internal turmoil and the war with Japan (1937–45), liberal democracy in China was not really able to assert itself.

E. Similarities between European and Chinese Law

Differences between the autochthonous European and Chinese legal cultures should not be overemphasised. The common humanness predominates. It should not be said that individual human rights are incompatible with ancient Chinese legal culture. They existed in ancient China not in the official legal texts, but in natural law which was embedded in the hearts of the Chinese. Sino-Western parallels in Chinese and European legal history should not be overlooked.

II. The Law of the People's Republic of China

A. A Complex Structure

The PRC comprises four legal systems:

- English common law essentially applies in the Hong Kong Special Administrative Region,[22] even after the Law of the PRC on Safeguarding National Security in the Hong Kong Special Administrative Region of 30 June 2020 (66 articles)[23] came into force.
- In the Macao Special Administrative Region, the Portuguese-continental legal system is essentially applicable.[24]
- In the Republic of China and Taiwan, there is a Western-liberal legal system shaped by German and American law.[25] Since the end of the twentieth century, lively legal communication between the PRC and Taiwan has developed in academia.[26]
- From the point of view of constitutional law, a Marxist-Leninist legal system applies in the core PRC (excluding Hong Kong, Macao and Taiwan).

[22] The Basic Law of the Hong Kong Special Administrative Region of the PRC, effective as of 1 July 1997, Arts 5 and 8, https://www.basiclaw.gov.hk/en/basiclaw/chapter1.html; 電子版香港法例 Hong Kong e-legislation: https://www.elegislation.gov.hk.

[23] 中华人民共和国香港特别行政区维护国家安全法, www.npc.gov.cn/npc/c30834/202007/3ae94fae8aec4468868b32f8cf8e02ad.shtml, English translation available at https://www.pkulaw.com/en_law/fa2c1a10e7be4780bdfb.html.

[24] The Basic Law of the Macao Special Administrative Regions of the PRC, effective as of 20 December 1999, Arts 5 and 8, https://www.refworld.org/docid/3ae6b53a0.html.

[25] 全国法规资料库 Laws & Regulations Database of the Republic of China (Taiwan): https://law.moj.gov.tw/ENG/LawClass/LawAll.aspx?pcode=A0000001; Lawbank 發源法律綱, https://www.lawbank.com.tw.

[26] The law of the PRC receives various impulses from the law taught and practised in Taiwan, especially on specific issues of private law that have not yet been researched as thoroughly in the PRC as in Taiwan, such as those

B. The Law of the Core PRC

i. Structures

The state structure of the PRC is centralised, with the central government based in Beijing. The core PRC has 22 provinces, five national minority autonomous regions (Tibet, Xinjiang, Inner Mongolia, Ningxia and Guangxi) and four cities directly controlled by the central government (Beijing, Tianjin, Shanghai and Chongqing).

The State Council (Guowuyuan) takes care of the affairs of state with the help of numerous ministries and other bodies. The highest organ of state power is the National People's Congress (NPC), a single-chamber legislature. The NPC is the largest parliament in the world, with up to 3,000 members.[27] Its size makes it quite cumbersome. It meets only once a year. The Standing Committee of the NPC (up to 200 members) is somewhat more flexible.

ii. Law

The law of the PRC is divided into a Constitution (*xianfa* 宪法), laws (*falü* 法律) and ordinances (*faling* 法令). In addition, there are legal enactments from central state bodies, in particular those of the State Council. These legal instruments can have different names, such as the following:

- 'Notice' (*tongzhi* 通知), eg, Notice of the Supreme People's Court on Citing the Order of Articles, Clauses, Items, and Items Listed in Laws and Decrees of 22 December 1956.
- 'Regulations' (*tiaoli* 条例), eg, the Regulations on Academic Degrees of 28 August 2004.
- 'Rules' (*guize* 规则), eg, the Rules Governing Operation of Foreign Civil Aircraft of 2019.

According to the Constitution of 2018, the NPC is – among other things – responsible for amending the Constitution and for enacting and amending criminal, civil, state institutional and other basic laws, such as the Civil Code of the PRC.[28] The Standing Committee of the NPC enacts laws that are not regarded as fundamental.[29] An example of such a law is the Environmental Protection Law passed by the NPC Standing Committee on 24 April 2014.

On the subnational level, Regional People's Congresses may enact and issue local regulations in light of the specific conditions and actual needs of the administrative region, provided that they do not contravene the Constitution, laws and administrative regulations. The regulations of the Regional People's Congresses must be submitted to the Standing Committee of the NPC and the State Council for recording.[30]

concerning questions of joint liability. See W Zejian, *Minfa Xueshuo Yu Panli Yanjiu* [*Civil Law Doctrine and Case* [*Law*] *Research*] (Beijing, 2009) 46 et seq, https://www.proz.com/kudoz/german-to-english/law-general/6804644-echter-und-unechter-solidarit%C3%A4t.html.

[27] Guinness World Records, https://www.guinnessworldrecords.com/world-records/65451-largest-parliament-legislative-body. See also https://www.worldatlas.com/articles/the-largest-legislatures-in-the-world.html.

[28] Constitution, Art 62 Nos 1 and 3.

[29] ibid Art 67 No 2.

[30] Organic Law of the Local People's Congresses at All Levels and the Local People's Governments at All Levels of the PRC of July 1, 1979, as amended on 11 March 2022, Art 10.

iii. Two Authorities in the PRC

The National Congress of the CCP and the Central Committee (CC) appointed by it are the supreme governing bodies of the Chinese Communist Party (CCP). The real power, however, lies with the two bodies that exercise the CC's powers between sessions: the CC's Politburo and the Standing Committee of the CC's Politburo, which currently consists of seven people (all men). The person or group of people who can gain the greatest influence in the Standing Committee of the Politburo of the CC will be the leader of the whole Chinese people.

The power of the Standing Committee of the Politburo results from the hierarchical structure of the CCP with its 96 million members and 4.936 million party organisations at the base (as of June 2022).[31] According to the party statute, the CCP is organised according to 'democratic centralism'.[32] The individual party members obey the party organisation, the minority obeys the majority, the subordinate organisations obey the superior organisations, and all party organisations and all party members obey the National Congress of the CCP and the Central Committee.

The core PRC has a Marxist-Leninist concept of governance. Accordingly, the law enacted at the state level is not the supreme normative authority; rather, the highest authority is the CCP. Article 1 of the Constitution sets this out clearly:

> The People's Republic of China is a socialist state governed by a people's democratic dictatorship that is *led by the working class* [which the CCP considers itself to represent] and based on an alliance of workers and peasants.
>
> The socialist system is the fundamental system of the People's Republic of China. *Leadership by the Communist Party of China is the defining feature of socialism with Chinese characteristics.* (Emphasis added)

Article 1 of the Constitution is the only Chinese law text to make mention of the CCP. More than 10 years ago, I read in a Chinese law journal the proposal of a professor of political science[33] concerning the enactment of a 'Law Concerning the Ruling Party (执政党法)', but the reaction to this proposal was complete and lasting silence. In the PRC, the state up to its highest level is subordinate to the CCP. Under the leadership of the CCP, the state legislator enacts law, which in turn serves as an instrument of the CCP to attain its political goals. The CCP itself and its members should adhere to the laws which (on the initiative of the CCP) the legislator had enacted. However, the CCP can at any time give the legislator the order to revise any law or to abolish it.

The Beijing party headquarters can neither oversee nor direct the daily and hourly management work to be carried out by the countless party cells under it. Nevertheless, it

[31] On 29 June 2022, statistics show that there are 96.712 million party members and 4.936 million party organisations (www.gov.cn/xinwen/2022-06/29/content_5698405.htm). See also 'Wie wurden die führenden chinesischen Politiker gewählt?' *China heute*, 29 September 2022, (http://german.chinatoday.com.cn/ch/politik/202209/t20220929_800308023.html.

[32] Statute of 2022, Art 10.

[33] Hua Xuecheng 华学成, 'Huaiyin Gongxueyuan Renwenxueyuan 淮阴工学院人文学院,' (2011) 7 *Zhengzhi Yu Falü* 政治与法律 [*Politics and Law*] 9 (the author was a professor at Huaiyin Technical College and Dean of the Faculty of Humanities).

wants all party cells and party officials to steer the 1.4 billion Chinese in uniform paths. To this end, the party headquarters issues certain guidelines, which I call 'party norms'. These 'party norms' are only aimed at about five per cent of the Chinese population, namely the party members, especially those in leadership positions. According to 'democratic centralism', they are obliged to follow the party norms.

The party norms of the CCP – the political line, the polarity norms and the policy norms – are therefore above state law. Just as the Chinese state is an instrument in the hands of the CCP, the law is an instrument for realising the Party's norms. All activities of the state are based on and limited by party norms.

C. A Sinomarxist Conception Driving CCP Party Norms: The Principal Contradiction

The national party headquarters in Beijing designs the party norms based on Sino-Marxism. This is German-Russian Marxism-Leninism, supplemented by contributions from (so far) five Chinese thought-leaders. The guiding function of Sino-Marxism is prescribed in all CCP statutes from the last few decades, as can be seen in the identical wording of the most recent statutes of 2017 and 2022:

> The Communist Party of China takes Marxism-Leninism, Mao Zedong Thought [since 1945], Deng Xiaoping Theory [since 1997] the important thought of Three Represents [formulated by Jiang Zemin, since 2002], the Scientific Outlook on Development [formulated by Hu Jintao, since 2012], and Xi Jinping Thought on Socialism with Chinese Characteristics for a New Era [since 2017] as its guide to action.[34]

It is not possible here to go into all the components of Sino-Marxism listed in the Statutes. Instead, the focus here is on the Sino-Marxist guide to action that still exerts the most important influence on shaping party norms and law: the method of defining and resolving a so-called 'principal contradiction'.

The concept of the 'principal contradiction' was theoretically established and powerfully put into political practice by Mao Zedong, who introduced the concept in 1937 in the context of the Second Sino-Japanese War (1937–45). Until that time, the 'class struggle' of the peasant and working class against the landlord class and the bourgeoisie, led by Generalissimo Chiang Kai-shek (the strongman of the Republic of China founded in 1911), had dominated the political activities of CCP. Mao recognised that China's struggle against Japan could not be settled by means of a 'class struggle' because the war effort required as many fighters against Japan as possible. Thus, Mao proclaimed that capitalists and large landowners had human rights (including a right to property)[35] and argued within the party that the

[34] Constitution of CCP of 22 October 2022, General Program, para 2, http://eng.chinamil.com.cn/CHINA_209163/TopStories_209189/10195159.html.

[35] '应规定一切不反对抗日的地主资本家和工人农民有同等的人权、财权、选举权和言论、集会、结社、思想、信仰的自由权.' Quoted from *Mao Zedong Xuanji* 毛泽东选集 [*Selected Works of Mao Zedong*], vol II (Renmin Chubanshe, 1969) 726. See also *Lun zhengce* 论政策 [*On* [*Our*] *Politics*], https://www.marxists.org/chinese/maozedong/marxist.org-chinese-mao-19401225.htm.

class struggle should be downgraded to being a secondary contradiction, while the national struggle of the entire Chinese people, including the 'class enemies', against Japan should be the highest priority. With his concept of the changing principal contradictions, Mao wanted to make the officials of the CCP, who were committed to the 'class struggle', understand why he was striving for a united front on the side of the class enemy Chiang Kai-shek.

Only with the help of human rights guarantees, among other things, could capitalists and large landowners be persuaded to make their contribution to resolving the principal contradiction, namely to make every effort to defeat Japan. Therefore, legal enactments were issued under Mao to protect individual human rights, for example:

> All [members] of the people who resist Japan shall enjoy freedom of speech, publication, assembly, association, domicile, change of residence and freedom of thought without distinction as to ethnic group, class, party, sex, occupation and religion and faith.[36]

D. The Goal-Oriented Dynamic Conception of Party Norms

Influenced by Mao's contradiction concept, the CCP is ruled by the idea that humanity – and Chinese society – is constantly developing. It is currently going through the 'primary stage of socialism' which will last 'over a century'.[37] This is to be a transition phase on the way to a classless communist society – a phase characterised by shared prosperity.[38] The development to this final goal is divided into consecutive stages, which differ from each other in relation to the particular principal contradiction each is to address.

The assessment of the principal contradiction made by the CCP headquarters and thus the political line of the party changed several times. Since its beginnings, the CCP has formulated the following five consecutive principal contradictions:

1. As already mentioned, the principal contradiction from 1937 to 1945 was the contradiction between the whole Chinese nation, including the anti-Japanese 'class enemies', and Japan, which wanted to conquer China. The main task was the defeat of Japan. The law, especially human rights law, served to solve this main task.
2. From 1945 to 1949, the principal contradiction was the contradiction between the CCP and Chiang Kai-shek's Guomindang government; the main task was to defeat Chiang Kai-shek. In this phase, Mao no longer protected the individual human rights and the property of rich farmers.

[36] Regulations for the Protection of Human and Property Rights in the Shanxi-Gansu-Ningxia Border Area, dated 17 November 1941, promulgated in February 1942, Art 2: 陕甘宁边区保障人权财权条例, 第二条 边区一切抗日人民，不分民族、阶级、党派、性别、职业与宗教，都有言论、出版、集会、结社、居住、迁徙及思想、信仰之自由，并享有平等之民主权利, https://wenku.baidu.com/view/5f9caf39f28583d049649b6648d7c1c708a10b82.html?_wkts_=1677525481104.

[37] Constitution of CCP of 22 October 2022, General Program, para 10.

[38] The following vision of Karl Marx is often quoted in the PRC: 'After the productive forces have also increased with the all-around development of the individual, and all the springs of co-operative wealth flow more abundantly – only then can the narrow horizon of bourgeois right be crossed in its entirety and society inscribe on its banners: From each according to his ability, to each according to his needs!' K Marx, *Critique of the Gotha Programme*, Part I, https://www.marxists.org/archive/marx/works/1875/gotha/ch01.htm.

3. From 1949 to December 1978, the principal contradiction was the 'class struggle' of the Chinese 'proletariat' versus the Chinese 'bourgeoisie'. Law in general and human rights in particular were neglected, as they disrupted the 'class struggle'. Human rights were said to be an intrigue of the bourgeoisie. The official view was that by expressing the concept of a human nature common to all human beings, the propagandists of human rights wanted to undermine the class struggle morale of the proletariat. This was based on the logic of the official view of society: according to the official opinion at the time, there was no common ground between the members of the enemy classes and of the proletariat. Moreover, the class enemies were bestialised, called 'niugui sheshen', ie, ox demons and snake spirits.[39] Human rights, then, could not be promoted, and nor could law.
   As a student at Beijing University, I lived through the last year of the 'Cultural Revolution' (1966–76) that focused on the 'class struggle'. At that time there was no talk of law. Whenever I asked about the role of law in the PRC, I was laughed at. When I once asked a person in charge at Beijing University why the lawyers active in the 1950s had been abolished, I received the answer that in lawsuits the lawyers always assisted criminals and that such work was considered superfluous. During my two years of study at Beijing University (1975–77), it was not until about a year after Mao's death (9 September 1976) that I first read a newspaper article about a Chinese legal enactment.[40]
4. From December 1978 to the autumn of 2017, the principal contradiction was 'the contradiction between the growing material and cultural needs of the people and backward social production'. To solve this principal contradiction, 'four modernisations'[41] were announced, namely of agriculture, industry, national defence, and science and technology. In the wording of the principal contradiction, in typical Marxist fashion, material needs come first and cultural needs come second. The satisfaction of 'the material needs of the people' has been interpreted very narrowly by the CCP for decades, with a total focus on double-digit economic growth rates. As a result, the PRC became the second-largest economy in the world in 2011.[42] However, healthy air, clean water, non-toxic food etc were not recognised as 'material needs of the people'. Legal norms concerning ecological care of the nature, such as those prescribed in the Environmental Protection Law of the People's Republic of China of 13 September 1979,[43] were neglected. Many other problems remained unsolved due to the one-sided focus on overall economic development.
5. The nineteenth CCP National Congress in October 2017 established a new principal contradiction: that between the ever-growing needs of the people for a satisfying and

[39] '横扫一切额牛鬼蛇神'[Sweep away All Ox Spirits and Serpent Spectres], Editorial l, *Renmin Ribao* [*People's Daily*], 1 June 1966, https://zh.wikipedia.org/zh-hans/%E6%A8%AA%E6%89%AB%E4%B8%80%E5%88%87%E7%89%9B%E9%AC%BC%E8%9B%87%E7%A5%9E.

[40] H von Senger, 'Erste Rechtsverordnung seit der Kulturrevolution' *Neue Zürcher Zeitung*, 4 August 1977, 2.

[41] H von Senger, 'Drei Welten und vier Modernisierungen' *Tages-Anzeiger*, 18 April 1978, 45.

[42] 'China löst Japan als zweitgrößte Kraft ab' *Manager Magazin*, 14 February 2011, https://www.manager-magazin.de/politik/weltwirtschaft/a-745374.html.

[43] 中华人民共和国环境保护法， https://www.pkulaw.com/en_law/fe5de82c03608a7dbdfb.html?way=textLawChange.

good life and unbalanced and inadequate development.[44] Herein, the CCP recognises that the Chinese people do not have a satisfying and good life. Significantly, too, under the fourth and fifth principal contradictions, the 'class struggle' has been downgraded in the same way as was the case under the first principal contradiction (1937–45). However, the class struggle has not been abandoned. The CCP Statutes of 2017 and 2022 state that:

> Owing to both domestic factors and international influences, a certain amount of class struggle will continue to exist for a long time to come, and under certain circumstances may even grow more pronounced, however, it is no longer the principal contradiction.

The role of law is heightened. Under the fourth principal contradiction, a true wave of codification started. This has continued under the fifth principal contradiction. On 1 March 2023, a statistic concerning legal acts of the core PRC noted that there are over 381,000 central legal acts in effect and nearly three million local legal acts.[45]

Such statistics should be viewed with caution, as the term 'law' is interpreted in an extremely broad sense,[46] but even if not entirely comparable to Western 'laws', there are a large number of legal acts that Chinese authorities have implemented. Laws were needed because the CCP leaders were convinced that without them, the fourth and fifth principal contradictions could not be solved. Without replacing the lawlessness of the 'class struggle' period with a certain legal order, it would have been impossible for the CCP to stabilise society and to motivate the people to strive for the four modernisations, and to combat the unbalanced and inadequate development.

Therefore, as under the first principal contradiction, an official acknowledgement of human rights was not surprising. In 2004, the Constitution was amended to say: 'The State respects and preserves human rights.'[47] Laws were also necessary in order to attract foreign investors and broaden commercial exchanges with foreign countries.

III. State Law as a Tool of Party Norms

In order to show how party norms of the CCP are substantiated by state law, I use as an example the 'Law of the PRC on Chinese-Foreign Equity Joint Ventures' of 1 July 1979 (hereinafter the 'Joint Venture Law').[48] This law was in force for 40 years[49] and made a significant contribution to the economic upswing of the PRC.

[44] Constitution of CCP of China of 22 October 2022, General Program, para 11.
[45] See PKU Law.com (https://pkulaw.com), with the headings 中央法规 [central legal enactments], 地方法规 [local legal enactments] and the subheading 时效性 [validity]. I owe this statistical information to 孙永亮 Sun Yongliang, Institute of Legal History, China University of Political Science and Law (中国政法大学法律史学研究院), who from 5 March 2022 to 28 February 2023 was an academic guest at the Swiss Institute for Comparative Law (email of 20 February 2023).
[46] Information given by Sun Yongliang, email of 1 March 2023.
[47] Constitution, Art 33.3, https://www.constituteproject.org/constitution/China_2004?lang=en.
[48] 中华人民共和国中外合资经营企业法, https://www.pkulaw.com/chl/44fe519756440da6bdfb.html?way=textLawChange.
[49] The Joint Venture Law was replaced by the Foreign Investment Law of the People's Republic of China (中华人民共和国外商投资法) on 15 March 2019, https://www.samr.gov.cn/djzcj/zcfg/fl/202003/t20200312_312860.html.

There is one polarity norm that regulates the contradiction between China and other countries in a general way: '洋为中用Make foreign things serve China [with China setting the course]!' The contradiction between self-sufficiency and help from abroad is regulated by the polarity norm: '自力更生为主，力争外援为辅 Rely mainly on one's own efforts while making external assistance subsidiary.'

In concrete terms, however, the following contradiction arises: 'Should the PRC use foreign advanced technology and foreign capital or not?' Concrete contradictions of this kind are regulated by the policy norms of the CCP. One policy norm, repeatedly invoked at the beginning of the so-called 'opening' era, determined that: 'Advanced foreign technology must be introduced and foreign capital used!' Jiang Yiguo, Wang Zumin and Jiang Baoqi devote a lengthy essay to this policy norm.[50] In particular, the authors clarify the relationship between the aforementioned policy norm, the political line and the polarity norm 'Rely mainly on one's own efforts while making external assistance subsidiary'.

The Chinese government, with its overview of the priorities to be set for the development of the Chinese economy, was able to steer foreign investment in the form of joint ventures in the desired direction at any time and to prevent their uncontrolled spread by means of state law wielded as a tool to implement the party norms.

First, Article 1 of the Joint Venture Law sets out that founding a joint venture requires the prior approval of the Chinese government. Article 2.2 then states that joint ventures must comply with the provisions of the laws, decrees and pertinent regulations of the PRC. 'In this way', writes a Chinese commentator on the law, 'the law-abiding partners who cooperate honestly with us can be protected, but the law-breakers who harm our country's interests can be promptly punished.'[51]

The legal requirements continue throughout to ensure official controls are built into the joint venture. The production and business operating plans of an equity joint venture shall be submitted to the competent authorities for the record and shall be implemented through economic contracts (according to Chinese law).[52] An equity joint venture shall have a board of directors with a chairman, whose office shall be assumed by the Chinese side, and one or two vice-chairmen, whose office(s) shall be assumed by the foreign joint venture partner(s).[53] In its purchase of required raw and semi-processed materials, fuels, auxiliary equipment etc, an equity joint venture shall give first priority to purchases in China.[54] An equity joint venture shall open an account with the Bank of China or a bank approved by the Bank of China.[55] The various kinds of insurance coverage of an equity joint venture shall be furnished by Chinese insurance companies.[56] The technology and equipment contributed by a foreign joint venture partner as its investment in kind must be advanced technology and equipment that really suit China's needs. In the case of losses caused by a foreign joint

[50] J Yiguo, W Zumin and J Baoqi, 'Jiakuai wo guo jingji fazhan sudu de yixiang zhongda zhengce – tantan yinjin xianjin jishu he liyong waizi wenti' [A Policy Norm Which is Important for Accelerating Our Country's Economic Development – Thoughts on the Question of Importing Advanced Technology and Using Foreign Capital] (1978) *Jingji Yanjiu* [*Economic Studies*] 10 et seq.

[51] W Baoshu, 'Tantan wo guo de zhongwai hezi jingying qiye fa' [Some Notes on the Law on Joint Ventures with Chinese and Foreign Investment Participation in Our Country], *Nanfang Ribao* [*Southern Daily*], Guangzhou, 8 August 1979, 3.

[52] Joint Venture Law, art 9.

[53] ibid art 6.1.

[54] ibid art 9.2.

[55] ibid art 8.1.

[56] ibid art 8.4.

venture partner practising deception through the intentional provision of outdated technology and equipment, it shall compensate for the losses.[57]

In general, the Chinese comments on the Joint Venture Law repeatedly emphasise that the 'fundamental economic interests' of the PRC must be safeguarded and that the independence and autonomy of the PRC are indispensable. Therefore, 'all conditions leading to enslavement' are to be rejected.[58]

The Joint Venture Law was only a first step towards concretising the party norms. Other regulations in special areas were gradually adopted, such as regulations on income tax, foreign exchange control, registration of industrial and commercial enterprises, a company law, a law on the protection of natural resources etc.

It is important to note that the Constitution of the PRC was used to implement the relevant party norms. Yet, it is not the Constitution, but the political line of the CCP that is dominant. When the political line for its implementing needs a law, this law can be enacted without a previous constitutional empowerment. The constitutional base for the Joint Venture Law of 1979 was only established three years later in the Constitution of 1982.[59]

The party norms, which gave unprecedented scope to the PRC foreign trade, required not only the enactment of legal norms but also changes in the traditional foreign trade structure of the PRC. Soon after the promulgation of the Joint Venture Law on 30 July 1979, new state bodies were created to implement this law: the 'PRC Foreign Investment Control Commission' (Zhonghua Renmin Gongheguo waiguo touzi guanli weiyuanhui),[60] the 'China International Trust and Investment Corporation' (Zhongguo guoji xintuo touzi gongsi))[61] and the 'PRC Committee for Import and Export Control' (Zhonghua Renmin Gongheguo jinchu-kou guanli weiyuanhui).[62] Moreover, the two provinces of Guangdong and Fujian, as well as the three cities of Beijing, Tianjin and Shanghai, were affected by the reforms. They have been given greater foreign trade autonomy than the rest of the PRC. Particularly generous new regulations applied to two special foreign trade zones which became later special economic zones. These have been set up in Shenzhen and Zhuhai in the vicinity of Hong Kong and Macao.[63]

[57] ibid art 5.2.

[58] Li Yangju, for example, emphasises this: 'Liyong waizi tong jianchi duli zizhu zili gengsheng fangzhen you maodun ma?' [Are the Use of Foreign Capital and the Polarity Norm "Independence and Self-Reliance, Trust in One's Own Strength" in Conflict with Each Other?], *Guangming Ribao* [*Enligthtment Daily*], Beijing, 11 July 1979.

[59] See Constitution of 1982, Art 18: 'The PRC permits foreign enterprises, other foreign economic organisations and individual foreigners to invest in China and to enter into various forms of economic cooperation with Chinese enterprises and other Chinese economic organisations in accordance with the law of the PRC. All foreign enterprises, other foreign economic organisations as well as Chinese-foreign joint ventures within Chinese territory shall abide by the law of the PRC.'

[60] 中华人民共和国外国投资管理委员会，https://baike.baidu.com/item/%E4%B8%AD%E5%8D%8E%E4%BA%BA%E6%B0%91%E5%85%B1%E5%92%8C%E5%9B%BD%E5%A4%96%E5%9B%BD%E6%8A%95%E8%B5%84%E7%AE%A1%E7%90%86%E5%A7%94%E5%91%98%E4%BC%9A/10478000.

[61] CITIC Limited, 中國中信股份有限公司, https://zh.wikipedia.org/zh/%E4%B8%AD%E5%9B%BD%E4%B8%AD%E4%BF%A1%E9%9B%86%E5%9B%A2.

[62] 中华人民共和国进出口管理委员会，https://www.baike.com/wikiid/2320157868421305412?view_id=244uyg2t8jk000.

[63] See 'Gu Mu fuzongli tan waimao tizhi gaige – ling Hu Jin zai waimao fangmian you jiao da zizhuquan [The Deputy Premier Gu Mu Comments on Reforms of the Foreign Trade System – Beijing, Shanghai and Tianjin Enjoy a Relatively Greater Autonomy in Foreign Trade], *Beijing Ribao* [*Beijing Daily*], 29 September 1979; 'Gu mu fuzongli zai dongjing jizhe zhaodaihui shang tan wo guo jianshe zijin wenti – zili gengsheng wei zhu ye yao yinjin waizi' [At a Press Conference in Tokyo, Vice Premier Gu Mu Answers Questions Regarding the Investment for the Development of Our Country – Trust in Our Own Strength as the Basis, But Also Foreign Capital Shoul Be Used], *Jiefang Ribao* [*Liberation Daily*], Shanghai, 7 September 1979.

IV. Final Remark

The law of the PRC has certain unique particularities. The most important is its dependence on the norms of the CCP. The content and even the existence of the law depends on the changing evaluation which the CCP makes according to the historical and political context.

3

The Structure and General Principles of Japanese Law

BÉATRICE JALUZOT

Japan's legal system is well known for having adopted the model of European laws and especially that of civil law systems. It has now been in existence for almost 150 years and Japanese law, the product of an economically successful country in East Asia, has long been a model that inspires many countries across Asia, exerting an especially strong influence on the law of South Korea and Taiwan. However, Japanese law remains largely unknown in the West, which means that it is hardly known at all and the widespread perception of it often leads to a distorted understanding that does not reflect the reality of contemporary law in Japan.

The purpose of this chapter is to introduce Japanese law in a holistic way, thus offering the public some essential keys to understanding it.

Japanese law was born at the end of the nineteenth century, at a time of political struggle with the Western powers.[1] Nowadays, in the first half of the twenty-first century, Japanese law is a comprehensive system based on parliamentary law produced by a centralised government. The legislative framework covers all human relations, whether in relation to the Japanese state and local authorities (constitutional, administrative and tax law) or between private individuals (personal, family and inheritance law etc). The law governs business relationships (commercial law, competition law, law of financial products etc) and regulates both non-profit legal entities (law of associations and foundations) as well as profit-making legal entities (company law). Labour relations are supervised by the law (labour law and social welfare law), as are the personal relationships to things and creations (property law, land law and intellectual property). Finally, Japanese law deals with the maintenance of public order (criminal law and criminal procedure law).

The primary features of Japanese law are complexity and efficiency. On the one hand, the system is complex, with the structure of the law being highly sophisticated. However, it is also efficiency-oriented, as legal policy choices are made in accordance with identified objectives, whether to resolve specific difficulties or to keep the system at the cutting edge of legal modernity.

The best way to understand the overall logic of Japanese law is to address it systematically from three perspectives: first, from the perspective of its genesis, in order to understand the historical logic of its inception; second, from the perspective of positive law in terms of the internal structure of the substantive law and core enactments; and, third, from the perspective of dispute resolution.

[1] See generally W Röhl (ed), *History of Law in Japan since 1868* (Brill, 2005).

I. The Genesis of Contemporary Japanese Law

Contemporary Japanese law was born in 1871, when the young Meiji government established the Japanese Ministry of Justice. Initially arising from the desire to create a legal system based on Western models, it subsequently underwent two major waves of reform: first, under the influence of American experts in the aftermath of the Second World War; and, second, from the 1990s onwards, as a result of the financial crisis that hit the country and whose consequences extended until nowadays.

A. The Historical Background

Until the nineteenth century, the Japanese administrative and political institutions at the state level were based on the Chinese model. Pressure from the imperialist Western powers then compelled the Japanese government to introduce a new legal system, mainly based on European models.[2]

As early as the Middle Ages, Japan had introduced the Chinese system of *ritsuryō* (律令). This system had been established in China during the Tang Dynasty and it provided the Chinese emperor with the ability to impose a single and unified law on the entire territory and thus govern it. As a result, codes of law, mainly criminal and administrative, were introduced in the sixth and seventh centuries. These later fell into disuse, but were rediscovered in the Edo era (1603–1867) when the Shogun, a military commander, took power away from the Japanese emperor. The *ritsuryō* system then served as the basis for the formulation of new laws, promulgated by the Shogun, who could lead the government of the country by means of a uniform law, even if he had to deal with the power of the feudal lords.[3]

Gradually, the Shogun implemented a closed-door policy for the country, the so-called 'seclusion' policy, which forbade any contact with foreigners.[4] During this era, Japan had no desire to import or to export its law. The Shogun government tried to avoid any disturbance and threat to its power that foreigners could bring – only the Dutch trading post was permitted, and even that was only permitted under very tight government control.

This hardline policy angered the Western powers, including the US. It was the US that was the first to decide to force the opening up of Japan. The arrival of the 'black ships', a military fleet of eight vessels, in the port of Edo on 13 February 1854 remains a turning point in Japanese history. The Treaty of Kanagawa, signed between representatives of the Shogun and US Commander Perry on 31 March 1854, was the first encounter of the Japanese with Western law. In the years that followed, Japan signed more than 15 treaties with the Western countries, the last of which was in 1869. These treaties, the so-called

[2] See B Jaluzot, 'Les traités inégaux japonais, de leur signature à leur renégociation' (2021) *Zeitschrift für japanisches Recht/Journal of Japanese Law* 1.

[3] See J Bourgon, Frédéric Constant and P-E Will, 'Aperçus sur le droit chinois comme *Jus commune* de l'Asie orientale' in M Delmas-Marty, K Martin-Chenut and C Perruso (eds), *Sur les chemins d'un jus commune universalisable* (Mare & Martin, Collection de l'Institut des sciences juridique et philosophique de la Sorbonne, 2021); Y Hiramatsu and DF Henderson (trans), 'Tokugawa Law' (1981) 14 *Law in Japan* 1.

[4] See MS Laver, *The Sakoku Edicts and the Politics of Tokugawa Hegemony* (Cambria Press, 2011).

'unequal treaties', were opposed by the state authorities throughout their negotiations. The jurisdiction clauses were among the points of particularly heated confrontations. These clauses provided for the jurisdiction of consular courts for all disputes concerning foreigners living on Japanese territory, including disputes involving Japanese subjects. The Japanese government viewed these provisions as an essential infringement on national sovereignty, whereas the Western authorities were only prepared to concede this point on the strict condition that Japan would adopt a Western-style legal system.

The Japanese government subsequently decided to create a legal system based on Western models and to move away from the previous system. From then on, the Japanese government decided to turn exclusively to European models, leaving behind old Japanese customs. Adoption of law became state policy.

However, the Japanese government had to deal with 15 powers, several of which had a deep-rooted legal tradition, such as the French and the British. As a result, Japanese lawyers were suddenly faced with the challenge of practising comparative law. However, the Japanese authorities turned this constraint into an advantage: initially guided by the desire to satisfy Western requirements, they decided to adopt the most favourable rules.

The task was therefore to understand the laws, to compare them and to select a model to follow. Comparing laws began to receive a tremendous work effort from then on. Japanese specialists were trained in the various foreign languages and laws, and foreign lawyers were invited to Japan to share their professional knowledge. The selection of rules was based on various objectives: to be the most 'modern', while at the same time best promoting the exercise of power by the government and the multiple public interests of the new Japanese society. The Meiji Constitution was promulgated in 1889 and was inspired by many models, mainly the German and British ones.[5]

In 1894, the British were the first to agree to rebalance their treaty with Japan, which led to the renegotiation of all treaties concluded with the Western powers. In 1899, the renegotiated treaties came into force in Japan, freeing it from Western control.

This era of the Meiji reforms laid the foundations of the Japanese legal system. It was the first of three waves of legal reform in Japan. As a legacy of this period, the comparison of laws became standard practice for Japanese lawyers, and this method is still consistently applied both in the production of new laws and in academic research. The Japanese legal doctrine is also shaped by this experience. It is divided between the various subjects, but also according to the countries of research: scholars usually belong to the German school, the French school or the English-American school.

B. The 'Three Waves' of Legal Reform

The Meiji era (1868–1912) is the founding period of contemporary Japanese law. The cornerstones of the legal system on which it is still based today were established during this period of time. As early as 1875, a judicial system and judicial professions were set up to provide for the handling of litigation. As far as legislation is concerned, a codified

[5] See T Kazuhiro, *The Meiji Constitution: The Japanese Experience of the West and the Shaping of the Modern State*, D Noble (trans) (Kodansha, 2007).

system was chosen very early on, as it was more likely to be introduced in a short time. The Napoleonic codification was the most modern system in the world at that time and it was chosen as a point of reference. In 1882, the Japanese government established a Code of Criminal Procedure and a Penal Code. In 1890, the first Civil Procedure Code was promulgated. It was the first piece of legislation in civil law to be influenced by German law.[6] These Codes were later thoroughly overhauled. Particular attention was paid to the Civil Code, which became the subject of heated debate among jurists and caused conflict between the different schools of thought. A first draft, drawn up by Gustave Boissonade (1825–1910),[7] suffered a setback when passed by parliament and it was replaced in 1896 by a draft prepared by the Japanese themselves, with no foreign support. This came into force in 1898.

In parallel with this process of introducing private law, the Japanese leaders decided to establish a constitution. The project began in 1881 and was completed in 1889 with the promulgation of the Meiji Constitution. The Meiji Constitution was strongly influenced by the German model of a parliamentary monarchy, whilst at the same time adopting a bicameral system and a British-style government. As a result, the Japanese Parliament is known as the Diet following the German historical tradition and the government is called the 'Cabinet' following the British tradition.

Regarding the models that inspired the Japanese legislator, the two countries to first strongly influence the Japanese law-makers were Britain and France. However, soon afterwards, the German model became dominant. At that time, German jurists were working on the renewal of legal science, which they wanted to become the cement of their young nation. At the same time, the Japanese authorities had discovered the Western countries and their reality through the Iwakura mission (1871–73), when a Japanese delegation visited all the countries that had been involved in the treaties. Japanese diplomats were then impressed by the quality of German law, especially constitutional law. The choice of German law as a constitutional model was a start; it was later adopted for administrative law, followed by commercial law and civil law, and thus it gradually extended to the whole of Japanese law. The most striking example of this change is the Japanese Civil Code. It was initially influenced by French law, however, during the drafting of the Code, scholars decided to take over many of the components of the first draft of the German Civil Code. After the Code's enactment and subsequent enforcement, its content further underwent a substantial change through the creative interpretation provided by the courts.

During this period, all the foundations of Japanese law were laid, as well as its operating structures: training of lawyers, a judicial system and administrative organisation. By 1912, it was fully established.

The second wave of influence on Japanese law occurred after the Second World War. The occupying forces were mainly American and they pursued a consistent policy of purging Japan of the reasons that had led to the war, the watchword being 'democratisation'.

[6] German law was very recent at the time as it followed the foundation of the German Empire in 1871.

[7] Gustave-Emile Boissonade de Fontarabie was Professor of Law at the Faculté de droit de Paris and an invited scholar in Japan from 1873 until 1895. He was recruited as a legal adviser for the Japanese government and stayed in Japan for more than 20 years. Among many tasks, he had been in charge with drafting codes such as a Criminal Code and a Criminal Procedure Code – drafting a Civil Code was his main achievement. The Boissonade draft is known in Japan as the 'old civil law' (*kyū minpō*, 旧民法.).

The Allied forces, under the aegis of Douglas MacArthur, undertook a large-scale institutional reform, where legal reform was central. It was carried out in a top-down process: the Allied forces rewrote the Constitution by involving German jurists who had fled Nazism. They prepared the new Constitution, called the Peace Constitution, which was promulgated in 1946. In line with the new institutions, the body of Japanese domestic legislation was thoroughly reformed. The major laws of Meiji were restructured, among them the law on local government,[8] the judicial system[9] and family law. New laws were introduced, including the Labour Standard Law,[10] the Trade Unions Act[11] and an anti-monopoly law (as part of the enactment of competition law).[12]

For the most part, the reformers endeavoured to remain faithful to the previous structures, thus maintaining the principles of monarchy and bicameralism. They revisited the content of the Codes whilst maintaining their shape. However, the introduction of an economic law, in line with Western capitalism, bears the hallmark of the US influence on Japanese law and is now a significant part of the Japanese legal system. The newly introduced structures contributed to the post-war recovery of Japan and to the emergence of Japan as a regional and global economic power.

The third wave of reforms followed the peak of Japanese economic success, that occurred between 1970 and the end of the 1980s. From 1989 onwards, the country fell into a crisis that jeopardised its financial system. A speculative bubble, largely concerning real estate assets, burst at the beginning of the 1990s, and a banking crisis ensued in 1997 when several banks defaulted. The state was compelled to step in so as to avoid a banking panic. The resulting distress prompted the necessity of institutional reforms to give the government room for manoeuvre to intervene. A new Ministry of Economy was launched and the Ministry of Finance was reorganised. This was followed by reforms in the banking sector and changes in the training of lawyers. There were also changes to numerous legal rules, including those concerning corporate insolvency, labour law,[13] intellectual property, civil procedure, company law,[14] securities law[15] and the law of legal entities (2006), culminating in the general reform of the law of obligations in 2017.

[8] Local Autonomy Act (*Chihō jichi hō*, 地方自治法) N° 1947, 67 promulgated on 17 April 1947, https://elaws.e-gov.go.jp/document?lawid=322AC0000000067.

[9] Court Act (*Saibansho hō*, 裁判所法) N° 1947, 59, promulgated on 16 April 1947, https://elaws.e-gov.go.jp/document?lawid=322AC0000000059 (Japanese version);, https://www.japaneselawtranslation.go.jp/ja/laws/view/4150 (English version).

[10] Labour Standards Act (*Rōdō kijun hō*, 労働基準法) N° 1947, 49, promulgated on 7 April 1947, https://elaws.e-gov.go.jp/document?lawid=322AC0000000049 (Japanese version);, https://www.japaneselawtranslation.go.jp/en/laws/view/3567/en (English version).

[11] Labour Union Act (*Rōdō kumiai hō*, 労働組合法) N° 1949, 174, promulgated on 1 June 1949, https://elaws.e-gov.go.jp/document?lawid=324AC0000000174 (Japanese version); https://www.japaneselawtranslation.go.jp/en/laws/view/3805 (English version).

[12] Anti-Monopoly Act (*Dokusen Kinshihō*, 独占禁止法) N° 1947, 54, promulgated on 14 April 1947, https://elaws.e-gov.go.jp/document?lawid=322AC0000000054_20220617_504AC0000000068 (Japanese version); https://www.jftc.go.jp/en/legislation_gls/amended_ama09/index.html (English version).

[13] See R Sakuraba, 'The Amendment of the Employment Measure Act: Japanese Anti-Age Discrimination Law' (2009) 6 *Japan Labor Review* 2, 56.

[14] See, for instance, F Baumgärtel, 'Role and Function of Independent and Outside Directors in Japan: After the 2015 Amendment of the Companies Act and the Implementation of Japan's Corporate Governance Code' (2018) 20 *Asian-Pacific Law and Policy Journal* 96.

[15] See AM Pardieck, 'The Formation and Transformation of Securities Law in Japan: From the Bubble to the Big Bang' (2001) 19 *UCLA Pacific Basin Law Journal* 1.

The third wave of reform has generally maintained all the previous enactments in force, but it has carried out in-depth overhauls. These changes are driven by several objectives: more efficient legal mechanisms in order to reduce risks, a commitment to modernise a system that seemed to be stagnant and had revealed its shortcomings, a quest for fresh impetus for the institutions, but also a concern with reducing state control and bringing in more political and economic liberalism. While the liberal intention of the early 2000s is less perceptible in 2023, reforms in this direction are still underway.

To conclude this section, contemporary Japanese law is the outcome of the confrontation with Western powers, the desire to follow their economic and social, and therefore legal, model. The comparison between the Western laws is the method that allowed for the development of the present legal system.

II. Japanese Positive Law

In order to provide the keys to an understanding of the Japanese legal system, the following discussion is a non-exhaustive account of the basic legal practices and legislation in Japan.

A. Organisation and Practice of Legal Studies

The architecture of legal education reflects the national ethos of the legal discipline. It addresses the needs of practitioners and is indicative of the inherent structure of the field, which may be significantly different from the statutory framework. It is something of an insider's view of the subject.

In Japan, law is taught at the undergraduate level for four years in faculties of law. Then the legal education may continue for two or three years in 'Law Schools' at the graduate level, with a view to specialising in legal professions. Faculties often combine the study of law and political science. The undergraduate legal subject matter, generally speaking (there are some variations between faculties' curricula), is approached through a 'funnel' pattern of education. In other words, it starts with basic subjects and gradually specialises. Constitutional law is taught throughout the first and second years. Civil law is taught throughout the first three years: the general part is given in the first year, the law of property and obligations in the second year, and family law in the third year. Furthermore, the basics of criminal law, the history of law, the basics of political science etc are also covered in the first year. During the second year, criminal law, administrative law, commercial law and political science are also covered. The third year includes civil procedure, labour law, international law and the sociology of law. In the fourth year, students have a wide choice of topics that vary according to the university – for example, tax law, international business law, intellectual property law, inheritance law, real estate law, environmental law, consumer law, Roman law, or the theory and philosophy of law, German law, French law, Chinese law and Muslim law.

As a result, the structure of legal education in Japan is very similar to that in France. However, there are a few notable differences. Japanese law faculties pay attention to the social sciences in general, especially emphasising sociology, quantitative methods and history. The teaching is very open to foreign legal systems too, and despite the fact that they have become a minor part of the curriculum, their visibility remains substantial.

As far as legal methods are concerned, a particular tool is used in Japan to deal with legislation: the *Roppō* 六法 or 'Code of the six laws'. The *Roppō* is a work in which the basic laws are published together. It is inspired by a textbook that was used in the nineteenth century at French law faculties to teach law, which has since fallen into disuse. In France, it included the French Constitution and the Napoleonic Codes (the Civil Code, the Civil Procedure Code, the Criminal Code, the Criminal Procedure Code and the Commercial Code), as well as the most important laws of the time, such as the Freedom of the Press Act of 1881. The Japanese *Roppō* presents the core of the Japanese legal system: the Constitution, the Civil Code, the Commercial Code, the Civil Procedure Code, the Criminal Code, the Criminal Procedure Code, some key legislation (such as the Labour Standard Law), and summaries of the main cases.

The Code of the six laws is the basic tool of every Japanese lawyer, whether student, teacher or practitioner. The various legal publishers release an updated version every year, ranging from paperback to extended versions for professional use. Because it remains a private compilation, the *Roppō* offers great flexibility. Hence, the basic format may be supplemented in the professional editions with more in-depth content and a coverage of the whole range of positive law: public law (the Constitution, international law, electoral law, judicial law, local authorities, administrative law, tax law, education, cultural law etc); civil law (the Civil Code, the Commercial Code, the Civil Procedure Code, private international law etc); criminal law (law and procedure, juvenile criminal law etc); social law (labour law, social protection law etc); corporate law (economic law, professional law, intellectual property law etc); and international conventions. Indeed, the very idea of a 'Code of six laws' tends to expand to refer to the basic statutory laws of a particular field, such as the publication of the 'six laws of intellectual property'.

In addition to this collection of texts, Japanese scholarship has developed a practice of compiling case law summaries which bring together the 100 most important court decisions in a given area. The most important cases of the Supreme Court, the Appeal courts or occasionally district courts are selected, summarised and commented on in these works. The comments are very synthetic and objective. These handbooks provide a better understanding of how court decisions supplement statutory law.

B. The Laws of the Japanese Legal System

The Japanese normative scheme takes the form of the Kelsen pyramid. At the top stands the Constitution, which is hierarchically superior to other laws in two ways. On the one hand, the fundamental rights stipulated in the Constitution are held to be rights of perpetual inviolability (Article 97). On the other hand, the Constitution (*Nihon Kenpô*, 日本憲法) is held to be the supreme legal instrument, with Article 98, § 1 providing that: 'This Constitution shall be the supreme law of the nation and no law, ordinance, imperial rescript or other act of government, or part thereof, contrary to the provisions hereof, shall have legal force or validity.' In force since 1947, the Constitution has never been amended. This is due to its Article 96, which locks the text and requires a two-thirds vote in each parliamentary chamber as well as popular ratification for any constitutional amendment.

International treaties (*kokusai yakusoku*, 国際約束) come second in the pyramid, according to Article 98, § 2 of the Constitution which provides that: 'The treaties concluded by Japan and established laws of nations shall be faithfully observed'. As a principle, international conventions do not have direct effect in Japanese domestic law. The Convention on the International Sale of Goods, which became effective in Japan in 2009, is one of the rare exceptions to this principle.

Parliamentary law is the main source of law in Japan and is mostly drafted by the Japanese government. These laws are supplemented by ministerial decrees and prime ministerial ordinances. Local governments have fairly broad regulatory powers in the areas assigned to them by law (Article 94 of the Constitution). Finally, the Japanese administration issues numerous circulars, which constitute one of the tools for 'administrative guidance'. Through this guidance, the Japanese government interacts and cooperates with the private sector in an incentive and non-binding manner, and such guidance was acknowledged by the Administrative Procedures Act in 1994 (Article 2).[16]

The entire legislative apparatus is anchored in two basic texts: the Constitution and the Civil Code. The Peace Constitution (*Heiwa kenpō*, 平和憲法) came into force in 1947 and has 103 articles and nine chapters. It contains two types of rules: institutional rules and fundamental rights. Concerning the institutional rules, the Constitution maintained the monarchy system, but with the sovereignty residing in the people, the role of the emperor is reduced to the role of the symbol of the state and the unity of the people (Article 1). Japan is a pacifist state that renounces war through Article 9; however, this provision is one of the most challenged and its scope has undergone significant change through a continuously developing official interpretation.[17] The Constitution establishes a bicameral parliament, with an upper and a lower house. Both appoint the Prime Minister, but the Lower House has the final say. In turn, the Prime Minister nominates the government. The Constitution provides the grounds for judicial organisation, public finance and local self-government for local authorities.[18]

With respect to fundamental rights, the law-makers assigned them a central place: inserted into Chapter III under the title 'rights and duties of the people', 31 fundamental rights are provided for (Articles 30–40). They include individual freedoms, such as: 'right to life, liberty, and the pursuit of happiness shall, to the extent that it does not interfere with the public welfare' (Article 13), freedom of religion (Article 20), freedom of association (Article 21) and academic freedom (Article 23). The fight against discrimination is another feature of these substantive rights, through the establishment of a broad principle of equality in Article 14: 'All of the people are equal under the law and there shall be no discrimination in political, economic or social relations because of race, creed, sex, social status or family origin.' This text was the first to provide for gender equality. Finally, these

[16] Administrative Procedure Act (*Gyōsei tetsuzuki hō*, 行政手続法) N° 1994, 88, promulgated on 12 November 1994, https://elaws.e-gov.go.jp/document?lawid=405AC0000000088 (Japanese version).

[17] See, among a large bibliography, E Seizelet, 'Le rôle du parlement japonais en matière de défense' (2019) 2 *Revue de droit public et de la science politique* 439.

[18] For an overview, see T Fukase and Y Higuchi *Le constitutionnalisme et ses problèmes au Japon: une approche comparative* (PUF, 1984); see also M Dean, *Japanese Legal System*, 2nd edn Cavendish Publishing, 2002).

rights provide for social rights such as the right and duty to work (Article 27), as well as the right of workers to organise themselves collectively (Article 28).

The Civil Code (*Minpōten*, 民法典) has been in force since 1898 and its structure is based on the German Civil Code. The Code is divided into five books: a general part, which includes all the institutions that are common to the entire civil law; followed by property; the law of obligations; family law; and inheritance law. The Code is gradually being reformed and updated. The reform of the law of obligations, which came into force on 1 April 2020, has amended more than 200 provisions of the Code, and the age of civil majority has been lowered from 20 to 18 (as of 1 April 2022). Furthermore, a law on the implementation of laws, revised in 2006, provides the basic rules of private international law (among other provisions).[19]

These rules are implemented by the Japanese courts in order to settle disputes.

III. Dispute Resolution in Japan

Dispute resolution in Japan is one of the most debated topics in the West. The practices used are either contentious, whereby disputes are brought before the courts, as is the case in Western traditions, or alternative dispute resolution, which has grown in terms of its diversity and sophistication. This is a characteristic feature of Japanese law.

A. The Japanese Court System

The Japanese court system was introduced in 1875 as one of the earliest achievements of the Meiji era, with the aim of resolving disputes according to Western standards.[20] It is focused on litigation and is not well suited to the small disputes of everyday life. Nevertheless, it allows for the resolution of significant disputes, especially those where legal or social issues are at stake. The organisation of the courts was completely overhauled after the Second World War, under the aegis of the Allied forces, and thus it shares some similarities with the federal judicial system in the US.

The Supreme Court (*saikō saibansho*, 最高裁判所) is at the top of the judicial hierarchy and is made up of 15 judges, including the President. Its assignments are to review the constitutionality of laws (Article 81 of the Japanese Constitution) and to act as the appellate authority in civil and criminal matters. In the latter context, it ensures the uniform interpretation of Japanese law. It is also responsible for overseeing the proper management of the judicial system. The Court seldom reviews the constitutionality of laws and when it declares a statute unconstitutional, the Court does not repeal it, but rather calls on the legislator to bring the law into conformity with the Constitution.

[19] Act on General Rules for Application of Laws (*Hō no tekiyō ni kan suru tsūsoku-hō*, 法の適用に関する通則法) N° 2006, 78, promulgated on 21 June 2006, came into force on 1 January 2007, https://elaws.e-gov.go.jp/document?lawid=418AC0000000078_20150801_000000000000000 (Japanese version), https://www.japaneselawtranslation.go.jp/ja/laws/view/3783 (English version).

[20] E Seizelet *Justice et magistrature au Japon* (PUF, 2002); JO Haley, 'The Japanese Judiciary: Maintaining Integrity, Autonomy and the Public Trust' in DH Foote (ed), *Law in Japan: A Turning Point* (University of Washington Press, 2007) 99–155.

Below the Supreme Court are the Courts of Appeal (*kōtō saibansho*, 高等裁判所), of which there are eight. Their assignment is to hear appeals from decisions of lower courts and to review decisions of summary courts. The Tokyo Court of Appeal is also the special appellate court for intellectual property and competition disputes.

There are a total of 50 courts of first instance, ie, the district courts (*chihō saibansho*, 地方裁判所): one per prefecture and four within Hokkaido. They have primary jurisdiction over cases with a value of more than 1,400,000 yen (Article 24 of the Courts Act) and in criminal matters for the most serious crimes, which are subject to the penalty of life imprisonment or death.

The system of the jury court was introduced in 2004. These courts are coupled with family courts (*katei saibansho*, 家庭裁判所), which have a special jurisdiction over family disputes and juvenile delinquency. Since 2014, the Tokyo and Osaka courts have jurisdiction over child abduction cases under the international Hague Convention. Judges there are assisted by family counsellors (*san'yo in*, 参与員) who are drawn from civil society and help resolve disputes. These courts also appoint specialised staff such as doctors and psychologists, who are in charge of social investigations.

Finally, the summary courts have jurisdiction in civil and criminal matters for small disputes. They hear cases in a single-judge formation.

Two administrative offices have jurisdictional powers: the Fair Trade Commission (*kōsei torihiki i'inkai*, 公正取引委員会) in matters of competition law, and the Central Labour Relations Commission (*chūō rōdō i'inkai*, 中央労働委員会). The latter is the common body for the commissions established by the Trade Union Act (Articles 19 et seq) and, in addition to various extra-jurisdictional competences, they are competent to settle disputes concerning unfair labour practices (Article 27).

This latter system, which is specific to labour relations, was introduced after the Second World War and has the distinctive feature of being a combination of contentious and non-contentious dispute settlement, the latter being particularly important in Japan.

B. Alternative Dispute Resolution (ADR)

Japan has a long tradition of settling disputes without referring to the formal court system, and this is encouraged by the state authorities and the law-makers.[21] Thus, judicial conciliation, carried out by a civil judge in the courts, is considered as an alternative to the contentious settlement of disputes. Provided for in land matters since 1922, it was extended by the legislator to various fields such as payment of debts or traffic accidents. Eventually, in 1951, a more general law was passed to consolidate the practice.[22] In parallel, a very similar procedure was introduced for family matters, such as divorce or adoption. The Family

[21] H Baum, 'Mediation in Japan: Development, Forms, Regulation, and Practice of Out-of-Court Dispute Resolution' in KJ Hopt and F Steffek (eds), *Mediation: Principles and Regulation in Comparative Perspective* (Oxford University Press, 2013, online edition) 1011–94, DOI:10.1093/acprof:oso/9780199653485.003.0020.

[22] Civil Conciliation Act (*Minji chōtei hō*, 民事調停法) N° 1951, 222, promulgated on 9 June 1951, https://elaws.e-gov.go.jp/document?lawid=326AC1000000222 (Japanese version), https://www.japaneselawtranslation.go.jp/ja/laws/view/2732 (English version of 2004).

Disputes Act 2011 has taken up and harmonised these procedures.[23] Judicial conciliation is a right for all litigants in Japan (Article 2 of the Law on Conciliation in Civil Matters) and is conducted by a judge assisted by two assessors from civil society, namely one man and one woman. Litigants and may be assisted or not by a lawyer. Conciliation seeks to bring the opposing parties together and, should this fail, the judge proposes an equitable solution which, if accepted, is legally binding and terminates the dispute.

In addition, mediation in labour law matters has been formalised in law: *assen* あっせん is designed to deal with individual labour disputes.[24] It takes place at the Local Public Administration in charge of labour issues, it is conducted by a mediation committee, consisting of members of the labour administration, company managers and employees, and the settlement must receive the employee's consent and in that case becomes a settlement contract (*wakai* 和解.).

With the reform of the justice system in 2004, the Japanese government sought to support ADR. Through the ADR law,[25] an accreditation system for dispute resolution centres was set up – these centres are especially involved in consumer issues. On the other hand, arbitration, particularly in commercial matters, is a form of ADR that has had little success in Japan and the public authorities are seeking to promote it.

IV. Conclusion

To conclude, the Japanese legal system is a relatively recent creation, established as it was in the late nineteenth century. However, the legal system remains a critical tool for the governance of the Japanese state, which maintains a monopoly over the design of the legal system. One of its key features is the overwhelming influence of comparative law,[26] which is still an essential reference for both legislators and legal researchers, Another key feature is a general concern for the social effectiveness of the law. This is a lesser-known but very important aspect of Japanese law: it is deployed in order to set up systems that allow society to operate more efficiently. Finally, Japanese law is highly regarded in far East Asia, serving as an inspirational model for Taiwan and South Korea. The Japanese government seeks to export Japanese legal know-how throughout East and South Asia

[23] Domestic Relations Case Procedure Act (*Kaji jiken tetsuzuki hō*, 家事事件手続法) N° 2011, 52, promulgated on 25 May 2011, https://www.japaneselawtranslation.go.jp/en/laws/view/2323/en (English version).

[24] Act on Promoting the Resolution of Individual Labour-Related Disputes (*Kobetsu rōdō kankei funsō no kaiketsu no kakushin hō*, 個別労働紛争解決促進法) N° 2001, 112, promulgated on 11 July 2001 (Heisei 13), https://elaws.e-gov.go.jp/document?lawid=413AC0000000112_20200401_429AC0000000045 (Japanese version), https://www.japaneselawtranslation.go.jp/en/laws/view/3804/en (English version).

[25] Act on Promotion of Use of Alternative Dispute Resolution (ADR Law) (*Saiban-gai funsō kaikestu tetsuzuki no riyō no suishin ni kan suru hōritsu*, 裁判外紛争解決手続の利用の促進に関する法律) N° 2004, 151, promulgated on 1 December 2004, https://www.japaneselawtranslation.go.jp/en/laws/view/3774 (English version), https://elaws.e-gov.go.jp/document?lawid=416AC0000000151_20220617_504AC0000000068 (Japanese version). See Kota Fukui 'The Diversification and Formalisation of ADR in Japan: The Effect of Enacting the Act on Promotion of Use of Alternative Dispute Resolution' in J Zekoll, M Bälz and I Amelung (eds), *Formalisation and Flexibilisation in Dispute Resolution* (Brill Nijhoff, 2014) 187–210.

[26] H Baum, 'Comparison of Law, Transfer of Legal Concepts, and Creation of a Legal Design: The Case of Japan' in JO Haley and T Takenaka (eds), *Legal Innovations in Asia* (Edward Elgar, 2014) 61–73.

through international cooperation and development assistance.[27] In 2013 it released a policy paper entitled 'Basic Policies on Legal Technical Assistance'[28] that states:

> It meets the reality and needs of recipient countries through dialogue and coordination with local counterpart organizations with the support of dispatched legal experts. When Japan conducts the assistance by utilizing its own experience and knowledge, the culture, history, development stage and ownership of the recipient country are respected. It is not limited to the drafting and amending of laws, but it is further extended to the development of foundations for operating and enforcing the legal institutions properly, to the training of legal professionals and legal education, and to the capacity-building in legal practices for appropriate legal operations.

Its objective is to 'contribute to capacity-building in developing countries, as well as to the strengthening of bilateral relations between Japan and the developing countries'. The most recent activity report was submitted in June 2022.[29] This stresses that the goal of 'legal diplomacy' is to promote the fundamental and universal values of the rule of law as well as the respect of human rights in the world.

[27] Y Kaneko, 'A Procedural Approach to Judicial Reform in Asia: Implications from Japanese Involvement in Vietnam' (2009–10) 23 *Columbia Journal of Asian Law* 313; I Giraudou, 'L'assistance juridique japonaise aux pays dits 'émergents' d'Asie. Contribution à l'approche pluraliste de la circulation du droit' [Japanese Legal Technical Assistance to Emerging Countries in Asia: A Contribution to the Pluralistic Approach to the Circulation of Law] (2009) *Transcontinentales* 47, doi.org/10.4000/transcontinentales.360.

[28] Ministry of Justice of Japan, 'Basic Policies on Legal Technical Assistance' (2013), https://www.moj.go.jp/content/000115321.pdf.

[29] Ministry of Justice of Japan, 'Activity Report: The 23rdAnnual Conference on Technical Assistance in the Legal Field 25 June 2022 International Affairs Division of the Minister's Secretariat the Ministry of Justice' (2022), https://www.moj.go.jp/content/001375171.pdf.

4

Legal Transfer and Law in Transition

Compulsory Share in Korean and Japanese Law

MARIE SEONG-HAK KIM

Korean law as a research field trails Chinese and Japanese counterparts. The reason for this, at least in part, is that Korea's traditional law has been seen as a recitation of Chinese Confucian precepts, whereas its modern law has regularly been dismissed as a rerun of Japanese law. Such characterisations are not accurate, but not entirely groundless either. In the early fifteenth century, Chosŏn Korea (1392–1910) undertook a comprehensive acceptance of the imperial Chinese code.[1] Some 500 years later, Korea's passage to the Romano-Germanic legal system took place under Japanese colonial rule (1910–45), and the first Civil Code of the Republic of Korea of 1960 was closely modelled after the Meiji and post-war Japanese code.[2] Yet, do similar examples of legal borrowing not abound in history? The reception of Roman law in the Holy Roman Empire at the end of the fifteenth century was no less sweeping than the Chosŏn case; the Turkish Civil Code of 1926 was a wholesale adoption of the Swiss Civil Code of 1907. The point of these deliberate oversimplifications is that scholars' breezy indifference to Korean law may be indicative of a larger problem of approaching legal transformation in East Asia from a static perspective.

The concept of legal transplant in the diffusion and transfer of law has been predominant in scholarship for some time. Normally, a distinction is made between receptive and unreceptive transplant: when a country voluntarily chose and adapted the imported law or had a population that was familiar with it, the process of transplantation was smooth and its legal order functioned relatively well; on the contrary, when the adjustment of foreign legal borrowings to local conditions was lacking, as in legal reception via colonisation, the recipient country suffered from negative transplant effect.[3] Few would object,

[1] The first article in the penal section of the *Kyŏngguk taejŏn* (Great Code for Administering the Country), promulgated in 1397 and revised in its complete form in 1471, explicitly stated that the *Ta Ming lü* (Great Ming Code) would be the basic law of the dynasty.

[2] The Korean Criminal Code came into force in 1954 and the Korean Civil Code, promulgated in 1958, took effect in 1960. The Japanese Meiji Civil Code was completed in 1898 and was revised in 1947.

[3] D Berkowitz et al, 'The Transplant Effect' (2003) 51 *American Journal of Comparative Law* 163. In the case of negative transplant, 'the mismatch between preexisting conditions and institutions and transplanted law' results in a weak public demand for the laws and for the institutions to enforce them, creating fewer sources for legal change (at 167–68 and 171).

initially, to placing Japan in the first category of transplant and Korea in the second. Meiji Japan (1868–1912) was not colonised by any country, and it carried out a remarkably successful transformation of its own laws in the style of French and German laws. But it is important to recall that its 'voluntary' reception of Western law had been precipitated by considerable pressure from outside: the enactment of a uniform corpus of civil law was a precondition for the revision of the much-deplored unequal treaties and the abolition of extra-territoriality.[4] For Korea, meanwhile, its modern legal system was unilaterally imposed by colonisers, but the laws and the legal system built by the Japanese were quickly accepted by the Korean population, and colonial law became the foundation for the modern state in South Korea.

These considerations reaffirm that, whereas borrowing is the principal way in which law develops, its actual process is subject to historical contingencies. Each legal tradition has a different way of adapting to change, and its nature can be best grasped through the examination of a vital strand of historical evidence. Scholars of late increasingly accept the idea that the disciplines of comparative law and legal history are one and the same.[5] While the concept of *legal transfer* is premised on the move of laws across national borders, the notion of *law in transition* engages changes at both internal and external levels. Korean law has been seriously influenced by outside forces, but its traditional norms grounded in Confucian philosophy have rarely been ousted by them. As such, Korean legal history poses a compelling topic in comparative law.

This chapter deals with the subject of compulsory share in inheritance law of Korea. The topic itself may seem to have limited relevance to private international law, which is the major theme of this volume, but it concerns questions that are essential for understanding the metamorphosis of Korean law in the context of the development of law in East Asia. As a snapshot that captures the process of ongoing influences and interactions between Japanese and Korean law, it offers an uncanny opportunity to examine the transformation of private law in East Asia in comparison with that in Europe.

Compulsory share (遺留分), also known under the various names of legal reserve, retained portion or forced heirship, refers to a statutory portion of testate inheritance. When the next of kin, such as children, spouse or parents, are excluded from inheritance by a last will, the law allows them a minimum share of the estate. Establishing an obligatory share of the estate was an idea embedded in Roman law and in medieval European custom, and it is preserved in German law (*Pflichtteil*) and French law (*réserve*). Similar concepts were absent in traditional East Asia. Compulsory share was first introduced to Japan in the late nineteenth century and was inserted into the Meiji Civil Code (*iryūbun*). It was not imposed on colonial subjects in Korea, as the Japanese colonial policy allowed private legal relations among Koreans to be governed by Korean custom instead of Japanese law.[6] After liberation, the institution of legal reserve was notably rejected and excluded from the Korean Civil Code of 1960, only to be included in Korean law in 1979 (*yuryubun*). Its convoluted history reveals the multifaceted nature of the country's inheritance law, deeply

[4] The promulgation of the Meiji Civil Code brought about the end of extra-territoriality.

[5] See 'Symposium: Legal History and Comparative Law: A Dialogue in Times of the Transnationalization of Law and Legal Scholarship' (2018) 66 *American Journal of Comparative Law* 727.

[6] M Kim, *Law and Custom in Korea: Comparative Legal History* (Cambridge University Press, 2012).

fused with the rhetoric of Confucian moral persuasion distilled in filial piety on the one hand and, on the other, powerfully driven by the forces of modernity.

Section I of this chapter provides a brief historical survey of Korean law from the Chosŏn dynasty to the postcolonial period.[7] Section II discusses the background of the enactment and contemporary interpretative issues surrounding the compulsory share laws. The concrete nature of legal diffusion should be identified through legislative as well as judicial courses, and selected judgments of the Korean courts will be examined.

The evolution of Korean law, as illustrated in the legal reserve provisions, constitutes a dialectical process. Korean people have exhibited their conscious choices to either adhere to or divert from the outside law, and these choices have shaped the way in which modern Korean law addresses central issues in private law relations. Compulsory share is a topic that continues to elicit heated discussion around the world because it curtails the principle of testamentary freedom. Examination of its evolution in Korean law in comparison with that of Japan can illuminate the nature and significance of legal transformation in East Asia.

I. Confucian Rhetoric to Civil Law Reasoning

Certain particular situations in the legal development of East Asia must be signalled at the outset. Meiji Japan pulled off what could be called a self-colonisation of its laws, and it subsequently brought to its colonies the laws that had undergone a thorough and identifiable course of *Japanisierung*.[8] A recipient of a filtered civil law under colonial aegis, Korea, along with Taiwan, underwent the process of legal modernisation with reduced unfamiliarity with the transplanted law. The fact that Japan and Korea belonged to the same cultural sphere of the Sinicised civilisation, not to mention the same race, sharing the same Chinese scripts, made their colonial encounter unique in history. The deep-rooted presence of Confucian tradition in the Chosŏn dynasty continued during Japanese rule and into the postcolonial period.

The Korean Civil Code (1960) states in Article 1: 'In civil trials, those matters for which there is no written law are governed by customary law, and those matters for which there is no customary law shall be adjudicated by inference from reason'.[9] Korea, a country of the

[7] In this chapter, Korea in the post-1945 context solely refers to the Republic of Korea (South Korea).

[8] The German-style Japanese Civil Code went through an identifiable process of 'Japanisierung' as it became adapted to Japanese normativity. See HP Glenn, 'The Grounding of Codification' (1998) 31 *University of California Davis Law Review* 765, 772.

[9] This language is similar to that in the Swiss Civil Code of 1907, which provided: 'In the absence of a provision, the court shall decide in accordance with customary law and, in the absence of customary law, in accordance with the rule which it would make as legislator. In so doing, the court shall follow established doctrine and case law' (art 1, secs 2 and 3). But the direct source of art 1 in the Korean Civil Code (and the Chinese Civil Code of 1929 and the Manchu Civil Code of 1938, which both included precisely the same language) was the Dajōkan proclamation of 1875 in Japan. Dajōkan (Council of State) decree, no 103, stipulated: 'In civil trials, those matters for which there is no written law are governed by custom, and those matters for which there is no custom shall be adjudicated by inference from reason' (art 3). If the Korean Civil Code was inspired by the Swiss Civil Code, which is quite possible, the underlying considerations for affirming the legal force of custom were rather divergent from each other. In the Swiss Code, custom as a source of law was viewed as necessary because a judge, who was not allowed to refuse to decide a case on the grounds that the statutory text was insufficient, needed to turn to other sources of law; custom was recognised as a formal source of law as a means to accommodate its history of

civilian tradition where all laws are written and judicial precedent is not law, thus recognises custom as an official source of law. Custom was what colonial authorities – judges working under the colonial legal order – declared to have legal force. Emphasis on custom in post-colonial law represented the efforts to preserve indigenous norms (particularly in family and succession relations) against the perceived onslaught of alien influences in Korean law's transition to civil legality.

A. Chosŏn Law

The Chosŏn dynasty was a model Confucian state. The interpretation of Confucianism by Zhu Xi (1130–1200), known as neo-Confucianism, was introduced and accepted as the state ideology. Neo-Confucian emphasis on ancestor memorial rites remained among the most principal elements of common identity in East Asia. Unlike in Europe, where the rites were traditionally construed in terms of church dogma, in East Asia they took the form of the veneration of deceased family members in individual households.[10] Korean literati, confident of their mastery of Confucian classics, were intransigent in their interpretation of rituals. It has been said that Koreans were more Confucian than Confucius. Orthodox neo-Confucian ideology was grafted onto the country's strong kinship-based social structure, resulting in thoroughly Koreanised property and inheritance practices.

In Europe, various legal instruments and strategies were devised to protect property and to facilitate its smooth succession. Marriage contracts, donations and wills constituted the cornerstone of what we call private law. Inheritance law was compulsory or mandatory law (*ius cogens*) rather than optional or default law (*ius dispositivum*). There was a distinct process of public institutionalisation of private law by the state. In pre-modern Korea, by contrast, the state remained disinterested in the regulation of inheritance – and was largely indifferent to legal relations among individuals for that matter. Filial piety and ritual propriety instead served as the nominal legal edifice, taking the place of legally enforceable property and succession rights. Disputes over inheritance distributions were routinely dismissed as violation of filial obligations.[11]

The duty of performing ancestral sacrifices was exclusively incumbent upon the eldest male in the family of the most senior line within the lineage. Confucian classics stipulate that ancestors enjoy a sacrifice only when it is offered by an agnatic descendant. Succession essentially meant succeeding the status as the presider of ancestor ritual, and the transfer of property occurred as incidental to ritual succession. The state code provided for equal distribution of property, but concerns arose that the partible distribution of slaves and land

disunity among different cantons. Korea, which neither had the history of multiple cantons like Switzerland nor was composed of different ethnic groups as in the Manchukuo, conferred an exalted status on custom in its Civil Code mainly to assert indigenous culture and nationalism. In 1907, Switzerland was composed of 22 cantons; currently, under the 1999 Constitution, there are 26.

[10] R Jacob, 'La coutume, les mœurs et le rite. Regards croisés sur les catégories occidentales de la norme non écrite' in J Bourgon (ed), *La Coutume et la norme en Chine et au Japon* (Presses universitaires de Vincennes, 2001).

[11] Magistrates approached civil matters exclusively as factual questions – specific fact situations, not legal principles, determined the outcome of disputes. In China, as the French legal historian Jérôme Bourgon has convincingly shown, contracts existed but contract law did not: J Bourgon, 'Ditan de tu'an: shilun Qingdai falü wenhua zhong de "xiguan" yu "qiyue"' [Figures in the Carpet: 'Customs' and 'Contracts' in Qing Legal Culture] in Q Pengsheng and C Xiyuan (eds), *Ming Qing falü lianzuo zhong de quanli he wenhua* (Lianjing Chuban Gongsi, 2009) 96–127.

would threaten the maintenance of the main descent line, jeopardising the observance of proper rituals.[12] From the seventeenth century, granting a special economic privilege to the primogenitary heir of a particular segment of the lineage became the standard for property inheritance. Ritual primogeniture thus engendered property primogeniture by necessity. In short, the obligation to perform ancestral ceremony led the transfer of material resources through generations without well-defined laws of property or inheritance.

B. Colonial Law

Korea was annexed by Japan in 1910. In March 1912, the colonial government issued the Chosŏn Ordinance on Civil Matters (*Chōsen Minjirei* in Japanese; *Chosŏn Minsaryŏng* in Korean), which became the basis of the colonial legal order. The Ordinance declared the Japanese Civil Code to be the governing law in Korea (Article 1), but it decreed that private law relations among Korean people be regulated by Korean custom as long as it was not in conflict with laws related to public order.[13] Article 11 stated: 'The provisions on capacity, family and succession in the laws listed in Article 1 do not apply to Koreans. The said matters involving Koreans are decided according to Korean custom'. Under this provision, family law and succession were subject to Korean custom even if there were contradicting provisions in statutes.

Most Korean customs were grounded in Confucian practices. The recognition of custom as a source of law smoothened out the transition of traditional patrilineal and agnatic ritual succession into a civil law regime of property succession. Colonial judges, like common law judges, abstracted from traditional Korean practices general rules and declared them to be Korea's customary law. The process was similar to what the Japanese judges had done in their country in the pre-codification years. In 1875, Japan declared custom to be an official source of law.[14] Subsequently, jurists proceeded to ascertain customary law that could be inserted into the Civil Code. An important, often overlooked, aspect of Japanese legal modernisation is the fact that Japanese received both civil law and common law. On the surface, Japan adopted the continental system, but in reality it followed the lines of English law, as judges expanded the use of precedents into areas that had previously not been governed by law. The same framework was imported into its colonies, where the dual operation of the Japanese code and indigenous custom facilitated the functioning of the legal order.

It has been claimed that colonial judges modified Korean custom in order to achieve the eventual assimilation of Korean law to Japanese law. But one must ask: why would the Japanese be interested in changing Korean family and succession practices that were

[12] In *Kyŏngguk taejŏn*, the article entitled *Pongsa* (compensation for performance of ancestral memorial rites) stipulated that successor of ancestral memorial rites receive one-fifth in addition to his lawful share of inheritance.

[13] For a discussion of the 1912 ordinance, see M Kim, 'Customary Law and Colonial Jurisprudence in Korea' (2009) 57 *American Journal of Comparative Law* 205. The Japanese colonial customary law policy in Korea borrowed heavily from those of the European imperial powers. Native custom were recognised insofar as it was compatible with the dictates of natural law and morality. The notion of *ordre public* in francophone Africa, the equivalent of the 'repugnancy clauses' in British colonies, served as a limitation to the application of local rules. For comparison of Japanese and European customary law policies, see Kim (n 6), especially ch 7.

[14] See n 9 above.

largely formulated of Confucian precepts? Any colonial power was aware of the daunting difficulties of forcibly changing indigenous custom. Further, in colonial management, the necessity to sustain the dominant moral system of the ruling class among the native population was of critical importance. Confucianism was an elite philosophy and its teaching was geared towards maintaining the established hierarchical social order. The colonial legal system broadly aimed to construe Korean laws and practices in line with modern legal concepts and principles in the Japanese Civil Code, but it does not lead to the conclusion that the Japanese manipulated Korean custom in order to exert tighter ideological control of the colonial citizenry.

C. Post-colonial Law

Immediately after Japan's defeat in the Second World War in 1945, the United States Army Military Government in Korea (USAMGIK) occupied the southern half of the Korean peninsula. The US forces preserved the colonial administrative and judicial structures, and also ordered the retention of most colonial laws in order to avoid a legal vacuum and ensure the uninterrupted operation of the courts.[15]

The continuing importance of the colonial legal order in liberated Korea can be illustrated in legal cases under American military rule. Among various judicial decisions rendered by the military government during this time, one opinion prepared by Ernst Fraenkel (1898–1975), the renowned German jurist who served as a legal advisor in Korea, is of particular interest. The question brought before him was: 'Whether U.S. personnel stationed in Korea legally may adopt a Korean child'. It prompted interpretation of Article 19 of the *Hōrei*, imperial Japan's private international law, which read: 'Requisites of adoption for each party concerned are governed by the law of his (her) country (*Lex Patriae*)'.[16] Fraenkel noted that under Article 11 of the Ordinance of Civil Matters, 'such family matters are controlled, not by the Japanese Civil Code, but by Korean customary law'. In Korean custom, 'there must be "male-side" – agnatic – blood-relationship between adopting parent and child. This requirement will be conclusive, unless perchance the prospective adoption parent is of Korean descent and related in fact to the child'. Thus, concluded Fraenkel, a legal adoption by an American as in this case could not take place.[17] This is but one example of how Korea's 'custom', the body of colonial jurisprudence grounded in Confucian norms, continued to dominate postcolonial society.

The legal force of colonial laws was affirmed by the Constitution of the Republic of Korea. Article 100 of the Constitution, promulgated on 17 July 1948, stated that the laws that were in effect at the time of the liberation would continue their force as long as they were not in conflict with the Constitution.[18] In this way, colonial laws that had governed

[15] USAMGIK Ordinance 21, Sec 1, Retention of Laws (2 November 1945).

[16] The *Hōrei*, the Law on the General Rules of the Application of Laws (Law no 10), was issued on 21 June 1898, a few weeks before the Civil Code. It was comprehensively amended in 2006. Korea's Private International Law, the *Kukche Sabŏp*, first issued in 1962, was wholly revised in 2022.

[17] United States Army Forces in Korea, *Selected Legal Opinions of the Department of Justice, United States Military Government in Korea*, Opinion # 712, 15 November 1946, 203–04.

[18] 'The current laws continue to have the force of law so long as such laws are not contradictory to this Constitution'.

Korea remained valid laws until they were replaced or abolished by the legislature or found unconstitutional by the courts.

The Civil Code of independent Korea drew heavily from the Japanese Civil Code as revised in 1947. It also borrowed from the Chinese Civil Code and the Manchu Civil Code, both of which had been drafted either by Japanese jurists or under their influence.[19] The Manchu Code was regarded as the culmination of mature Japanese legal theories. The first generation of judges and lawyers in postcolonial Korea, including the drafters of the Civil Code, had been educated and trained during the colonial period, and it was normal that most theoretical and methodological tools in postcolonial law came from Japanese legal science. A critical aspect of legal transfer resides in translation, at the cultural as well as linguistic levels. Translation in the Korea-Japan context is more than a metaphor; it involves a literal borrowing of legal vocabularies and terminologies. Legal modernisation in East Asia relied on the Japanese neologism. When the Meiji scholars translated the Napoleonic Code (1804), they had to come up with a whole new set of lexicons in Chinese characters to convey the meanings of those Western terms that had no equivalents in Sino-Japanese civilisation. The glossary composed by them constitutes the basis of modern legal nomenclature in East Asia.[20]

Colonial law spared postcolonial Korean legislators and scholars the trouble of reinventing the wheel but, nonetheless, conscious efforts were made by them to distinguish Korean law from Japanese law. The evolution of the compulsory share laws in legislation and jurisprudence illustrates the nexus between the laws of the two countries.

II. Compulsory Share and Inheritance Law

The idea of compulsory legal share was not an unfamiliar concept for Korean jurists who lived under Japanese colonial law, although it was not imposed on Korean subjects. Explanation of why legislators initially rejected the reserved portion in inheritance but eventually accepted it some 20 years later captures key aspects of Korea's succession rules.

A. The Concept of Legal Reserve

The origins of modern compulsory portion laws can be traced back to two separate sources in European history. In Germanic custom prevalent in medieval and early modern France, the *réserve coutumière* referred to the portion of the decedent's estate that was reserved for the heir as part of the latter's legal right to inheritance. In the *pays de droits coutumiers*, custom considered a part of the estate family property, or the

[19] See n 9 above.

[20] The Japanese often regrouped the Chinese characters to give old Chinese terms new meanings. This was the case with the term 'custom': *shūkan* 習慣 (*xiguan* in Chinese; *sŭpkwan* in Korean) denoted a habit or practice; the newly created term, *kanshū* 慣習 – the same characters in reverse order – designated custom, with legal notions. See J Bourgon, 'La coutume et le droit en Chine à la fin de l'Empire' (1999) 54 *Annales HSS* 1091–92. Another example of this 'lexical innovation' is *ritsuhō* 律法, referring broadly to a law in traditional Asia, and *hōritsu* 法律, meaning a legislative enactment.

propres, to preserve in the family. It was different in nature from *légitime* in Roman law that was in force in the *pays de droit écrit*.[21] While the doctrine of the *réserve* stood on the premise of defending family property against disposal, *légitime* was based on a perceived moral duty of the decedent who enjoyed complete testamentary freedom. *Légitime* was neither about the inherited property nor about an inheritance right; the testator's prerogative was not challenged. It was simply a method of guaranteeing the welfare of close relatives who were disinherited, by giving them a monetary claim of a certain value in the property against the designated heir. The customary law regions in France had adhered to a strict system of limiting the testator's ability to alienate property. However, as Roman law increasingly penetrated into these regions, many *coutumes* were reformed in the sixteenth century to add the features of *légitime* to the conventional *réserve coutumière*.

Traditional Asia did not have the concept of compulsory share in favour of the heirs. The notion was introduced into Japan by the French jurist Gustave Boissonade de Fontarabie (1825–1910), who came to Japan in 1873 to serve as a legal adviser to the Meiji government. Boissonade had been well known in France for his work on the system of *réserve héréditaire*, and it was no coincidence that he paid attention to reforming Japanese law on this issue.[22] Boissonade needed to devise measures that would not seriously disrupt Japan's unique system of the house (*ie* 家) succession. The house, a kind of legal entity, functioned as the basic unit constituting society and formed the foundation for the inheritance system. Boissonade highlighted the practical utility of the legal reserve in maintaining the existing house structure and the family business through restrictions on the will of the deceased to dispose of the property outside the house. He stressed that the primary duty of the house head was to support the members belonging to the house, and that the reserve system allocated a portion of the inherited property for the house successor so that the latter could fulfil his responsibility in line with the natural law principle.[23]

Under Boissonade's design, the property of the decedent was divided into a discretionary portion, which could be freely disposed of by will, and a reserved portion, which passed to the decedent's next of kin. In the event that the decedent had disposed of the property to a third person beyond the discretionary portion, infringing on the heir's reserved shares, the heir could claim a reduction in the excess free portion. The civil code Boissonade drafted, known as the Old Civil Code (*Kyū Minpō*), failed to come into effect, but the reserve system was expressly stipulated in the Meiji Code.[24]

As seen above, the compulsory share provisions in the Japanese Civil Code were not applied in colonial Korea.[25] Traditional Korea had no notion of reserved share.

[21] M Kim, *Custom, Law and Monarchy: A Legal History of Early Modern France* (Oxford University Press, 2021) 126–27. See also M Kim, 'Droit coutumier' and 'Droit écrit' in *Münsteraner Glossar zu Einheit und Vielfalt im Recht* (Käte Hamburger Kolleg Münster, 2023) 18–23.

[22] G Boissonade, *Histoire de la réserve héréditaire et de son influence morale et économique* (Guillaumin, 1873); G Boissonade, *Histoire des droits de l'époux survivant* (Guillaumin, 1873); G Boissonade, 'Législation comparée des droits du conjoint survivant' (1873) 3 *Revue de Législation ancienne & moderne française et étranger* 261. For recent work on Boissonade's role in the making of the Japanese Civil Code, see, among others, M Ikeda, *Bowasonādo to sono minpō* [*Boissonade and His Civil Law*], revised edn (Keiō Gijuku Daigaku Shuppankai, 2021).

[23] K Nishi, 'Iryūbun seido no saikentō' [Re-examination of the Compulsory Share System] (2007) 124 *Hōgaku kyōkai zasshi* 1854, 2090–92 and 2319–25.

[24] Articles 1130–46 ('Legal Portions') in the 1898 Civil Code; following the revision of the Code in 2018, the reserve system is currently provided in arts 1042–49.

[25] For comparisons between Japanese and Korean laws of the compulsory share, see S Pak, 'Ilbon yuryubun chedo ŭi doip kwa goyu ŭi sangsok pŏp wŏlli wa ŭi chohwa' [The Introduction of the Japanese Compulsory

In the Chosŏn dynasty, heirs were legally determined, and property could not be given to someone other than blood relatives.[26] The general practice was that the decedent's property was received by the ritual heir at the end of the three-year mourning period, who would divide and distribute it to other heirs. The ritual heir held significant control over the actual partition of the property. In this sense, Korea's traditional inheritance system could be distinguished from the division of family property in China. In China, a large portion of family land consolidated into corporate ancestral estates in order to minimise its disintegration from partible inheritance. Collective ritual initially served as a cement among lineage group members, but the function of lineage for ancestral worship gradually diminished.[27] In Korea, neo-Confucian rituals were taken far more seriously. The literati, self-styled guardians of Confucian philosophy, elevated ancestor worship to a religion. Seniority in line of descent, through which genealogical headship passed, carried extreme significance in family organisation, which dictated succession matters in the main line of lineage. The hierarchy in the blood relationship within the family was absolute. Scholars have long debated whether inheritance in Chosŏn predominantly took place in equal partition or whether a broad freedom of disposition was allowed. The law code provided for equal distribution, but many scholars are of the opinion that it applied only in the absence of a last will.[28] In either case, there was no reason to institutionalise a reserved share of the estate, because family property was not allowed to flow out of the family and the scope of those to receive inheritance was strictly limited to blood kin.

B. Compulsory Portion in Korean and Japanese Law

The most reliable descriptions of Chosŏn succession custom come from the *Customs Survey Report* compiled by the colonial government in 1910, which stated:

> Since there is no clear custom regarding the portion of inheritance to be received by the heir, when the inheritance was reduced through bequest or gift, the heir cannot claim a reduction of the gift or bequest, even if it is minimal compared with the total amount of intestate inheritance the heir would be entitled to. Therefore, the claim for the return of the reserved portion was also not accepted.[29]

The *Report* indicated that, in the case of succession in the stem line of descent within the lineage, 'the household head must leave all the property for the heir and cannot take such

Share System and Its Harmonisation with the Principles of the Traditional Inheritance Law] (2018) 58 *Pŏpsahak yŏngu* 237.

[26] P Pak, *Hanguk pŏpchesa ko* [*A Study of the History of Korean Law*] (Pŏmmunsa, 1983) 147.

[27] A recent study has argued that corporate lineages in China were the institutional means that local families adopted to make themselves suitable agents to the central government. See D Faure, *Emperor and Ancestor: State and Lineage in South China* (Stanford University Press, 2007). This explanation is applicable to the Korean situation as well, although the importance of ancestor veneration in lineages was much more prominent in Korea.

[28] See P Ch'oe and S Yi, '*Kyŏngguk taejŏn* kwa yuŏn ŭi chayu' [*Kyŏngguk taejŏn* and Testamentary Freedom] (2018) 59 *Seoul Taehakkyo Pŏphak* 1 (arguing 'Korea was a land which allowed freedom to make a will absolutely, even without requiring formalities in making a will as long as its authenticity was secured'). It appears, though, that while wills were prevalent, there was no development of the 'law' of the will. See n 11 above and accompanying text.

[29] Question # 180, Chōsen Sōtokufu, *Kanshū chōsa hōkokusho* (Chōsen Sōtokufu Torishirabe Kyoku, 1912 [1910]; reprint Ryukei Shosha, 1995). The 1912 edition is available at http://dl.ndl.go.jp/info:ndljp/pid/1028317.

measures as not letting it be succeeded by the heir in whole or in part (however, if there is no heir, this is waived)'.[30] The Chōsen Kōtō Hōin, the highest colonial court, ruled in 1930 that 'there is a custom among Koreans regarding the distribution of property in the event that the decedent dies without a will, but there is no legal share requirement as long as there is a will. When property is bequeathed through a will, there is no custom to annul the bequests or accept claims for their reduction'.[31] Close family member had no claim when they were disinherited.

In 1933, the Chōsen Kōtō Hōin abolished ritual succession as a jural act, declaring that it was a mere practice of acquiring an ethical status to perform ancestor ceremonies.[32] But the colonial courts continued to implement – as Chosŏn's custom – that property was exclusively inherited by the eldest son, who would retain about half of the property and divide the rest in equal shares to younger siblings when they got married and left the house. The presumption was that the new household head would split and distribute the property in an equitable manner. The system was based on the basic premise of Confucian ethics: the ritual successor, whose sacrosanct duty to perform ancestral rituals justified exclusive succession, had moral obligations to take care of other family members who were the descendants of the common ancestors. These long-held Confucian succession practices were preserved by postcolonial jurists.

Relying in part on the customs survey report that denied the existence of the notion of reserved share in traditional law, the drafters of the Korean Civil Code chose not to provide for a compulsory portion. There was deep scepticism about the ideology behind the reserved portion system in Japanese law – at least in the way it had been perceived by them. Many postcolonial Korean jurists viewed the legal reserve as the vestiges of feudalism.[33] In Meiji Japan, the measure was tightly connected to the continuation of the house property, just like the *réserve* system in late medieval and early modern France. Both societies, with their feudal past, placed strong emphasis on lineage property which was valued as a sociological foundation of the family. The desire to ensure the continuity of the family and patrimonial integrity is a universal phenomenon. In Korea too, social importance attached to family estate was paramount.[34] The uniqueness of the Korean case, then, resided in the fact that ritual purposes legitimated lineage properties, placing permanent injunction against alienation. The ritual heir inherited a disproportionate portion of the family property for the sake of performing ancestral ceremonies. The need to preserve family property and bequeath it to the heir only indirectly hinged on the desire to preserve the family wealth or business. In this context, the argument that a minimum share of inheritance was needed for the maintenance and support of the family members carried relatively little urgency because it was supposedly something intrinsically assumed in ritual succession. The whole apparatus stood on the ethical values of ancestor devotion and blood ties in kinship ideology.

[30] Ibid, Question # 166.

[31] Chōsen Kōtō Hōin, judgment of 25 February 1930, in *Chōsen Kōtō Hōin hanketsuroku*, vol 17, 64.

[32] Chōsen Kōtō Hōin, judgment of 3 March 1933, in *Hanketsuroku* (n 31), vol 20, 154–62.

[33] T Yi, 'Yuryubun pŏp ŭi kaejŏng panghyang' [Directions of the Revision of the Compulsory Share] (2019) 33 *Kajokpŏp yŏngu* 159.

[34] M Kim, 'Rites and Rights: Lineage Property and Law in Korea' (2020) 22 *L'Atelier du Centre de recherches historiques*, http://journals.openedition.org/acrh/11667.

In Japan, the house headship succession system was removed from the Civil Code in 1947, but the existing compulsory portion laws were preserved. In both *réserve coutumière* in late medieval France and *iryūbun* in Japan, the original focus was not on the preservation of the quantitative value of the property, but on the preservation of its qualitative *propres* or house assets. Gradually, its purpose shifted to protecting the exchange value (quantitative) rather than the use value (qualitative).[35] In Japan, the weakening of the concept of house property prompted the revision of the legal reserve laws to allow prior renunciation.[36] In return for relinquishing in advance the claim to the entitled portion, the rights holder could receive an amount equivalent in value. This change was reportedly introduced to compensate for the abolition of the house headship succession. Following the 2019 revision of the Civil Code, a person whose legally reserved portion has been encroached upon can now claim money equivalent to the infringed portion.[37]

Apart from backlash against the Japanese house system, there were genuine concerns among Korean legislators that the compulsory share system would cause undue restraints on individual property rights. The dominant doctrinal and jurisprudential consensus in the postliberation years was that the will of the testator must be respected. An often inadequately appreciated aspect of the Korean Civil Code is that it placed a strong emphasis on freedom of the testator and on property ownership in general. There were widespread sentiments during the legislative process that the suppression of the freedom to dispose of private property would conflict with the constitutional guarantee of the citizens' rights to property. Respect for testamentary freedom was seemingly consistent with the preservation of the Confucian patriarchal order. Above all, it is important to recall that the idea of the testator's prerogative and the absence of reserved portion in Korean ancient custom were solidly grounded in the moral duties of the ritual heir to support family members. Unlike in Japan, the concept of family property was not a major concern at the time of the making of the civil law. Instead, the Civil Code highlighted the notion of ritual propriety of the lineage and the discretion of the ritual successor, which were regarded as conforming to public policy (*ordre public*). The ruling of the Supreme Court of Korea in 1958, rendered shortly after the first Civil Code was proclaimed, summed it up: 'our country does not have a custom of the compulsory share' and the Civil Code excluding the reserved share system was reasonable as it 'goes against the trend of the times'.[38]

The belief that the duty to maintain and support the kin members was one of a moral rather than a legal nature was an idea suffused with Confucian precepts and patriarchal family ethics. The problem was that the household head, given broad control over property division, did not always live up to the expectations to fulfil his ethical obligations toward the family members who were excluded from inheritance. Succession disputes under colonial custom illustrate the difficulties. When the courts heard disputes over property

[35] T Takagi, 'Kindai-teki iryūbun seido josetsu: iryūbun no kachika o chūshin to shite' [Introduction to Modern Reserve System: Focusing on the Valuation of the Reserved Portion] (1957) 7 *Kōbe hōgaku zasshi* 230, 236.

[36] Civil Code (Japan) (1947), art 1043 (art 1049 of the Civil Code amended on 1 July 2019).

[37] Civil Code (Japan) (2019), art 1046(1).

[38] Supreme Court (Korea), 3 April 1958, 4290MinSang643. See S Yi, 'Yuryubun chedo ŭi kaesŏn pangan e kwanhan ippŏmnon jŏk yŏn'gu' [A Legislative Study on the Improvement of the Compulsory Share System], PhD dissertation (Chŏnbuk Taehakkyo, 2022) 171–72.

division in which succession had occurred before the Civil Code took effect in 1960, they were compelled to rule 'in accordance with the old civil law', that is, colonial custom.[39] The Supreme Court of Korea wrote in 1969:

> Even when the household head does not divide the property in equal shares and the division ratios become somewhat skewed, no objection can be raised. Normally the division of inheritance is done in kind, but where the division in kind is not feasible, it can take place through monetary conversion, as such is the custom according to the Civil Ordinance that was in force under the old civil law.

The household headship successor was expected to follow the conventional division ratio, but 'he is allowed some latitude' and 'which property should be given to which son is within his discretion'.[40]

With the Civil Code in 1960, the era of sole inheritance by the eldest son came to an end. Still, succession laws remained tightly tied to gender, marriage status or status as the next household head, favouring male heirs to the disadvantage of other heirs. Under the civil law, the new household head, the eldest son, received an additional half of the intestate share; the share of female heirs, including the wife, was one half of the male heirs. A married daughter received one-quarter of a male heir's portion.[41] The continuing assumption was that the members of the family were to receive minimum economic protection from the head of the household, but the absence of a compulsory portion could leave the surviving spouse and daughters in a precarious state.

The gender-discriminatory inheritance laws were the subject of much grievance. The Supreme Court wrote as late as 1973:

> When a head of household dies, all his property is transferred to his heir, and the second son and other heirs below him have the right to claim the distribution of property within the scope of the existing property against the household head, but they have no right to claim property beyond that. Since they have no right to claim, they do not have a legal interest in inheritance property.[42]

It was in this situation that women's rights advocates pushed for a revision of the Civil Code to incorporate the compulsory portion system. Guaranteeing reserved shares for women was viewed as a critical step toward the goal of abolishing the household headship system, in which the eldest male exercised preponderant power over other family members. In December 1977, the National Assembly passed the bill to introduce compulsory share into law, to take effect on 1 January 1979.[43]

[39] The Korean Civil Code officially replaced Japanese codes and declared the retroactive effect of its provisions, but it provided that legal acts that had taken place before 1 January 1960, which was the date that the Civil Code came into effect, were not affected by the new law: Supplementary Provision, art 2. The Code specifically pronounced that the matters of succession would continue to be governed by preexisting laws: Supplementary Provision, art 25, sec 1.

[40] Supreme Court (Korea), 25 November 1969, 67Mŭ25.

[41] Civil Code (Korea) (1960), art 1009.

[42] Supreme Court (Korea), 12 June 1973, 70Ta2575. Similar judgments: 23 December 1975, 75Ta38; 19 January 1988, 87TaK'a1877; 30 October 1990, 90TaK'a 23301; 18 November 1994, 94Ta36599.

[43] Civil Code (Korea), arts 1112–18 ('Legal reserve in inheritance').

C. Legislative and Jurisprudential Adaptations

The discussion above shows that the main consideration in enacting compulsory share laws was different between Korea and Japan. In Japan, there was a broad consensus on the need to prevent the loss of family property, such as businesses handed down through generations. Designating a portion of estate and dividing it equally among the heirs were seen as a means to maintain the house system and prevent the fragmentation of property. It was a compromise between the idea that one should be able to dispose of one's property freely and the conventional belief that property should be left in the house as much as possible. In Korea, preserving family property, including continuing family business, was not the reason for implementing the guaranteed share laws. The paradox was, then, that the Korean system of compulsory portion borrowed substantially from the old form of Japanese law from almost 100 years earlier, instituted under dissimilar considerations and circumstances.[44] Certain problems lay in wait.

The Japanese system, based on the house succession, aimed to resolve disputes between the house successor and a third party who was not the heir. By contrast, disputes in Korea took place predominantly among co-heirs. The majority of the ever-increasing legal proceedings concerned situations where the testator treated male and female heirs differently or disproportionately favoured the eldest son. When the reserve system was inserted into the Civil Code in 1979, the legislators did not provide for the measure of value reduction.[45] Japanese law allowed the advance waiver of the rights to the reserved share, but a similar mechanism did not become part of Korean law.

Compulsory share in Korea has operated in such a way as to grant the heirs rights akin to property ownership to a portion of the estate. Whether legal share is construed as the right to property or is treated as the right to claim in obligations has important differences.[46] In the former case, the original property must be returned to the right's holder at the expression of his or her intention to request the return of the reserved portion, which is at the expense of the freedom of the decedent to dispose of property.[47] The general doctrinal opinion is that it would be reasonable to presume that those who hold the rights to compulsory share are more interested in acquiring the economic value of the inherited property than in securing the original property at inheritance. In Korea, nevertheless, the return of the original property is the rule and compensation for its value an exception. This means that, when the property had been transferred through gift or bequest prior to the exercise of the right to claim the return of the reserved portion, putting such a right into effect could void the transaction, seriously jeopardising the interests of the transferee.

The range of people entitled to the legal reserve in Korean law is quite broad. Under the current law, legal share is allowed for lineal descendants and spouses (each entitled to one-half of the statutory share of inheritance), lineal ascendants (one-third), and brothers and

[44] Pak (n 25).

[45] The Meiji Civil Code provided that value reimbursement could be made in all cases (art 1144).

[46] In Roman law, the claim for the return of the reserved portion was treated not as a guarantee of the right to inheritance, but as a simple monetary claim.

[47] Article 1115 of the Korean Civil Code only stipulates that a claim for the return of the property can be made if there is a shortage in the reserved portion.

sisters (one-third).[48] This is in contrast to the Japanese law that does not entitle brothers and sisters to a compulsory share. Inclusion as in Korea of not only the direct ascendants but also the siblings has equivalents in few other countries.[49] This is but one example of the still-strong presence of Confucian tradition emphasising kinship relations. In April 2022, a bill was introduced in the National Assembly to exclude siblings from those covered under reserved portion. Most scholars expect the revision of the law to take place, but they predict that debate on the compulsory share laws will continue.[50] As late as 2022, specific compulsory share provisions were challenged on the ground that they infringed upon testamentary freedom in violation of the Constitution.[51] Several constitutional petitions contesting the system are pending at the Constitutional Court.

The topic of compulsory share is at the centre of ongoing discussion worldwide. Many argue that there is no convincing reason to restrict the testator's prerogative so as to entitle family members to an obligatory share of the estate regardless of their economic needs.

For our purposes, it suffices to note that different societies place different levels of normative values on the regulation of social and economic affairs, which shape their inheritance laws. Many laws in Korea have taken on a dimension of national identity, with attendant emphasis on the country's historical and cultural legitimacy, but it is essential to avoid the danger of reifying national stereotypes.

III. Conclusion

The history of compulsory portion illustrates the dialectical quality of Korean law. In the post-war years, both Japan and South Korea have had to deal with the problems of mediating between traditional Confucian tenets and modern civil law principles. Today they share aspects of their laws and legal systems more closely than any other country. Yet, consideration of public policy behind the reserve system differed in Japan and in Korea. The absence of compulsory portion was not viewed as contrary to morality and public order in traditional Korean society; the system was legitimated in modern Korea in terms of gender equality. In sum, its evolution in Korea bears witness as much to the imprints of outside laws through legal transfer as to the equally powerful internal social and ideological transition of law. A distinctive process of acculturation was at work by law-makers, legal scholars and

[48] Civil Code (Korea), art 1112.

[49] Article 1042 of the current Japanese Civil Code allows the compulsory share of one third for a direct ascendant and one-half for all others, like art 2303 of the German Civil Code. In Switzerland, the old clause recognising one-quarter of the statutory share of inheritance for siblings was abolished in 1984. Under the current Swiss Civil Code (amended in January 2023), the descendants and the spouse (including the same-sex partner), but not the parents, of the deceased are entitled to a compulsory share. The French Code, amended in 2006, also excluded lineal ascendants from the protected holders.

[50] Siblings can succeed only when the deceased did not leave the spouse, direct descendants or parents; even in such cases, siblings cannot, under the proposed bill, claim the reserved share. The Ministry of Justice reportedly considered the exclusion of the parents as well, but this was deleted from the bill of April 2022.

[51] The Supreme Court rejected the claim that the laws violated arts 23(1) and 37(2) of the Constitution. Supreme Court (Korea), 10 February 2022, 2020Ta250873. Constitution (Korea) (1987), art 23(1): 'The right of property of all citizens shall be guaranteed. The contents and limitations thereof shall be determined by Act'; art 37(2): 'The freedoms and rights of citizens may be restricted by Act only when necessary for national security, the maintenance of law and order or for public welfare'.

judges, across the pre-modern Confucian legal tradition and modern civil law originating from colonial custom and law.

The development of Korean law has layers of complexity, as efforts to bring Korean law out of the shadows of foreign influence have been overcast with nationalistic sentiments. Confucian law was criticised for its role in upholding discriminatory social relations, while colonial law was denounced for being an instrument of imperial domination and ethnic discrimination. Modern civil law introduced by Japan eroded confidence in Confucian legal tradition, but colonial rule spurred the idea of 'our Korean law', harking back to indigenous culture and law. For some, Confucianism was the vestige of a bygone era, reactionary cultural remnants; for others, it was the embodiment of traditional values that needed to be shielded from the forces of modernism brought on by colonialism.

Confucian-inspired laws and customs still carry an immense normative force in society. Korea is the only place in the world where a substantial percentage of ordinary citizens perform ancestor memorial services in private households several times a year. The ritual property succession laws attest to the uniquely Korean sensibility of filial piety, which remains at the basis of both ethical obligations and cultural pride. The vestiges of Confucian injunctions for moral rectification are found not only in civil law but also in penal law. For example, Korean criminal laws prohibit the filing of a criminal complaint against one's lineal ascendants such as parents and grandparents.[52] The Criminal Code also imposes enhanced punishment for crimes (such as murder and assault) committed against lineal ascendants.[53] Neither the current Chinese nor Japanese penal codes have analogous laws.[54] Perceived as the expression of the nation's identity, these laws have so far survived constitutional challenges of equality and proportionality, as the court ruled that they promoted the legitimate legislative purpose of filial piety.

Incidentally, Max Weber (1864–1920) ascribed the absence of 'rational spirit' in Chinese law to the all-comprising and all-pervading Confucian tenet of filial piety. According to him, 'the duties of a Chinese Confucian always consisted of piety toward concrete people whether living or dead, and toward those who were close to him through their position in life', and that this 'adherence to unconditional discipline' discouraged the rise of individual rights.[55] His Protestant bias notwithstanding, Weber rather perceptively pointed out that concerns for one's own family and ancestors – what he called 'family egoism' – suppressed the development of private law in East Asia. Weber did not mention Korea in

[52] Criminal Procedure (Korea), arts 224 and 235. The constitutionality of art 224 was challenged in 2011. Five justices found it unconstitutional, while four justices found it constitutional. In Korean law, the declaration of unconstitutionality of a statute by the Constitutional Court requires a minimum of six votes, so the constitutional contest failed. Constitutional Court (Korea), 24 February 2011, 2008Hŏn-Pa56. See M Kim, 'Confucianism That Confounds: Constitutional Jurisprudence on Filial Piety in Korea' in S Kim (ed), *Confucianism, Law and Democracy in Contemporary Korea* (Rowman & Littlefield, 2015) 62–64.

[53] Criminal Code (Korea), art 250, and arts 257–60. The constitutionality of art 259(2), imposing aggravated punishment for assaults of lineal ascendants, was challenged in 2002, and that of art 250(2), imposing aggravated punishment for the murder of lineal ascendants, in 2013. Each law was upheld. Constitutional Court (Korea), 28 March 2002, 2000Hŏn-Pa53; Constitutional Court (Korea), 25 July 2013, 2011Hŏn-Pa267.

[54] Japan had aggravated penalty provisions, but abolished them in 1995, in the aftermath of the famous *Aizawa* case in 1973, Supreme Court (Japan), Shōwa 45(A) 1310, 4 April 1973. Taiwan has laws similar to those in Korea: punishment is increased up to one-half – for example, 15 years instead of 10 years.

[55] M Weber, 'Die Wirtschaftsethik der Weltreligionen: Konfuzianismus und Taoismus' in *Gesammelte Aufsätze zur Religionssoziologie*, vol 1, translated as *The Religion of China: Confucianism and Taoism* (Free Press, 1951) 158 and 236.

his writings; it is doubtful whether he was aware of differences between China and Korea. If he had based his discussion on Confucianism in Korea, his thesis may have carried more credibility. At any rate, it is important to stress that historical Confucianism in Korea was not the same as historical Confucianism in China. Coercive commands of 'muscular Confucianism' for moral regeneration in traditional Korea evolved to neither 'Confucian fascism' nor, conversely, 'Confucian communism'.[56]

Finally, the process of *Koreanisierung* of Japanese law in the twentieth century can be juxtaposed with the *Japanisierung* of European law in the nineteenth century. In both cases, what set the dialectical process in motion were the forces of persuasion. Had colonial law been viewed unreasonable and unprofitable, it would not have taken root in postcolonial Korea. This chapter has argued that a successful legal borrowing takes place when the new law is internally accepted by those who are subject to it. Korean law has the potential in the twenty-first century to serve as a model and inspiration for laws in other jurisdictions to help meet their own local needs. A powerful process of legal diffusion continues in East Asia, which calls for a more fluid and dynamic approach.

[56] See JB Palais, *Confucian Statecraft and Korean Institutions: Yu Hyŏngwŏn and the Late Chosŏn Dynasty* (University of Washington Press, 1996); F Wakeman, Jr , 'A Revisionist View of the Nanjing Decade: Confucian Fascism' (1997) 150 *China Quarterly* 395; DA Bell, 'From Communism to Confucianism: Changing Discourses on China's Political Future' in *China's New Confucianism: Politics and Everyday Life in a Changing Society* (Princeton University Press, 2010).

5

Influence of Japanese Law on Taiwanese Law

YING-HSIN TSAI

I. Introduction

This chapter introduces the formation and subsequent influence of Japanese law on the Taiwanese civil law. The close relationship between Japan and Taiwan stems from three important factors. First, the territories are in close geographical proximity to each other. Second, both use the Chinese-character cultural circle. Third, from a historical context, Taiwan was under Japanese rule from 1895 to 1945. Based on these factors, Taiwan's society, culture, economy and legal system have long been influenced by Japan. Japan's influence, in turn, was itself influenced by European (mainly German) civil law to a considerable extent, because Japan adopted this civil law at home and consequently also exported it to its colonial territory.

Taiwan's legal system, however, was not only influenced by Japan and German law. First, as a part of China prior to Japanese colonisation and following the Second World War, Chinese law has left its imprint on Taiwan. After Japanese colonial rule, the Republic of China (ROC) implemented all the statutory laws on the mainland; like Japanese law, Chinese law was itself partly a product of adoption from European legal rules, taking ideas from the German, but also Swiss legal traditions. Taiwan's other influence came after the Second World War, when US company laws were taken as models.

Significantly, the influence of the various systems of law in Taiwan was – even when the foreign ruling powers insisted upon the rules – particularly deep because of the impact of the Taiwanese legal educators. By the end of the Second World War, the development of some special areas of civil law was influenced by American law due to the alliance between Taiwan and the US. Yet, even if Japan's political influence on Taiwan was not as strong as that of the US, the Japanese civil law still wielded a significant influence over Taiwan's civil law. This is because most of the first-generation Taiwanese legal scholars after the war came from China and were deeply influenced by the pre-war Japanese jurisprudence – itself based on the European civil law system – that had been dominant in China at the time. Furthermore, some Taiwanese legal scholars went to Japan to study law during Japanese colonial rule. Many years later, these second-generation Taiwanese legal scholars directly introduced post-war European civil law systems and theories from Germany, while continuing to import ideas from Japan. With many students studying abroad or learning from foreign professors, the adopted rules were internalised and became the basis for Taiwan's own adaptations. Thus, the theory and practice of the Taiwanese civil law were still influenced by the thinking and operation methods of the European civil law system, especially German law. Even today, the Taiwanese civil law scholars who have studied in Japan serve as a bridge, introducing the theories of the Japanese civil law to interpret Taiwan's civil law.

The relationship between Taiwan and Japan's legal systems thus presents a special case of adoption, adaptation and exportation by one (Japan) onto another system (Taiwan's) that itself adapted the incoming law and mixed it with both its own traditions and the influences imitated and adapted both by and from other (mainly Chinese, but also Swiss and US) legal systems.

The following section explains the different influences throughout Taiwan's modern history. Many details have had to be left out due to space constraints, but the complexities are, we hope, apparent.

II. The Early Period of Japanese Colonial Rule (1895–1922)

Before coming into Taiwan, Japan had adopted a large number of Western legal systems and actively formulated a civil code in their image.[1] In 1873, the Japanese Ministry of Justice recruited Professor Gustave Boissonade from the University of Paris and began to formulate the civil code in 1880. This version of the civil law was compiled using the French civil law format. However, due to a controversy over the appropriate model for a civil code in 1890, Japanese scholars who majored in British legal systems thought that French civil law was not the only civil law model that should be followed; rather, they believed that British and German laws should be also considered. Therefore, in 1893, the Japanese government decided to postpone the implementation of the civil law on which it had been working.[2] Subsequently, the Japanese government formed a code investigation committee to compile and modify the current version of the Japanese Civil Code. The compilation of this new civil code was based on the *Pandekten* system of general principles, rights *in rem*, obligations, family and inheritance, while abandoning the adoption of the institutional system. The new civil law became effective on 16 July 1898.

During Japan's first period of colonial rule over Taiwan (1895–1922), the Japanese Imperial Government chose to respect Taiwan's local customs by not fully applying this new civil law to Taiwanese society immediately. This decision can be attributed to the fact that the Taiwanese civilian armed forces fought against the regular Japanese army. As they did so, the Imperial Government realised that the Taiwanese people were different from the Japanese in terms of race and culture, so it decided to adopt a 'special rule' policy.[3] In other words, the Imperial Government decided to use Taiwanese customary law as the applicable law for handling local civil matters.

[1] T-C Chen, *Taiwan Civil Law and the Modernization of Japanese Contract Law* (National Taiwan University Law Series, 2011), 332.

[2] ibid 337.

[3] T-S Wang, 'The Reception of Continental European Civil Law in Taiwan: From the Transition of Japan and China to Direct Adoption' (2017) 68(4) *Law Monthly* 1, 3.

In November 1895, Taiwan's Governor-General announced the 'Taiwan Residents' Civil Procedure Order' by military order. Article 2 specifically stipulated that 'judges are allowed to adjudicate lawsuits according to local customs and legal principles'. In 1896, the Japanese Imperial Government first enacted the Six-Three Act, which endowed Taiwan's Governor-General with legislative powers. Two years later, the Governor-General promulgated the 'Civil and Commercial Laws' stipulating that Taiwanese residents and Qing people involved in civil and commercial matters should follow local customs and legal principles. Meanwhile, the civil and commercial matters of the Japanese living in Taiwan, as well as those of foreigners other than the Qing people, were governed by the provisions of Japanese civil and commercial laws, except for one provision: all civil matters involving land rights were still handled in accordance with local customs in Taiwan.

On the one hand, to accord Taiwanese customs a position in positive law, Taiwan's Governor-General formulated the Taiwan Civil Order, which recognised Taiwan's existing customs in terms of positive law and used existing customs to regulate various legal relationships in Taiwan society. It also re-affirmed the notion that the civil matters of the Taiwanese and Qing people should be handled in accordance with Taiwan's customs. Furthermore, the Taiwan Civil Order stated that the civil and commercial matters of Japanese people living in Taiwan, as well as those of foreigners other than the Qing people, should be covered by the Japanese civil law, except for land rights.

On the other hand, with the goal of understanding Taiwan's civil customs, the Japanese Imperial Government established a temporary Taiwan Old Customs Investigation Committee in 1901, under the supervision of Shinpei Goto, the Civil Affairs Chief of the Taiwan Governor-General's office. Santaro Okamatsu, a civil law scholar who had studied in Germany, was in charge of investigating the legal customs of Taiwan and the Qing Dynasty. The results of this investigation were published in a report entitled 'Taiwan's Private Law' (1909–11), which was divided into four parts in terms of layout: real property, personnel, personal property, and commercial affairs and obligations. This structure differed from the five parts adopted by Japan's new civil law (general principles, rights *in rem*, obligations, family and inheritance), although it had similarities. For one thing, both were the result of systematisation based on German conceptual jurisprudence and used the core concept of 'rights' in continental jurisprudence to typify various legal relationships. The 'Taiwan's Private Law' report had consciously cooperated with the classification standard of the Japanese civil law.[4] This meant that the 'Taiwan Private Law' report compiled by Shinpei Goto used the concept of European law to explain the civil customs of the Taiwanese people during the Qing Dynasty. The fact that the report analysed and systematised Taiwan's civil customs during the Qing Dynasty was significant in confirming the old customs of this period through the court to achieve the status of customary law.[5]

At the beginning of the twentieth century, the Qing Dynasty also hired the Japanese scholar Yoshimasa Matsuoka to supervise the drafting of a Civil Code. In 1911, he completed the 'Great Qing Civil Law Draft' (hereinafter 'the Draft'), which included five volumes: general principles; obligations; rights *in rem*; family; and inheritance. The Draft was largely an imitation of the civil laws of Germany and Japan.

[4] ibid 5.
[5] T-S Wang, *General Discussion on Taiwanese Legal History*, 3rd edn (Angle Publishing, 2009) 281.

When the ROC government was formally established (1912), the Beiyang Government (1912–1928) proposed the 'Second Civil Law Draft', completed in 1925. The Second Draft maintained the five volumes of the original version. The contents of general principles and rights *in rem* in the two drafts were quite similar, while the obligation volume of the latter version adopted the Swiss debt law. Moreover, the two volumes of family and inheritance of the second draft are partly incorporated into the precedents of Chinese courts.[6]

When the National government established by the Kuomintang unified China in 1928, it was eager to complete the enactment of the civil law. Therefore, the general provisions of the civil law were promulgated and implemented in 1929, the obligations and rights *in rem* were promulgated in 1930 and implemented in 1931, and the rules on family and inheritance were promulgated in 1930 and became effective in 1931.[7] The National government completed the formulation and implementation of the civil law in such a short time based on the 'Great Qing Civil Law Draft' of the previous Qing Dynasty and the subsequent 'Second Civil Law Draft' under the Beiyang Government.

The civil law implemented by the National government did not completely imitate the layout style of the Japanese civil law; rather, it had exactly the same layout style as the German civil law. Furthermore, it is also very similar to the German civil law in terms of its content related to regulations. Nevertheless, there are still some differences between this civil law and its German counterpart. The most important feature is that the Kuomintang's civil law referred to the provisions of the Swiss debt law and some provisions of the Japanese civil law. For example, the civil law implemented by the National government adopted the integration rather than the separation of the civil and commercial laws adopted by Germany and Japan.

The reason why this civil law adopted the integration of civil and commercial laws is because the 'Second Civil Law Draft' imitated the Swiss debt law in terms of the integration of civil and commercial laws. For this reason, civil law incorporates many contents belonging to the norms of commercial law into civil law. (Indeed, until now, the provisions of Taiwan's civil law have almost inherited those of the Swiss debt law rather than those of the German civil law.) In addition, the method of identifying real estate in the Taiwanese civil law adopts the method stipulated in the Japanese civil law (ie, land and buildings are identified as different objects of real rights) instead of the German civil law, which regards buildings as an important part of the land.[8]

III. The Latter Period of Japanese Occupation (1923–45)

In the latter period of Japanese colonial rule in Taiwan (1923–45), the Japanese Imperial Government adopted the 'inland law extension doctrine' for Taiwan's rule policy. This doctrine refers to the political measures adopted by Kenjiro Den, the first Japanese civil governor of Taiwan, to resist the national sentiments of self-determination and democracy

[6] Wang (n 3) 9.
[7] ibid.
[8] Chen (n 1) 340.

that permeated the world after the First World War. Instead, the Japanese civil and commercial laws that had been adapted from the European civil law system were made directly applicable to Taiwanese society. The Japanese government promulgated 'Civil Laws Concerning Implementation in Taiwan' in 1922, which designated 19 types of Japanese civil, commercial and related laws to be directly implemented in Taiwan. While this meant that Taiwan's existing customs should no longer have the effect of positive law, local Taiwanese customs were nevertheless still applied in matters of family and inheritance.[9]

Regarding property law, under the Japanese civil law, it was still officially implemented in Taiwan, representing the way in which European civil law took root in Taiwan. In fact, Taiwan-born legal scholars played an important role in deepening the reach of European civil law-influenced the Japanese civil law in Taiwanese society. In the early days of the Japanese occupation, Taiwanese youth with Japanese language skills travelled to Tokyo to study law, their numbers gradually increasing in the 1920s.[10] The law these Taiwanese youths learned was a version of the Japanese civil law inherited from the European civil law system before the war. In addition, upon the establishment of the Faculty of Arts and Political Science at Taipei Imperial University in 1928 by the Japanese Imperial Government, a small number of Taiwanese students were able to take up law in Taiwan. These students were under the tutelage of professors who were mostly Japanese scholars. Thus, the legal education taught by these professors was exactly the same as that taught by the law departments of universities in Japan.

Regarding family and inheritance matters, these were still settled by Taiwanese customs during this period. Nevertheless, the customary laws of Taiwanese family and inheritance matters were also somehow influenced by European civil law. This can be explained by the fact that in the early days of Japanese colonial rule, almost all the judges of the colonial courts were, in principle, Japanese. These Japanese judges, intending to assimilate the Taiwanese, brought in many relative inheritance provisions in the Japanese civil law when identifying Taiwanese customary laws in individual cases. Through the exercise of judicial power, the Imperial Government brought concepts or institutions, such as parental rights, guardianship, kinship meetings, individualistic marriage, adoption, succession by subrogation, limited succession and abandonment of succession, into Taiwanese society.[11]

IV. The Kuomintang Takeover of Taiwan up to the Present

A. The Early Post-Second World War Years: Chinese Civil Law with Japanese Influence

On 25 October 1945, the Kuomintang came to Taiwan and officially implemented the civil law of the ROC in Taiwan. This civil law was no stranger to the Taiwanese, because during

[9] Chen (n 1) 334.

[10] T-S Wang, *Legal Reform in Taiwan under Japanese Colonial Rule*, 2nd edn (University of Washington Press, 2014) 370.

[11] ibid 371.

the period of Japanese colonial rule, the Japanese Imperial Government had expanded the scope of enforcement of the Japanese civil law, thereby also transplanting European law systems from mainland Japan to colonial Taiwan. Thus, the Taiwanese were already familiar with the relevant systems of the European civil law system before 1945. Given that the civil law of the ROC was mainly based on German civil law, it was similar to the Japanese civil law to a certain extent. After this civil law was implemented in Taiwan, it was naturally integrated into the lives of the Taiwanese. In addition, when Japan ruled Taiwan, it left accurate household registration and cadastral records for the latter, providing a solid foundation for the implementation of the civil law of the ROC in Taiwan. This also introduced the Japanese style of revolving mortgages to Taiwan – a system that was retained until after the Kuomintang came to power.[12]

Nevertheless, some issues caused by differences in legal norms still emerged during the transition from the Japanese civil law to the application of the ROC civil law in Taiwanese society. The change of real rights in the Japanese civil law, for example, did not adopt the principle of personal property delivery and real estate registration effective in German civil law; instead, it adopted the doctrine of the French legal system (especially the doctrine of confrontation of real estate registration for the transaction of real estate) and did not take registration as a validation requirement. Under this premise, during the period of Japanese colonial rule, if there was a change in property rights in real estate transactions, as long as the parties concerned had the intention of transferring ownership, the real estate ownership would be transferred and would not need registration for validity. Sometimes even the owner listed in the registration book (who may not be the real owner under the registration provisions) would be directly listed as the owner in the ROC law. This affected the civil rights of many Taiwanese people at that time.[13]

When the Kuomintang government came to Taiwan, the ROC civil law continued to be implemented in Taiwan, where it became known as the 'Taiwan civil law'. As mentioned previously, although the Taiwanese civil law was mainly based on the German civil law, it was still largely influenced by the Japanese civil law. Aside from the fact that the late Qing government hired Japanese scholar Yoshimasa Matsuoka to oversee the drafting of the 'Great Qing Civil Law', the number of overseas students studying in Japan who were sent by the Qing government exceeded the number of overseas students studying in other countries. This can be explained by the fact that there were far more legal scholars in Taiwan who were proficient in Japanese than in German. Moreover, in 1946 the Kuomintang government re-named Taipei Imperial University (which was established during Japanese colonial rule) the 'National Taiwan University'. Most of the law professors were Taiwanese with Bachelor of Laws degrees from Tokyo Imperial University. Therefore, these Japanese-educated Taiwanese legal scholars naturally quoted Japanese civil law theories to teach and interpret the Taiwanese civil law.[14]

Japan also offered a one-year legal and political course for Chinese students. Of these, the more famous course was the one taught by Professor Kenjiro Ume, an authoritative Japanese civil law scholar from Hosei University. In addition, China and Japan belong to

[12] T-C Chen, 'Taiwan's Civil Law in a Century' (2010) 186 *Taiwan Law Review* 181.
[13] Wang (n 3) 10.
[14] Wang (n 5) 224–38.

the same culture guided by Chinese characters. Thus, for Chinese civil law scholars who aimed to understand or explain the contents of this civil law, the easiest way to interpret its provisions was to translate Japanese civil law theories. Therefore, civil law scholars at that time often ignored the differences between the civil law systems of Taiwan and Japan, and completely transplanted Japanese civil law theories.

B. The 1950s to the Present: US Company Law but Mainly German and Japanese Influences

Beginning in the 1950s, due to changes in the political situation in Taiwan, the US and Taiwan – both fighting against communist forces – established a close military and economic alliance, through which the latter received economic assistance from the former from 1951 to 1965.[15] In this way, the US considerably influenced Taiwan's economic and trade law system, as well as the development of special civil laws in Taiwan. For example, when the Company Law, a special civil law, was revised in 1966, it was influenced by the concept of the 'separation of ownership and control' emphasised by American law, which strengthened the function of the board of directors. Furthermore, in 1968, Taiwan's civil law imitated American law to formulate securities law.

However, despite this fact, the German and Japanese civil laws still held greater influence over Taiwan's civil law. The possible reason behind this is that, after the 1960s, many Taiwanese legal scholars who studied in Germany and Japan returned to Taiwan to teach. Although the number of Taiwanese legal scholars who studied in Japan was not as large as those who studied in Germany, many continued to refer to the Japanese civil law theories to interpret Taiwan's civil law.

Regrettably, since the 1990s, the number of the Taiwanese civil law scholars studying in Japan has dropped sharply, and the influence of Japanese civil law theories on Taiwan's civil law has gradually declined.

V. Conclusion

There is no doubt that the Japanese civil law has influenced the development of the Taiwanese civil law over the past 30 years. From a historical context, Japan has undoubtedly contributed to Taiwan's contact with and acceptance of the European legal system, as well as to the modernisation of Taiwan's legal system. From the early period of Japanese colonial rule, the Japanese Imperial Government stabilised its rule over Taiwan by respecting Taiwan's customs and endowing them with the status of positive law. During this time, the Imperial Government exercised legislative and judicial power to incorporate the concepts of the European civil law system into Taiwanese customs.

In the latter period of its rule, the Imperial Government changed the way it governed Taiwan. Except for the part wherein inheritance still respected Taiwan's customs, it directly

[15] W-T Chen, *Law and Economic Miracle: Interaction between Taiwan's Development and Economic Laws after WWII* (Angle Publishing, 2000) 110–18.

applied the Japanese civil law, thereby allowing the Taiwanese to experience European continental law for the first time. When the Kuomintang government took over Taiwan in 1945, it took the civil law implemented in China to Taiwan for implementation.

Meanwhile, the civil law of the ROC was mainly inherited from the German civil law, while some provisions were inherited from the Swiss debt law. This civil law was somewhat similar to the Japanese civil law that was in force in Taiwan before 1945, facilitating easier adaptation among the Taiwanese. Furthermore, Japanese-educated Taiwanese legal scholars frequently used Japanese civil law theories to explain the Taiwanese civil law. In this way, the Japanese civil law continued to have an indirect influence on the Taiwanese civil law. However, such an influence has gradually weakened over the years as the number of Taiwanese legal scholars studying in Japan has decreased.

At the same time, there is another trend to which we should pay attention. After the lifting of martial law in Taiwan in the 1990s, Taiwanese society became more democratic than ever before. Based on this context, the contents of the Taiwanese civil law regarding family and inheritance have been revised many times to pursue gender equality and respect for same-sex marriage. These changes have made Japanese legal scholars rethink their position regarding the need for changes in Japanese civil law.[16]

[16] K Suzuki, *Birth of Taiwan's Same-Sex Marriage Act* (Nippon Hyoron Sha, 2022).

PART 2

Rules on Private International Law

6

On the Process of China's Private International Law in the Past Decade

JIN HUANG

Over the past 10 years, the theory and practice of private international law in China have undergone a remarkable progress. Three issues deserve particular notice.

The Law of the People's Republic of China on the Application of Law for Foreign-Related Civil Relationships is a milestone in the history of Private International Law in China. On 28 October 2010, the Standing Committee of the National People's Congress (NPC) in China examined and adopted the Law of the People's Republic of China on the Application of Law for Foreign-Related Civil Relationships (LALFCR, or 'the Law'), which came into force on 1 April 2011.[1] The LALFCR consists of eight chapters (and 52 articles): namely General Provisions, Civil Subjects, Marriage and Family, Inheritance, Property Rights, Creditor's Rights, Intellectual Property Rights and Supplementary Provisions.

The passage and implementation of the LALFCR is of significance in the history of private international law in China. First, the LALFCR put an end to a history characterised by no separate and unified law on the application of law for foreign-related civil relationships.

In the history of China, the then-Government of the Republic of China promulgated a Regulation on the Application of Law in 1918.[2] The Regulation had seven chapters divided into 27 articles, and was the first statute of private international law in China, as well as one of the earliest statutes in the field of private international law in the world. The Regulation was repealed after the founding of the People's Republic of China. In more than 60 years, there had been no separate statute of private international law in Mainland China. This was not compatible to the status of the country as a major power, and failed to meet the needs of its reform and opening-up and participation in global governance. The formulation of the LALFCR ended this history.

The LALFCR was designed to meet the needs of the country's opening up to the outside world and the ever-expanding international civil and commercial exchanges. It sums up China's own experience of more than 30 years of reform and opening-up, drawing on international practices and focusing on the issues concerning the application of law. This reduces controversy surrounding the frequently recurring foreign-related civil disputes.

[1] Full text available at www.gov.cn/flfg/2010-10/28/content_1732970.htm.

[2] See H Ma, *Private International Law* (4th edn, in Chinese) (Hanlu Publishing House, 2022) 47; W Chen, *Comparative Private International Law* (in Chinese) (Law Press, 2022) 88.

In addition to general provisions, the LALFCR has laid down systematic provisions on the subject of foreign civil relations, marriage and family, inheritance, property rights, creditor's rights and intellectual property rights. It is an important achievement in the construction of China's foreign-related legal system, as well as an improvement of the socialist legal system with Chinese characteristics.

Second, the LALFCR is to some extent an innovation of China's system concerning the application of law for foreign-related civil relationships. In the process of drafting and enacting the LALFCR, drafters paid more attention to summarising the experience in foreign-related civil legislation, justice, law enforcement and legal services over the past 30 years of reform. They were open to incorporating the viable rules and practices, and to drawing lessons from the other countries' successful experience in the formulation of private international law legislation and international conventions. They referred to international practices and the latest developments in private international law. At the same time, efforts were made in light of China's conditions to innovate in the application of law of foreign-related civil relationships. The innovations include new structures, new principles and new rules:

(1) In terms of the structure of the LALFCR, the 'personal law' parts (the three chapters 'civil subjects', 'marriage and family' and 'inheritance') are placed before 'property law' and 'debt law', reflecting the people-first orientation, highlighting the subjectivity and rights of people, and optimising the structure of the legislative system.
(2) The LALFCR adopts the principle of the most significant connection as the principle for the application of law in all foreign-related civil relationships that are not provided for by the LALFCR. This avoids loopholes in the application of law for foreign-related civil relationships.[3]
(3) The LALFCR also adopts the law of habitual residence as the personal law, supplemented by the law of the country of nationality.[4] Generally speaking, traditionally, the civil law countries adopt the law of the country of nationality (the national law) as the personal law, and the common law countries adopt the law of domicile law as the personal law. In order to coordinate the differences between the two legal systems in personal law, the Hague Conference on Private International Law adopted the law of habitual residence as the personal law in many Hague Conventions on Private International Law. This approach is one of the reasons for the success of these conventions. China has bravely and firmly adopted the law of habitual residence as the personal law in domestic legislation, which is outstanding and noticeable.
(4) The LALFCR expands the scope of the choice of law by parties involved in foreign-related civil relationships, which also broadens the scope of application of the principle of parties' autonomy.[5] Taking into account the fact that parties have the right to dispose of civil rights, and in light of the international trend that parties have expanding possibilities for choosing the applicable law on their own, the LALFCR stipulates that parties

[3] Article 2, paragraph 2 of the LALFCR: 'If there are no provisions in this Law or other laws on the application of any laws concerning foreign-related civil relations, the laws which have the closest relation with this foreign-related civil relation shall apply.'

[4] See Chapters 2, 3, 4 and 6.

[5] See Chapters 2, 3, 5, 6 and 7.

can choose the applicable law in the fields of marriage and family, property rights, creditors' rights and intellectual property rights.

(5) For the first time, the LALFCR stipulates that the mandatory provisions imposed on the foreign-related civil relationships shall be directly applicable.[6] It has actually absorbed this while using for reference of the theory of 'loi d'application immédiate' in the world in consideration of China's reality.

(6) In terms of the application of law of movable property rights, the LALFCR allows the parties to agree on the choice of the applicable law for movable property rights.[7] This is a pioneering initiative that fully takes into account the wide varieties of movable property rights, the close association between the changes in movable property rights with commercial transactions, and the diversity in conditions and means of transactions.

(7) The Law adopts the internationally advanced principle of 'the law of the place where protection is requested' in the application of law of intellectual property rights. This is conducive to the application and protection of intellectual property rights in the course of handling the frequent disputes concerning intellectual property rights' confirmation,[8] transfer[9] and infringement.[10]

Third, the LALFCR is people-oriented and people-friendly, and its openness has shown the world an image of China's further openness. The Law, which mostly adopts bilateral conflict rules, adheres to the parallelism of internal and external laws, equally protects the lawful rights and interests of internal and external parties, promotes harmonious international civil relations and seeks to resolve foreign-related civil disputes more fairly, equitably and reasonably. The Law's provisions on adoption, support, guardianship, consumer contracts, labour contracts and product liability fully reflect its people-orientation and protection of the interests of disadvantaged parties. The provisions of the LALFCR avoid obscure vocabulary and terminologies often used in private international law, and try to be as concise and clear, and easy to approach and understand as possible.

I. Aspects for Improvement

Of course, the LALFCR is far from perfect, and there are some points that deserve further discussion. There are also some shortcomings and some regrets, which are mainly

[6] Article 4 of the LALFCR: 'If there are mandatory provisions on foreign-related civil relations in the laws of the People's Republic of China, these mandatory provisions shall directly apply.'

[7] ibid art 37: 'The parties concerned may choose the laws applicable to the right over the movables by agreement. If the parties do not choose, the laws at the locality of the movables when the legal facts take place shall apply.' Article 38: 'The parties concerned may choose the laws applicable to any change of the right over the movables taking place in transportation by agreement. If the parties do not choose, the laws at the destination of transportation shall apply.'

[8] ibid art 48: 'The laws at the locality where protection is claimed shall apply to the ownership and contents of the intellectual property right.'

[9] ibid art 49: 'A party may choose the laws applicable to the assignment and licensed use of intellectual property right by agreement. If the parties do not choose, the relevant provisions on contracts of this Law shall apply.'

[10] ibid art 50: 'The laws at the locality where protection is claimed shall apply to the liabilities for tort for intellectual property, the parties concerned may also choose the applicable laws at the locality of the court by agreement after the tort takes place.'

manifested in the following aspects. First, the LALFCR is not yet a truly unified, systematic and comprehensive law on the application of law for foreign-related civil relationships, and it has incorporated neither the provisions concerning the application of the law in the Negotiable Instruments Law, the Maritime Law and the Civil Aviation Law, nor the mature provisions in the judicial interpretations. Second, regarding the relationship between the new law and the old laws, Article 2 of the LALFCR stipulates that 'if other laws have special provisions on the application of law concerning foreign-related civil relationships, [the applicable law will be determined] in accordance with their provisions' and more can be referred to in its Article 51. Still, the relationship concerning the application of law has not been clearly stated between the LALFCR and the laws beyond the Negotiable Instruments Law, the Maritime Law and the Civil Aviation Law, Articles 146 and 147 of the General Principles of the Civil Law and Article 36 of the Inheritance Law. If the relationship between them is explained in accordance with Article 2 of the LALFCR, it means that the new improvements of the Law are meaningless. For example, Article 150 of the General Principles of Civil Law stipulates: 'The application of foreign laws or international practices in accordance with the provisions of this chapter shall not violate the public interests of the People's Republic of China.' Article 5 of the new Law provides that 'if the application of foreign laws will harm the public interest of the People's Republic of China, the laws of the People's Republic of China shall apply'. The biggest difference between the two is that the former can exclude the application of international practices by the principle of public order, while the latter does not provide such a provision. The two conflict with each other. Should the new law or the old one be applied? If the old law is applicable in accordance with Article 2 of the new law, then there is no need for the new Law to re-regulate public order issues. Third, the LALFCR fails to provide for certain contents that should be stipulated, such as the definition of foreign-related civil relationships, evasion of law, preliminary questions, the application of international treaties and international practices, the classification of point of contacts, and the interpretation of applicable laws. Fourth, there are improprieties in the structural arrangement and logical sequence of the provisions. For example, the 'Intellectual Property Rights' chapter should not be placed after the 'Creditors' Rights' chapter, but should be placed after the 'Property Rights' chapter and before the 'Creditors' Rights' chapter. For another example, it is also inappropriate to place the application of law of the arbitration agreement in the 'Civil Subjects' chapter. Moreover, there are also problems with the sequential order and logical structure of the articles in the chapter, and there is room for adjustment. Fifth, some provisions of the law can be further simplified and optimised. For example, Article 3 of the LALFCR stipulates that 'the parties may expressly choose the applicable law for foreign-related civil relationships in accordance with the law', which is completely redundant, because since the law has clearly stipulated that the parties may expressly choose the applicable law for a foreign-related civil relationship, there is no point in repeating the rule.

In short, the formulation and improvement of China's applicable law of foreign-related civil relationships is a gradual process. It is a process that blends theory and practice, a process in which Chinese legal and Western legal cultures meet, a process of transformation from the past to the present, a process of weighing up the present and the future, and a process of gaming between the conservative and the innovative. This is actually a microcosm of contemporary Chinese legislation. In this process, China's private international law legislation has undergone a bumpy journey, but has taken a steadfast step towards a bright future. Following the implementation of the Law in April 2011, China's legislation on the application of law for foreign-related civil relationships entered a brand-new period.

II. The Supreme People's Court Judicial Interpretations of the LALFCR

In a sense, private international law is mainly formulated for the courts responsible for handling foreign-related civil cases, therefore making it the 'law of judges'. The Supreme People's Court (SPC) in China has attached great importance to its application in the court's foreign-related trial practice, and immediately after the LALFCR entered into force, the SPC began to draft judicial interpretations for the application of the LALFCR. After nearly a year of hard work and several revised drafts, the 'Interpretation of the Supreme People's Court on Several Issues Concerning the Application of the Law of the People's Republic of China on the Application of Law for Foreign-Related Civil Relationships (1)' (hereinafter 'the LALFCR Interpretations (1)') was finally discussed and approved at the 1,563th meeting of the Judicial Committee of the SPC on 10 December 2012.[11] The 21-article judicial interpretations were promulgated by the SPC on 28 December 2012, and took effect on 7 January 2013.

After the passage of the Civil Code of the People's Republic of China (hereinafter 'the Civil Code') in 2020, the 1,823th Meeting of the Judicial Committee of the SPC passed the amendment to the LALFCR Interpretations (1), deleting Articles 4 and 5, and reducing it to 19 articles.

The LALFCR Interpretations (1) mainly concerns the most significant issues that exist in the implementation of the LALFCR, as described below.

A. Defining Foreign-Related Civil Relationships

This is a fundamental issue of private international law and a prerequisite for the application of the LALFCR, because only when the disputed legal relationship is a 'foreign-related civil relationship' can there be room for application of the law (purely domestic civil cases are not governed by the LALFCR). The LALFCR provides that its purpose is to clarify the application of laws in foreign-related civil relationships, reasonably resolve foreign-related civil disputes, and safeguard the lawful rights and interests of the parties. However, the LALFCR did not clearly define what 'foreign-related civil relations' meant, making judicial interpretation necessary. Article 1 of the LALFCR Interpretations (1) stipulates as follows:

> If a civil relationship has one of the following circumstances, the people's court may determine it as a foreign-related civil relationship:
>
> (1) One or both parties are foreign citizens, foreign legal persons or other organisations, stateless persons;

[11] The full text is available at https://www.court.gov.cn/shenpan-xiangqing-5273.html.

(2) The habitual residence of one or both parties is outside the territory of the People's Republic of China;
(3) The subject matter is outside the territory of the People's Republic of China;
(4) The legal facts concerning the creation, alteration or extinction of the civil relations occur outside the territory of the People's Republic of China;
(5) Other circumstances that can be identified as foreign-related civil relationships.

It can be seen from the above that the core analytical framework in the rules is still the 'three-element theory', which is designed to examine whether the three elements of the subject, object and content of the legal relationship are related to foreign countries, but the scope of the subjects are slightly expanded to include 'other foreign organisations'. Interestingly, 'foreign-related' is taken in its broadest sense, transcending looking only at a country's borders or at cross-border transactions. In addition to the 'nationality' point of contact, the 'habitual residence' point of contact is valued and has become the basis for determining whether the civil relation in question is 'foreign-related'.

B. The Relationship between the New Law and the Old Laws

Regarding how to deal with the relationship between the LALFCR and other conflict rules in China's legal system, even though Articles 2 and 51 of the LALFCR provide a way in principle, it still makes judges feel bewildered when dealing with foreign-related civil cases. Therefore, it is necessary to further clarify the relationship between the LALFCR and the conflict rules in the General Principles of Civil Law, the Negotiable Instruments Law, the Maritime Law, the Civil Aviation Law and other laws. Otherwise, it is easy to make mistakes when applying the Law. Article 2 of the LALFCR Interpretations (1) stipulates:

> For foreign-related civil relationships that occurred before the implementation of the Law on the Application of Law for Foreign-Related Civil Relationships, the people's courts determine the applicable law in accordance with the law in force when the civil relation occurred; if there was no provision in the law at that time, it can be determined by referring to the provisions of the Law on the Application of Law for Foreign-Related Civil Relationships.

Article 3 states:

> [I]f the Law on the Application of Law for Foreign-Related Civil Relationships is inconsistent with other laws on the same foreign-related civil relationship, the provisions of the Law on the Application of Law for Foreign-Related Civil Relationships shall apply, except for the special provisions of the Negotiable Instruments Law of the People's Republic of China, the Maritime Law of the People's Republic of China, the Civil Aviation Law of the People's Republic of China and other intellectual property rights-related laws.
>
> If the Law on the Application of Law on Foreign-Related Civil Relationships does not provide for the application of laws for the foreign-related civil relationships, while other laws contain such provisions, the provisions of other laws shall apply.

These two provisions reflect the legal principles concerning the relationship between the new law and the old law, ie, the non-retroactivity of law, *lex posterior derogat priori*, *lex specialis derogat generali* and no legal vacuum for the covered subject matters, thus properly dealing with the connection between the new law and the old ones.

C. Application of International Treaties and International Practice

Article 6 of the Foreign Economic Contract Law of the People's Republic of China, which was enacted by the NPC Standing Committee in 1985 at the beginning of the reform and opening up stipulated:

> International treaties related to contracts concluded or acceded to by the People's Republic of China have different provisions from the laws of the People's Republic of China, the provisions of the international treaties shall apply, except for the provisions over which the People's Republic of China has declared reservations.

For the first time, it clearly spelled out the relationship between China's international treaty obligations and China's domestic laws. The General Principles of Civil Law formulated by the NPC in 1986 extended such provisions from the field of contract law to the entire civil law field. Article 142 clearly states:

> [W]here the international treaties that the People's Republic of China has concluded or acceded to are different from the civil laws of the People's Republic of China, the provisions of international treaties shall apply, with the exception of the provisions over which the People's Republic of China has declared reservations.
>
> If there are no provisions in the laws of the People's Republic of China and international treaties to which the People's Republic of China has concluded or acceded to, international practices may apply.

Article 95 of the Negotiable Instruments Law, Article 268 of the Maritime Law, Article 184 of the Civil Aviation Law and Article 238 of the Civil Procedure Law all have similar provisions. Such provisions show that in the field of civil and commercial matters, China adheres to the principle of giving priority to the application of international treaties and the principle of filling vacancies by international practices. Since the introduction of reform and opening up, practice has proved that in the field of civil and commercial affairs, adherence to such principles has been instrumental in the formation of a good, legalised and internationalised business environment for China, and has made great contributions to China's reform and opening up.

In view of the fact that the LALFCR does not provide for the application of international treaties and international practices, and that foreign-related judicial practice often involves the application of international treaties and international practices, Articles 4 and 5 of the LALFCR Interpretations (1) respectively provide guidance on the application of international treaties and international practices, quoting relevant provisions of other laws as the legal basis.

What needs to be pointed out here is that due to the principle of universal recognition of territoriality of intellectual property rights and the principle of independent protection by various countries, China has adopted a transformation approach for the application of the Agreement on Trade-Related Aspects of Intellectual Property Rights (hereinafter TRIPS Agreement) under the World Trade Organization (WTO), and with respect to international intellectual property rights treaties beyond the TRIPS Agreement, it usually stipulates minimum protection standards rather than unified specific rules. Therefore, in judicial practice relating to intellectual property, if domestic laws and international treaties have different provisions, the provisions of international treaties may not necessarily be applied. In view of this, Article 4 of the Judicial Interpretation (1) has added an exception provision for international treaties in the field of intellectual property which have been transformed or need to be transformed into domestic laws. It provides that international treaties in the field of intellectual property, which have not been transformed into domestic laws, could not been applied directly in a Chinese court.

Regrettably, after the Civil Code was promulgated and implemented, the General Principles of the Civil Law ceased to be effective, and its Article 142 no longer had legal effect. At the same time, the SPC revised the 'LALFCR Interpretations (1)' and directly deleted its Articles 4 and 5.[12] This has left questions about how to deal with the application of international treaties and international practices in judicial practice in the future.

D. Expansive Application of the Parties' Autonomy

One of the highlights of the LALFCR is to extend the application of the parties' autonomy principle from the traditional field of contracts to the many aspects of foreign-related civil relationships in terms of the application of law. However, how to perform specific operations in judicial practice, including when the parties can choose the law, how to choose the law and the scope of the laws to be chosen, all required further clarification. Articles 4–7 of the LALFCR Interpretations (1) provide answers.

It can be said that where the Chinese law does not clearly stipulate that the parties may choose the applicable law for the foreign-related civil relationship, if the parties do choose an applicable law, the people's court shall determine that the choice is invalid.

Second, the LALFCR Interpretation (1) clarifies that the law chosen by the two parties does not need to be related to the disputed foreign-related civil relationship to be applicable.

The third clarification regards the time when the parties agree to choose the applicable law. In other words, the parties may choose or change the applicable law before the end of the debate in first-instance trial; moreover, the implicit choice of law by the parties shall be supported, and if the parties invoke the law of the same country without raising an objection, the people's court may determine that the party concerned has made a choice regarding the law applicable to a foreign-related civil relationship.

Fourth, it is clearly stipulated that the parties may invoke an international treaty that has not yet entered into force for China as the applicable law in their contract. The people's court may determine the rights and obligations between the parties based on the content of the international treaty, unless it violates the public interest of the People's Republic of China or the mandatory provisions of the laws and administrative regulations of the People's Republic of China.

E. The Direct Application of Mandatory Provisions

In recent years, more and more national laws stipulate that certain foreign-related civil and commercial relationships must be subject to certain special laws, mandatory laws

[12] The amended text is available at https://cicc.court.gov.cn/html/1/218/62/84/2131.html.

and prohibitive norms, thereby excluding the application of foreign laws. This is a sharp reflection of the strengthened state intervention in social and economic life in the international arena, through the application of private law. For example, competition law, foreign exchange control law, foreign trade law, price law, social security law and consumer protection law are generally designed to protect the country's economic order or provide special protection for certain types of interests, and each has a major impact on foreign-related civil relationships. Article 4 of the LALFCR provides for the direct application of mandatory provisions in Chinese laws. However, which provisions in the Chinese legal system fall into the category of mandatory provisions needs to be made clear. Otherwise, Article 4 of the LALFCR could lead to judicial abuse and compromise the effectiveness of private international law. Article 8 of the latest LALFCR Interpretations (1) provides:

> [I]n any of the following circumstances involving the public interest of the People's Republic of China, where the provisions of the laws and administrative regulations that the parties cannot exclude the application by agreement, and must be directly applied to foreign-related civil relationships without going through with the conflict rules guidance, the people's courts shall recognise the provisions as the mandatory provisions stipulated in Article 4 of the Law on the Application of Law for Foreign-Related Civil Relationships:
>
> (1) Involving the protection of labour rights;
> (2) Involving food or public health safety;
> (3) Involving environmental safety;
> (4) Involving foreign exchange control and other financial security;
> (5) Involving anti-monopoly and anti-dumping;
> (6) Other circumstances that should be deemed mandatory.[13]

This judicial interpretation defines 'mandatory provisions' in general terms: provisions of laws and administrative regulations that involve national and social public interest, that the parties cannot exclude the application through agreement, and that do not need to go through the guidance of the conflict rules, but that are directly applicable in foreign-related civil relationships. It also lists the relevant mandatory regulations by way of enumeration, which is convenient for operation and implementation.

F. Evasion of Law

The system of evasion of law is a traditional system in private international law, which is clearly stipulated in the private international law legislation of many countries. The LALFCR itself does not provide for the issue of evasion of the law, but Article 9 of the LALFCR Interpretations (1) makes corresponding provisions, emphasising that if one party intentionally creates a point of contact of a foreign-related civil relationship which circumvents the mandatory provisions of the laws and administrative regulations of the People's Republic of China, the people's court shall determine that it does not have the effect of leading to the application of foreign laws. Such judicial interpretations provide a tool for judges to safeguard China's social public interest in handling foreign-related civil cases.

[13] This was art 10 before the SPC revised the LALFCR Interpretations (1).

G. Preliminary Issues and the Application of Law where Various Relations are Involved

In judicial practice, preliminary questions and the application of law where the case involves different legal relationships appear from time to time. The LALFCR does not provide for this, but the LALFCR Interpretations (1) provide a corresponding judicial interpretation. Article 10 stipulates that where the settlement of a foreign-related civil dispute must be based on the confirmation of another foreign-related civil relationship, the people's court shall determine the law to be applied according to the nature of the preliminary question itself. Article 11 stipulates that where a case involves two or more foreign-related civil relationships, the people's courts shall determine the applicable laws separately. In fact, the applicable law is also determined separately according to the nature of the two or more foreign-related civil relationships involved in the case.

Regarding the application of the law of the arbitration agreement, Article 18 of the LALFCR stipulates that the parties may agree to choose the law applicable to the arbitration agreement; if the parties do not choose, the law of the location of the arbitration institution or the law of the place of arbitration shall apply. Article 12 of the LALFCR Interpretations (1) provides for a supplementary explanation. Where the parties neither choose the applicable law of the foreign-related arbitration agreement nor agree on the arbitration institution or place of arbitration, or if the agreement is unclear, the people's court may apply the law of the People's Republic of China to determine the validity of the arbitration agreement.

H. Interpretation of Habitual Residence

Habitual residence referred to in the LALFCR is similar to the habitual residence mentioned in the Hague Conventions on Private International Law. These regard 'habitual residence' as an important point of contact in order to bridge the differences between the nationality principle and the domicile principle in determining the personal law of various countries, and are a product of the unification movement of private international law. The LALFCR puts the natural person's 'habitual residence' in a more prominent position as a point of contact in the personal law, but it and other civil laws in China do not define what constitutes a 'habitual residence'. Article 13 of the LALFCR Interpretations (1) is thus useful, clearly stipulating that if a natural person has lived in a place continuously for more than one year and had it serve as the centre of his life at the time of the creation, change or termination of a foreign-related civil relationship, the people's court may determine that it is the habitual residence of the natural person as referred to in the Law on the Application of Law for Foreign-Related Civil Relationships.[14]

The second paragraph of Article 14 of the LALFCR stipulates that the habitual residence of a legal person shall be its main place of business. The LALFCR is devoid of 'place of registration' of a legal person, which needs to be further clarified, because the law of the place of registration applies to matters such as the capacity for civil rights, capacity for civil conduct, organisational structure, and shareholder rights and obligations of legal persons and their branches. Article 14 of the LALFCR Interpretations (1) stipulates that the people's

[14] There are exceptions for medical treatment, labour dispatch, official duties etc.

courts shall recognise the place of registration of the establishment of legal persons as the registration place of the legal persons as referred to in the LALFCR.

I. The Ascertaining and Application of Foreign Law

In the practice of foreign-related judicial trials in China, the ascertaining and application of foreign laws has always been a 'bottleneck' that restricts the efficiency of foreign-related civil trials. How will the foreign law be ascertained when the foreign law should be applied? Important questions arise, including the following: what are the ways to ascertain foreign laws? Do various channels need to be exhausted to determine that 'foreign laws cannot be ascertained'? What should the judge do when the parties have different understandings of foreign laws? These have always been difficult questions for judges, and they all need to be explained clearly.

Article 10 of the LALFCR consists of two paragraphs. The first is that foreign laws applicable to foreign-related civil relationships shall be verified by the people's court, arbitration institution or administrative agency *ex officio*, but if the parties choose to apply foreign laws, they shall provide the laws of the chosen country. Second, if the foreign law cannot be ascertained or the country's law does not provide for it, the laws of the People's Republic of China shall apply. Article 15 of the LALFCR Interpretations (1) lists the methods commonly used in judicial practice concerning the ascertaining of foreign laws, including those provided by the parties and provided for in international treaties which the People's Republic of China has concluded or acceded to, and provided by Chinese and foreign legal experts. It also clearly stipulates that if 'foreign laws cannot be obtained through these reasonable channels', then the judge may regard the foreign laws as not ascertainable. In the event that the parties should provide foreign laws, the people's courts should assign a reasonable time limit to the parties. If the parties fail to provide foreign laws without justifiable reasons or cannot provide foreign laws within the reasonable time limit, the people's courts can determine as 'unable to ascertain foreign laws'.

Since the judges who hear cases are not necessarily familiar with foreign laws, it is necessary in judicial practice to guide the judges in how to determine the content of foreign laws and how to correctly understand them. In accordance with the guidelines of Article 16 of the LALFCR Interpretations (1), for foreign laws that should be applied, whether it is provided by the parties or ascertained by the people's courts *ex officio*, the court shall listen to the comments by the parties on the content of the foreign law and its interpretation and application. If the parties have no objection to the content, understanding and application of the foreign law, the people's court can confirm it; if either party has any objection, the people's court shall review and determine it.

J. Inter-regional Conflict of Laws: Hong Kong and Macao in the LALCFR

According to the principle of 'One Country, Two Systems', after the return of Hong Kong and Macao to China, their original laws were to remain basically unchanged. This means that the legal system practised in Hong Kong and Macao is different from the legal system implemented in Mainland China. Hong Kong and Macao are both independent 'jurisdictions' or 'law districts' in China. China is a multi-jurisdictional country, a pluri-legal country or a country with inconsistent legal systems. Strictly speaking, the conflict of laws between the Mainland China, Hong Kong SAR China and Macao SAR China is a conflict of laws between different jurisdictions within one sovereign country, an inter-regional conflict of laws, not an international conflict of laws. So, in judicial practice, how do courts in the mainland resolve the application of law issue when handling cases involving Hong Kong and Macao? The laws of the country have no provisions on the application of law concerning civil relations involving Hong Kong and Macao. During the drafting of the LALFCR, it was suggested that China's inter-regional conflict of laws should be stipulated. However, due to the consideration of various factors, the LALFCR ultimately did not address this issue.

However, in judicial practice, the courts have always handled cases involving Hong Kong and Macao in the same way as they do foreign-related cases. Therefore, Article 17 of the LALFCR Interpretations (1) clearly stipulates:

> For issues concerning the application of law in civil relations involving the Hong Kong Special Administrative Region and the Macao Special Administrative Region, this provision shall be applied as reference.

III. Promoting the Settlement of International Commercial Disputes by Constructing an International Commercial Court System

In the tide of economic globalisation, international commercial courts have been established one after another in response to the needs of international commercial dispute resolution. For example, the United Arab Emirates, Singapore, Kazakhstan, the Netherlands and other countries have successively established international commercial courts. As China deepens its reform and opening up, actively promotes the construction of the 'Belt and Road',[15] continuously integrates into economic globalisation, and extensively participates in the reform and construction of the global governance system, it is indeed necessary to explore the establishment of a fair, just and reasonable international commercial dispute settlement mechanism in China that can provide more efficient, convenient, and affordable solutions for international commercial disputes. On 23 January 2018, the Central Leading Group on Comprehensive Deepening of Reform, hosted by Chairman Xi Jinping, reviewed and approved the 'Opinions on the Establishment of "Belt & Road" International Commercial Dispute Resolution Mechanism and Institutions' (hereinafter 'Opinions'). On 27 June 2018, the General Office of the Central Committee of the Communist Party of China and the General Office of the State Council issued the 'Opinions'. These 'Opinions' established the core concept and designed the basic model for China's international commercial dispute resolution mechanism, namely, the establishment of an international commercial court, of an international commercial expert committee and of a diversified dispute resolution

[15] It refers to 'the Silk Road Economic Belt and the 21st-Century Maritime Silk Road', in short, it is called 'the Belt and Road Initiative (BRI)', which was proposed by China in 2013, aiming at promoting inclusive development by encouraging the integration of more countries and regions into economic globalisation.

mechanism that integrates litigation, mediation and arbitration. It thus forms a convenient, fast and affordable 'one-stop' dispute settlement centre. The SPC has successively issued judicial interpretations to ensure its functionality. These include the 'Provisions of the Supreme People's Court on Several Issues Concerning the Establishment of International Commercial Courts', the 'Procedural Rules for the China International Commercial Court of the Supreme People's Court (for Trial Implementation)' and the 'Working Rules of the Supreme People's Court International Commercial Expert Committee'. The SPC has also established and improved relevant rules and systems.

On 28 June 2018, President Zhou Qiang of the SPC appointed the first eight judges of the International Commercial Court.[16] On the same day, the First and the Second International Commercial Courts were launched in Shenzhen and Xi'an respectively, and were officially inaugurated.

A. The Basic Principles for the Establishment of an International Commercial Court System

China has established its international commercial dispute settlement mechanism and institutions according to the following principles.

i. Adhering to the Principle of Extensive Consultation, Joint Contribution and Shared Benefits

The characteristics of internationalisation are highlighted in the court system, and the spirit of extensive consultation, joint contribution and sharing of benefits is reflected by maintaining an open and inclusive atmosphere. The institutions encourage experts from relevant countries who are proficient in both international law and their domestic law to actively participate in proceedings, and the judges value the right of parties to choose domestic and foreign legal experts to resolve disputes.

ii. Adhering to the Principle of Fairness, Efficiency and Convenience

Measures including learning from the useful practices of the existing international dispute settlement mechanisms and establishing a widely accepted new international commercial dispute settlement mechanism and institutions that conform to relevant nations' conditions have been taken to facilitate the settlement of cross-border commercial disputes in a fair and efficient manner.

iii. Adhering to the Principle of Respecting the Parties' Autonomy

This principle requires respecting the right of the parties to choose the method of dispute resolution by agreement. It also includes allowing them to agree to apply their familiar

[16] See China International Commercial Court, available at https://cicc.court.gov.cn/html/1/index.html.

domestic law or the law of a third country or international treaties and practices. Finally, it means ensuring the equal protection of the legitimate rights and interests of all parties.

iv. Adhering to the Principle of Diversified Dispute Resolution Methods

In order to effectively satisfy Chinese and foreign parties' diversified needs for dispute resolution, the SPC has fully considered the diversity of participants in international commercial activities, the complexity of dispute types, and the differences in national legislation, justice and rule of law culture. It has thus actively cultivated and improved a dispute settlement mechanism that integrates litigation, arbitration and mediation. Through the establishment of the international commercial dispute settlement mechanism and institutions, a stable, fair, transparent and predictable business environment under the rule of law will be created.

B. Jurisdiction of the International Commercial Courts

The International Commercial Court accepts the following five types of cases:

(1) first-instance international commercial cases in which the parties have (pursuant to Article 34 of the Civil Procedure Law) agreed to choose the SPC as the forum and in which the amount at stake is more than RMB 300 million;[17]
(2) first-instance international commercial cases under the jurisdiction of the High People's Court that are deemed necessary to be tried and approved by the SPC;
(3) first-instance international commercial cases that have a significant national impact;
(4) cases where applications for arbitration preservation, for cancellation or for enforcement of international commercial arbitration awards have been filed in accordance with judicial interpretations at the 'one-stop' dispute resolution mechanism for arbitration; and
(5) other international commercial cases that the SPC believes should be heard by the International Commercial Court.

Major jurisdictional innovations have been made within the framework of the current Civil Procedure Law. Through such systems as agreed-upon jurisdiction, transferred jurisdiction and elevated jurisdiction, the International Commercial Court is capable of handling difficult and complicated disputes of significant importance, while maintaining the stability of the current jurisdiction system for foreign-related civil and commercial cases.

C. International Commercial Expert Committee

In order to improve the professional level of international commercial trials, strengthen international exchanges and cooperation, and facilitate and promote the trial work of the International Commercial Court, the SPC decided to establish the International Commercial Expert Committee (ICEC). This committee is composed of Chinese and

[17] This is equivalent to £35 million.

foreign experts appointed by the SPC. Members should all be well-regarded and upstanding experts with profound knowledge in international trade, investment and other international commercial law fields, and have an international reputation. On 26 August 2018, the SPC appointed 31 experts as the first batch of members of the ICEC for a four-year term. On 8 December 2020, the SPC appointed 24 experts as the second batch of members of the ICEC. Thirty-one foreign experts were appointed as the two batches of members of the Expert Committee. The two batches of expert members come from different countries and regions with different legal systems, including leaders of important international organisations, legal experts, eminent scholars, experienced judges and outstanding lawyers. The composition of the Committee reveals a broad representation in respect of both geographical region and professional field. The expert committee members may be entrusted by the International Commercial Court to undertake the following duties: (1) preside over the mediation of international commercial cases; (2) provide advisory opinions on international treaties, international commercial rules, ascertainment and application of extra-territorial laws and other specialised legal issues involved in the trial of cases by the International Commercial Court and other people's courts at all levels; (3) provide opinions and suggestions on the development plan of the International Commercial Court; (4) provide opinions and suggestions on the formulation of relevant judicial interpretations and judicial policies by the SPC; or (5) other matters requested by the International Commercial Court. This institutional innovation demonstrates China's emphasis on its internationality and professionalism in dealing with international commercial disputes, as well as its open stance and inclusive mentality.

D. Construction of the One-Stop Dispute Resolution Mechanism

The International Commercial Court facilitates parties' access to a dispute resolution platform that organically links mediation, arbitration and litigation, who may choose the method they deem appropriate for the resolution of international commercial disputes. After taking into full consideration the number of international commercial dispute cases accepted by various institutions in the early stage, their international influence, their arbitral capacity and other factors, the SPC designated a first batch of arbitration and mediation institutions to be incorporated in the 'one-stop' mechanism: the China International Economic and Trade Arbitration Commission (CIETAC), the Shanghai International Economic and Trade Arbitration Commission (SIETAC), the Shenzhen Court of International Arbitration (SCIA), the Beijing Arbitration Commission (BAC), the China Maritime Arbitration Commission (CMAC), the China Council for the Promotion of International Trade Mediation Center and the Shanghai Economic, Trade and Commercial Mediation Center. For cases involving international commercial disputes brought to the International Commercial Court, the parties may agree to choose the mediation institutions above. After the mediation institution presides over the mediation and the parties reach a settlement, the International Commercial Court may prepare and issue a mediated settlement in accordance with the law. If the parties request a judgment, it may prepare a judgment based on the content of the settlement and serve it to the parties. For cases of international commercial disputes accepted by the arbitration institutions incorporated in the mechanism, the parties may apply to the International Commercial Court for evidence, property or behaviour preservation before filing the arbitration application or after the initiation of the arbitration procedure; after the arbitration award is made, the parties may apply to the International Commercial Court to enforce the arbitral awards or to annul it, if applicable.

E. Reform of the Evidence System

From the standpoint of facilitating litigation, the SPC has introduced a number of reforms in the evidence mechanism involved in the International Commercial Court litigation. For the first time, the SPC issued a judicial interpretation to remove the mandatory requirements for notarisation and authentication of extra-territorial evidence. In response to the time- and labour-consuming translation of a large number of English-language evidence materials in the trial practice of the International Commercial Court, it is stipulated that, with the consent of both parties, the Chinese translation of the English evidence materials need not be furnished. At the same time, it is stipulated that the International Commercial Court may use information network methods to investigate and collect evidence, organise cross-examination and make full use of the achievements of smart court construction in the country.

IV. Concluding Thoughts

The last thing to mention here is that with the establishment and operation of the International Commercial Court of the SPC and the International Commercial Expert Committee, various institutional innovations in China's international commercial dispute settlement mechanism are being realised. Although promising, there are also some difficulties to overcome, problems to be solved and shortcomings to be fixed. In the future, it will be necessary to continuously optimise and improve the various mechanisms of the International Commercial Court and the International Commercial Expert Committee. Full implementation of the measures and plans for diversified dispute resolution, and effective use of the fair, convenient, fast and low-cost 'one-stop' dispute resolution centre will help secure high-quality and efficient legal services for Chinese and foreign parties, providing Chinese solutions and Chinese wisdom for the settlement of international commercial disputes.

Even now, China is further exploring and improving the international commercial court system. On 26 September 2019, with the approval of the SPC, the Hainan First and Second Foreign-Related Civil Tribunals were launched in Haikou and Sanya, respectively. On 29 November 2020, the Suzhou International Commercial Tribunal was established in Suzhou Industrial Park, making it the first international commercial tribunal established in a local court with the approval of the SPC. Since 2020, 12 international commercial tribunals have been established in local courts with the approval of the SPC.[18] With these new institutions, the adoption, adaptation and innovation of commercial dispute resolution continues.

[18] They are in the cities of Nanjing, Qingdao, Ningbo, Hangzhou, Nanning, Wuxi, Quanzhou, Xiamen, Changchun, Chengdu, Beijing and Suzhou.

7

New Developments of Private International Law in Japan and East Asia

YUKO NISHITANI

I. Introduction

Since Savigny established modern private international law or conflict of laws in civil law systems in the nineteenth century, international harmony of decisions has been considered its primary objective.[1] While the unification of applicable law rules has often turned out to be difficult to achieve, it is helpful to conduct a comparative study on conflict of laws to find harmonised solutions, to establish an international framework of cooperation and to develop a workable, functioning system of conflict of laws at the domestic, regional and international levels.[2]

This chapter examines recent developments in private international law in Japan from a comparative perspective, indicating features specific to Japan and East Asia, and differences and commonalities with other legal systems. With a view to analysing changing and evolving conflict of laws in Japan, the following three main streams will be discussed. First, the 'nationalisation' trend encompasses a series of statutory reforms in Japan since early 2000s in accordance with the judicial reform (section II). Second, the 'regionalisation' trend extends to recent developments in East Asia, which reflect colonial history and intricate political and economic relationships in the region (section III). Third, the 'internationalisation' trend expounds the commitment and desirability for Japan to take part in international legal framework to facilitate cross-border dispute resolution and enhance cooperation (section IV). Some final remarks with future perspectives will conclude (section V).

[1] FC von Savigny, *System des heutigen römischen Rechts*, vol 8 (Bei Veit und Comp, 1849) 23 et seq.

[2] Y Nishitani, 'Comparative Conflict of Laws' in M Siems and PJ Yap (ed), *The Cambridge Handbook of Comparative Law* (Cambridge University Press, forthcoming, 2023).

II. 'Nationalisation': Domestic Legislation from a Comparative Perspective

A. Background

In Japan, the first codification of conflict of law rules goes back to *Hôrei* of 1898 during the Meiji era.[3] Japan was seeking to boast itself as a modern, independent state in response to disparity treaties that Japan had been forced to sign with the US, Britain, France, Russia and other major foreign powers since 1858. To renegotiate these treaties and fully regain its sovereignty, Japan needed to establish a progressive, reliable legal system. This is how codification work was instituted.[4] Japan proceeded to transplant the most advanced Western legal systems including conflict of laws from France, Belgium, Italy, Switzerland and Germany. The structure of *Hôrei* followed the 'Pandekten' system, while the individual conflict of laws rules, accommodating the principle of nationality in family and succession law and party autonomy in contract law, were the results of meticulous comparative work.[5] Later, *Hôrei* was entirely reformed in family law in 1989[6] to realise gender equality in marital relationships and to install the 'favour principle' grounded on alternative connecting factors in legal parenthood.[7]

Since 2001, the Japanese government has carried out deregulation and substituted the *ex ante* control of the administration by the *ex post* control of the judiciary. The wave of legislative work extended to almost all areas of law, including private international law. This chiefly touched upon the amendments and transposition of *Hôrei* into the Act on General Rules for Application of Laws (AGRAL) in 2006,[8] and the adoption of new international jurisdiction rules in 2011 and 2018 (see below, section II.C). Furthermore, the 2000 Act on the Recognition of Foreign Insolvency Proceedings[9] and the 2003 Arbitration Act[10] implemented the respective United Nations Commission on International Trade Law (UNCITRAL) Model Laws[11] to adhere to international instruments and facilitate cross-border commercial transactions. The Arbitration Act was further amended in April 2023 (see below, section IV.B).

Even today, preparatory work for legislation conducted by the Ministry of Justice in Japan is largely based on a comparative law study. Yet, the focus has shifted from transplanting advanced foreign legal systems to achieving internal consistency and incorporating case law, practice and doctrine in Japan. The path of Japan differs from that followed in

[3] *Hôrei* (Act No 10 of 21 June 1898).

[4] Y Nishitani, 'Lawmaking in Japan' in J Basedow, H Fleischer and R Zimmermann (eds), *Legislators, Judges, and Professors* (Mohr Siebeck, 2016) 4.

[5] See Y Nishitani, 'Mancini and the Principle of Nationality in Japanese Private International Law' in H-P Mansel et al (eds), *Festschrift für Erik Jayme zum 70. Geburtstag*, vol 1 (Sellier, 2004) 627 et seq.

[6] Act No 27 of 28 June 1989.

[7] J Torii, 'Revision of Private International Law in Japan' (1990) 33 *Japanese Annual of International Law* 54; see M Nagata, ch 13 in this volume).

[8] Act on General Rules for Application of Laws (AGRAL) (Act No 78 of 21 June 2006).

[9] Act on Recognition of and Assistance for Foreign Insolvency Proceedings (Act No 129 of 29 November 2000).

[10] Arbitration Act (Act No 138 of 1 August 2003).

[11] UNCITRAL Model Laws on Cross-Border Insolvency of 30 May 1997, and on International Commercial Arbitration of 21 June 1985, as amended on 7 July 2006 (www.uncitral.un.org).

Europe,[12] where the Brussels and Lugano system[13] and a series of European Union (EU) regulations have enacted rules on jurisdiction and the recognition and enforcement of foreign judgments, judicial assistance and insolvency, as well as conflicts rules in contractual and extra-contractual obligations (Rome I and II Regulations) and some family and succession matters.

B. Choice-of-Law Rules

In 2006, Japanese legislature replaced *Hôrei* with the AGRAL. The amendments chiefly concerned conflicts rules in contractual and extra-contractual obligations and the assignment of receivables, whereas the family law part and the general part upheld the provisions of *Hôrei* that had been adopted in its 1989 reform.[14]

Notably, the AGRAL still adheres to the principle of nationality in family and succession law (Articles 24–37). This is because nationality is considered in Japan to generally reflect the individual's customs, culture and religion, unlike in other countries that largely accept double nationalities and combine *jus sanguinis* and *jus soli*. Nationality is also advantageous, as it hardly changes and is easily ascertainable for judges and civil registrar officers.[15] The principle of nationality is still followed by the Republic of Korea (South Korea), the Republic of China (Taiwan), the Philippines, Vietnam, Indonesia, Thailand and Mongolia owing to their colonial past.[16] This clearly contrasts with the Hague Conference on Private International Law (HCCH) instruments and common law jurisdictions, as well as the EU and its Member States, Switzerland and Mainland China, which adhere to the principle of habitual residence or domicile respectively. Notably, European countries have gradually given up the principle of nationality to focus on the person's habitual residence in view of practicality, predictability, closeness and equality among EU citizens and various immigrants. Mainland China followed suit in 2010, mainly to solve interregional conflicts of laws in relation to Taiwan, the Hong Kong Special Administrative Region (SAR) and the Macao SAR.[17]

Furthermore, the AGRAL has some specific features in contractual and tortious conflict of laws. In contracts, the primary principle is party autonomy since 1898 (Article 7 of *Hôrei*),[18] so parties are free to choose any law to govern their contract (Article 7 of the AGRAL).

[12] For further details, see www.europarl.europa.eu/factsheets/en/sheet/154/judicial-cooperation-in-civil-matters.

[13] Regulation (EU) No 1215/2012 of the European Parliament and of the Council of 12 December 2012 on jurisdiction and the recognition and enforcement of judgments in civil and commercial matters (recast) [2012] OJ L 351/1; Convention on jurisdiction and the recognition and enforcement of judgments in civil and commercial matters, signed at Lugano on 30 October 2007 [2007] OJ L 339/3).

[14] See Y Nishitani, 'Die Reform des internationalen Privatrechts in Japan' (2007) *IPRax* 552 et seq; Y Okuda, 'Reform of Japan's Private International Law: Act on the General Rules of the Application of Laws' (2006) *Yearbook of Private International Law* 145 et seq; K Takahashi, 'A Major Reform of Japanese Private International Law' (2006) 2 *Journal of Private International Law* 311 et seq; see also contributions in J Basedow, Y Nishitani and H Baum (eds), *Japanese and European Private International Law in Comparative Perspective* (Mohr Siebeck, 2008) and (2007) 50 *Japanese Annual of International Law* 3 et seq.

[15] Y Nishitani, 'Global Citizens and Family Relations' [2014] 7(3) *Erasmus Law Review* 136 et seq.

[16] Nishitani (n 2).

[17] Nishitani (n 15) 139 et seq.

[18] Y Nishitani, *Mancini und die Parteiautonomie im Internationalen Privatrecht* (Winter-Verlag, 2000) 206 et seq.

Absent parties' explicit or tacit choice of law, the closest connection test applies (Article 8 of the AGRAL), whereby habitual residence of the debtor, who carries out the 'characteristic performance' of the contract, is presumed to have the closest connection.[19] Enacted in 2006, two years before the EU Rome I Regulation,[20] the AGRAL relied on previous Article 4 of the 1980 Rome Convention[21] and differs from the detailed objective connecting factors enumerated in Article 4 of the Rome I Regulation.

For the protection of weaker party, the AGRAL incorporated special rules for consumer and employment contracts. When foreign law is chosen, the consumer or employee may invoke the relevant mandatory rules of the place of the consumer's habitual residence or the place where the employee regularly carries out their work (Articles 11 and 12 of the AGRAL).[22] This rule is, however, contradictory as it places the burden of referring to the mandatory rules on the weaker party, with a view to alleviating the judge's burden to compare two laws and pick the more favourable one.[23] Unlike in Japan, the Rome Convention and the Rome I Regulation require an *ex officio* comparison of the relevant mandatory rules to effectively protect the weaker party (Articles 6(2) and 8(1) of Rome I).

For torts, conflicts rules of the AGRAL largely coincide with the 2007 EU Rome II Regulation.[24] Notably, however, the AGRAL upheld the conventional 'double actionability' rule (Article 22 of the AGRAL) emanating from English case law. Even though foreign law governs the tort, the judge always applies Japanese law cumulatively. It is not obvious why Japanese law should systematically intervene without due regard to the link with the case. It also contradicts the closest connection test or party autonomy (Articles 20 and 21 of the AGRAL) when the application of the designated foreign law is automatically thwarted by Japanese law. Despite criticism, the 'double actionability' rule was upheld to exclude US punitive damages claims by restricting the category and extent of damages claims to those accepted by Japanese law.[25]

[19] Y Nishitani, 'Party Autonomy and its Restrictions by Mandatory Rules in Japanese Private International Law' in Basedow, Baum and Nishitani (n 14) 77 et seq; Y Nishitani, 'Party Autonomy in Contemporary Private International Law: The Hague Principles on Choice of Law and East Asia' (2016) 59 *Japanese Yearbook of International Law* 300 et seq; Y Nishitani, 'Japan' in D Girsberger, T Kadner Graziano and JL Neels (eds), *Choice of Law in International Commercial Contracts: Global Perspectives on the Hague Principles* (Oxford University Press, 2021) 537 et seq.

[20] Regulation (EC) No 593/2008 of the European Parliament and of the Council of 17 June 2008 on the law applicable to contractual obligations (Rome I) [2008] OJ L 177/6.

[21] Convention on the Law Applicable to Contractual Obligations, signed at Rome on 19 June 1980 (80/934/EEC) [1980] OJ L 266/1.

[22] Pursuant to arts 11 and 12 AGRAL, the consumer or employee as the weaker party is required to invoke themselves the relevant mandatory rules of the state, in which the consumer habitually resides or the employee usually carries out his or her work (in its absence, the location of the employer's establishment which hired the employee). The problem can be alleviated by applying overriding mandatory rules. See Y Nishitani, 'New Private International Law of Japan: Protection of Weaker Parties and Mandatory Rules' (2007) 50 *Japanese Annual of International Law* 41 et seq; K Nishioka and Y Nishitani, *Japanese Private International Law* (Hart Publishing, 2021) 26 et seq.

[23] Nishitani (n 22) 46 et seq.

[24] Regulation (EC) No 864/2007 of the European Parliament and of the Council of 11 July 2007 on the law applicable to non-contractual obligations (Rome II) [2007] OJ L 199/40.

[25] Nishioka and Nishitani (n 22) 125 f.

C. Rules on International Jurisdiction

i. *Civil and Commercial Litigation*

As for international jurisdiction in civil and commercial matters, Japan adopted new rules in the 2011 amendment of the Code of Civil Procedure (CCP) (Articles 3-2 et seq).[26] These jurisdiction rules largely relied on case law since the 1981 *Malaysia Airlines* decision.[27] The case law was grounded in domestic territorial jurisdiction with a possible dismissal of the claim under 'special circumstances', which caused considerable uncertainty and unpredictability.[28] While in the 1990s the Japanese government waited for the possible completion of the HCCH Judgments Project, it decided to prepare domestic legislation after the envisaged 'Mixed Convention' project failed and reduced its scope to the exclusive choice of court agreements by the 2005 HCCH Convention.[29]

Under the current CCP, general jurisdiction of the Japanese courts is granted at the defendant's domicile or main establishment (Article 3-2(1)(3)). Special jurisdiction is provided, among others, at the place of performance for contractual obligations (Article 3-3 No 1), the place of the branch office for disputes over its transactions (No 4), the place of continuous business activities (No 5) and the place of tort (No 8). Choice-of-court agreements are also accepted to a large extent, insofar as giving effect to the choice-of-court agreement at hand does not run counter to exclusive jurisdiction grounds or public policy (Article 3-7).[30]

Notably, compared with the fixed, restrictive jurisdiction grounds under the Brussels and Lugano system,[31] Japan allows for a more extensive exercise of jurisdiction. In addition to the above-mentioned special jurisdiction grounds, there are also the *situs* of assets jurisdiction (Article 3-3 No 3 of the CCP) and joinder of claims and parties (Article 3-6). Moreover, there is no exclusive jurisdiction for disputes over rights *in rem* in immovable property (Articles 3-3 No 11 and 3-5), which is comparatively unique and opens jurisdiction at the defendant's domicile. To deter exorbitant jurisdiction, an exceptional dismissal of the claim is provided for, as under the previous case law. The 'special circumstances' test allows the judge to dismiss the claim when granting jurisdiction is inappropriate in view of fairness between parties and proper and prompt administration of justice (Article 3-9 of the CCP). It is rather unusual for a civil law system to provide for extensive jurisdiction grounds in general and restrict their scope by the 'special circumstances' test on a case-by-case basis, comparable to the *forum non conveniens* doctrine in common law jurisdictions.[32]

[26] Act No 36 of 2 May 2011, amendments to the CCP (Act No 109 of 26 June 1996, as amended); see Y Nishitani, 'International Jurisdiction of Japanese Courts in Comparative Perspective' (2013) 60 *Netherlands International Law Review* 251 et seq; K Takahashi, 'Japan's Newly Enacted Rules on International Jurisdiction: With a Reflection on Some Issues of Interpretation' (2011) 13 *Yearbook of Private International Law* 146 et seq; D Yokomizo, 'The New Act on International Jurisdiction in Japan: Significance and Remaining Problems' (2013) 34 *Zeitschrift für Japanisches Recht/Journal of Japanese Law* 95 et seq; see also contributions in (2011) 54 *Japanese Yearbook of International Law* 260 et seq. and (2012) 55 *Japanese Yearbook of International Law* 263 et seq.

[27] Supreme Court, 16 October 1981, *Minshû* 35-7, 1224.

[28] Supreme Court, 11 November 1997, *Minshû* 51-10, 4055.

[29] HCCH Convention on Choice of Court Agreements of 30 June 2005; for the background of legislation, see, inter alia, Nishitani (n 26) 252 et seq.

[30] See Nishitani (n 26) 264 et seq.

[31] See n 13 above.

[32] See Supreme Court, 10 March 2016, *Minshû* 70-3, 846, (2017) 60 *Japanese Yearbook of International Law* 488.

ii. International Jurisdiction in Status and Family Matters

In 2018, Japan's legislature further enacted rules on international jurisdiction in status and family matters.[33] These rules are provided in Articles 3-2 et seq of the Personal Status Litigation Act (PSLA) for contentious cases (divorce, nullity of marriage, establishment of parenthood etc)[34] and in Articles 3-2 et seq of the Domestic Relations Case Procedure Act (DRCPA) for non-contentious cases (adoption, parental authority, guardianship etc).[35] These jurisdiction rules primarily rely on previous case law.[36]

For cross-border contentious status cases including divorce, the PSLA provides for four major jurisdiction grounds: (i) the defendant's domicile (Article 3-2 Nos 1–4); (ii) both spouses' Japanese nationality (No 5); (iii) both spouses' last common domicile (No 6); and (iv) the plaintiff's domicile under 'special circumstances' when, *inter alia*, the defendant is missing, or a judgment rendered at the defendant's domicile cannot be recognised in Japan (No 7). This 'special circumstances' test presupposes weighing up the interests of the parties and ensuring access to justice. This will apply, for example, when the defendant has been extradited, or legal or factual hindrances prevent a suit at the defendant's domicile.[37] The DRCPA, on the other hand, provides for limited jurisdiction grounds for each category of non-contentious family and succession matters. For example, jurisdiction for adoption is granted at the adoptive parents' and the child's domicile (Article 3-5), and jurisdiction for parental authority at the child's domicile (Article 3-8).[38] Due to limited party disposition, submission or choice-of-court agreement is not accepted, except for division of estate and family court conciliation (Articles 3-11(4) and 3-13(1) No 3).[39]

The jurisdiction grounds under the PSLA and the DRCPA are narrower than those of the CCP, aiming to satisfy the respondent's right to be heard and balance the parties' interests. Still, jurisdiction can be denied under 'special circumstances' in view of fairness between parties and proper and prompt administration of justice (Article 3-5 of the PSLA and Article 3-14 of the DRCPA). As a result, the 'special circumstances' test is used both to positively justify jurisdiction at the plaintiff's domicile (Article 3-2 No 7 of the PSLA) and to negatively exclude jurisdiction (Article 3-5 of the PSLA). This unusual construct may compromise legal certainty and predictability. Given the limited jurisdiction grounds under the PSLA and the DRCPA, the 'special circumstances' test to deny jurisdiction should only be sparely used.[40]

Notably, the EU and Switzerland grant jurisdiction on much broader grounds in status and family matters. In particular, jurisdiction in matrimonial cases is provided when the

[33] Act No 20 of 25 April 2018; see contributions in (2019) 62 *Japanese Yearbook of International Law*; Y Okuda, 'New Rules on International Jurisdiction of Japanese Courts in Family Matters' (2020) 50 *Zeitschrift für Japanisches Recht/Journal of Japanese Law* 217 et seq.

[34] Personal Status Litigation Act (PSLA) (Act No 109 of 16 July 2003, as amended).

[35] Domestic Relations Case Procedure Act (DRCPA) (Act No 52 of 25 May 2011, as amended).

[36] For divorce cases, see Supreme Court, 25 March 1964, *Minshû* 18-3, 486; Supreme Court, 24 June 1996, *Minshû* 50-7, 1451.

[37] Y Nishitani, 'International Adjudicatory Jurisdiction in Matrimonial Matters in Japan' (2019) 62 *Japanese Yearbook of International Law* 162 et seq.

[38] Y Nishitani, 'New International Civil Procedure Law of Japan in Status and Family Matters' (2019) 62 *Japanese Yearbook of International Law* 130 et seq.

[39] Nishitani (n 37) 151 et seq; Nishitani (n 38) 119 et seq.

[40] Nishitani (n 37) 187 et seq; Nishitani (n 38) 137 et seq.

plaintiff habitually resides or is domiciled in the forum state at least for one year, or when the plaintiff is a national of the forum state and resides there for at least six months.[41] Unlike in commercial disputes, granting jurisdiction at the plaintiff's domicile makes sense in terms of honouring his or her right to petition for divorce etc. Japan should have followed the European model to facilitate access to justice across borders.

III. 'Regionalisation': Dynamism and Challenges in East Asia

A. Diverse Jurisdictions in East Asia

The second major trend in Japanese private international law concerns 'regionalisation'. East Asia is diverse in terms of its political and economic aspects and entails different legal systems. While most jurisdictions in East Asia like Japan, Mainland China, Taiwan, Macao, North and South Korea, Vietnam and Indonesia are embedded in the civil law tradition, Hong Kong and Singapore belong to the common law system. The Philippines is characterised as a mixed legal system. Malaysia, Singapore, Indonesia and Myanmar are split between different personal laws in family relationships, depending on the individuals' religion, race or tribe. These diverse pictures in East Asia reflect the Western and Japanese colonialism. Even today, the colonial past and the developments after the Second World War raise specific conflict of laws questions.[42]

B. Non-recognition of the State or Government

i. Legal Consequences of Non-recognition: Taiwan

A number of countries, including Japan in 1972,[43] switched official recognition of the legitimate government from the Republic of China (Taiwan) to the People's Republic of China. This diplomatic move has had repercussions on various conflict of laws issues.

a. The *Kôkaryô* Case

In the famous *Kôkaryô* case, the Republic of China purchased a student dormitory named *Kôkaryô* from a private company in 1952. The dormitory, constructed in 1931, was run for Chinese students in Kyoto. Following conflicts with dormitory residents, the Republic of China instituted court proceedings in 1967 – as the legitimate government of China at that time – against the residents to recover the property in Japanese courts.

[41] For divorce cases, see art 3 of Council Regulation (EU) 2019/1111 of 25 June 2019 on jurisdiction, the recognition and enforcement of decisions in matrimonial matters and the matters of parental responsibility, and on international child abduction (recast) [2019] OJ L 178/1; art 59 of the Swiss IPRG (Private International Law Act).

[42] See Nishitani (n 2).

[43] Joint Communiqué of the Government of Japan and the Government of the People's Republic of China, 29 September 1972, www.mofa.go.jp/region/asia-paci/china/joint72.html.

The Osaka High Court acquiesced to the claim in 1987, considering that the procedural entitlement for private law disputes is not affected by the Japanese government switching the state recognition to the People's Republic of China. The judges characterised the situation in China as an 'incomplete government succession', which left leeway to validate the acts of the unrecognised government. Following leading academics, the judges reasoned that the plaintiff could pursue its legitimate interests in a private law dispute over a property that was not purchased for diplomacy or the exercise of state power.[44] The Supreme Court, however, reversed and remanded the case to the Kyoto District Court in 2007.[45] Without addressing who owned the property, the Justices simply declared that the plaintiff had lost the diplomatic authority to represent China in 1972 and hence the procedural entitlement to petition for recovery of the property.[46]

This Supreme Court decision is arguably flawed. First, it took the Supreme Court 20 years to render a judgment. This unusual delay thwarted the legitimate expectation of Taiwan after having pursued the lawsuit for over 40 years. Second, the Supreme Court decision was solely based on the argument of state recognition without ascertaining the ownership of the property. Yet, the dispute would be unsolvable if the lower courts confirmed the ownership of Taiwan. Third, the reasoning of the Supreme Court was inconsistent, as state recognition works retroactively only to validate acts of the recognised state, but not to invalidate acts undertaken by the de jure government prior to its derecognition.[47] Considering the frequent commercial transactions of Japanese enterprises in Taiwan, it would be contradictory to deny the Taiwanese government procedural entitlement to sue Japanese companies in Japan.

Because the People's Republic of China was not interested in pursuing the ownership of *Kôkaryô* or taking over the dispute, the dormitory has been left as a ruin without anybody preserving, managing or cleaning the property. It is a regrettable loss of cultural heritage, as the building has high value as modern, pre-war architecture in Japan.

b. The *Entô Kôkû* Case

The lack of diplomatic relationship between Japan and Taiwan may also hinder the proper administration of justice. This was demonstrated in the *Entô Kôkû* (*Far Eastern Air Transport*) case decided by the Tokyo District Court in 1986.[48]

After an aircraft operated by Entô Kôkû crashed following departure from the Taipei Songshan Airport in August 1981, Japanese bereaved family members petitioned for damages before the US District Court in the Northern District of California. They sued Boeing for product liability and United Airlines for negligence in selling the defective second-hand plane to Entô Kôkû. In April 1982, the US District Court dismissed the case on grounds of *forum non conveniens*. The Court ordered the plaintiffs to go to Taiwanese courts, confirming that both Boeing and United Airlines would not invoke the statute of limitations and abide by a judgment to be rendered by the Taiwanese courts to pay damages.

[44] Osaka High Court, 26 February 1987, *Hanrei Jihô* 1232, 119; see also Osaka High Court, 14 April 1982, *Hanrei Jihô* 1053, 115 (affirming the procedural entitlement of the Republic of China).

[45] Supreme Court, 27 March 2007, *Minshû* 61-2, 711, (2008) 51 *Japanese Yearbook of International Law* 512.

[46] See T Kitamura, 'Japanese Supreme Court Judgment in the So-Called "Kokaryo" Case' [2008] 7(3) *Chinese Journal of International Law* 713 et seq.

[47] Chun-i Chen, 'Special Report: Kuang Hua Liao (Kokaryo) Case' (2007) 25 *Chinese (Taiwan) Yearbook of International Law and Affairs* 140.

[48] Tokyo District Court, 20 June 1986, *Hanrei Jihô* 1196, 87.

Despite this backstory, the plaintiffs brought the same lawsuit to the District Court of Tokyo in Japan. However, the crucial evidence and witnesses on the cause of the accident were concentrated in Taiwan. Absent diplomatic relationship with Taiwan, Japanese courts could not have requested access to the evidence or judicial assistance. The judges therefore dismissed the claim under the 'special circumstances' test in 1986,[49] opining that Taiwanese courts were better placed to hear the case. The result would be the same under the current Article 3-9 of the CCP, when the necessary evidence located abroad is unavailable to the Japanese courts for lack of diplomatic relationship.[50]

ii. Legal Consequences of Non-recognition: North Korea

Over 30 countries including Japan do not recognise the Democratic People's Republic of Korea (North Korea) as an independent 'state', despite its membership of the UN. This had legal consequences on copyright protection in Japan.

The 2011 Supreme Court decision[51] underlay the following facts. The North Korean authority (X2) owned the copyright of several movies and licensed their exclusive use in Japan to a Japanese company (X1). A Japanese TV company (Y) took over the entire business of a Japanese company (A), which had made a TV programme on propaganda in North Korea and used a two-minute section of footage of the movies without the permission of X1 and X2. Thus, X1 and X2 sought an injunction and damages against Y and achieved partial success before the Tokyo High Court.

Upon appeal, the Supreme Court considered that Japan became party to the amended Berne Convention (1971 Paris Act)[52] on 24 April 1975, and North Korea on 28 April 2003. According to the Justices, Japan does not automatically obtain rights or incur obligations towards an unrecognised state joining a multilateral treaty subsequently. Rather, Japan can select whether to establish a treaty relationship with that state, unless universal obligations are set out in general international law. This is not the case with the Berne Convention, which solely protects copyrights of works created by a contracting state national or published in a contracting state. Nor did Japan enter a declaration in favour of North Korea. Thus, the Justices denied copyright protection and dismissed the claims.[53]

Notably, Japan grants the protection of intellectual property for Taiwan pursuant to the Agreement on Trade-Related Aspects of Intellectual Property Rights (hereinafter TRIPS Agreement) of the World Trade Organization (WTO),[54] to which Taiwan is party as a Separate Customs Territory. Yet, the Supreme Court treated North Korea differently by relying on the precedent of the Berne Convention, where treaty obligations towards the then Democratic Republic of Germany (DDR, or East Germany) were denied for lack of state recognition.[55]

[49] For previous case law, see n 28 above.
[50] Nishitani (n 26) 270.
[51] Supreme Court, 8 December 2011, *Minshû* 65-9, 3275.
[52] Berne Convention for the Protection of Literary and Artistic Works, done at Berne, 9 September 1886, as amended by the Paris Act, 24 July 1971, www.wipo.int/wipolex/en/text/278718.
[53] N Kobayashi, 'Case Note' (2012) 1437 *Jurist* 7.
[54] Agreement on Trade-Related Aspects of Intellectual Property Rights, done at Marrakesh, 15 April 1994, www.wto.org/english/docs_e/legal_e/27-trips_01_e.htm.
[55] M Yamada, 'Case Note' (2011) *Saikô Saibansho Hanrei Kaisetsu Minjihen* 731 et seq.

iii. *The Principle of Nationality*

In terms of conflict of laws, North Korea and Taiwan are treated as independent legal systems despite the lack of state recognition. Because conflict of laws aims to determine the law applicable to a private law relationship regardless of state interests, both North Korean law and Taiwanese law are held eligible. Suffice it to say that the unrecognised state exercises authority over its territory and has an administrative body and its own legal system.[56]

For the principle of nationality, a further question arises as to whether a 'Korean' national belongs to North Korea or South Korea, or a 'Chinese' national to Mainland China or Taiwan. For the equality of foreign legal systems, priority should not be given to the law of South Korea or Mainland China as the recognised state. The focus should be placed on the individuals' belongings in regulating family relationships. Thus, these split states have been assimilated either as a juxtaposition of two independent states or two regions within a federal state. Accordingly, the national law was determined by reference to the rules on double nationality (Article 38(1) of the AGRAL) or multi-unit state (Article 38(3) of the AGRAL) respectively. In the case law, the former position prevailed in North-South Korea cases,[57] whereas the latter position was preferred for the China-Taiwan divide.[58] In both legal constructs, the judge generally sought the individuals' closest connection based on their own and family members' habitual residence, the origin of their ancestors, the place of their family registration, and their place of birth. The membership of fellow citizens' organisations, ie, 'Mindan' for South Korea[59] and 'Chongryon' for North Korea,[60] was also decisive. In order to determine personal law, the individual's identity and sense of belonging was given critical weight.[61]

C. Reparations after the Second World War

Japan's colonialism has left some delicate issues unresolved until today. Victims of the Second World War – former conscripted soldiers, forced workers and comfort women from Korea, China and the Philippines – claimed damages against the Japanese government, but were generally unsuccessful.[62] The Japanese courts opined that: (i) the victims' individual claims

[56] The initial position of the Japanese government to only apply the law of a recognised state was gradually given up. See A Kunitomo, 'Article 38 of the AGRAL' in Y Sakurada and M Dôgauchi (eds), *Chûshaku Kokusaishihô* [*Commentary on Private International Law*], vol 2 (Yûhikaku, 2011) 266 et seq; Y Tameike, *Kokusaishihô Kôgi* [*Lecture on Private International Law*], 3rd edn (Yûhikaku, 2005) 183 et seq. For cases applying the law of Taiwan, see Supreme Court, 8 March 1994, *Minshû* 48-3, 835. For the difficulties of ascertaining North Korean law *ex officio*, see Y Nishitani, 'Treatment of and Access to Foreign Law in Japan' (2018) 46 *Zeitschrift für Japanisches Recht/Journal of Japanese Law* 81 f.

[57] Tokyo District Court, 7 June 2011, *Hanrei Times* 1368, 233.

[58] Tokyo District Court, 12 December 2013, 2013WLJPCA12128006; Tokyo District Court, 19 October 2016, 2016WLJPCA10198016.

[59] www.mindan.org/index.php.

[60] www.chongryon.com.

[61] Kunitomo (n 56) 268 et seq; Tameike (n 56) 192 et seq.

[62] For Korean victims, see Supreme Court of Japan, 29 November 2004, *Saibansho Jihô* 1376, 14 (comfort women); Supreme Court of Japan, 1 November 2007, *Minshû* 61-8, 2733; K Teraya, 'Consideration of the So-Called Comfort Women Problem in Japan-Korea Relations: Embracing the Difficulties in the International Legal and Policy Debate' [2013] 6(1) *Journal of East Asia and International Law* 195 et seq. For Chinese victims, see Supreme Court, 27 April 2005, *Saikôsaibanshû Minji* 224, 325; Supreme Court of Japan, 27 April 2007, *Minshû* 61-3, 1188 (unsuccessful against Japanese company *Nishimatsu*); Tokyo High Court, 19 April 2005 and 13 May 2005, *Shômu*

were excluded by the 1965 Korea-Japan Reparation Agreement[63] and the 1972 China-Japan Joint Communiqué;[64] (ii) state liability did not exist in the pre-war era; and (iii) damages claims grounded in torts were barred by the statute of limitations.

After Korean former forced workers sought damages against a Japanese company before the Supreme Court of Japan in vain,[65] the case was brought to the Korean Supreme Court. The Justices condemned Shin-Nittetsu Jûkin (today Nihon Seitetsu) on 30 October 2018, and Mitsubishi Jûkôgyô on 29 November 2018. The Court opined that the 1965 Korea-Japan Reparation Agreement unduly limited Japan's compensation to US$300 million without ascertaining the illegality of its colonialism. This agreement could not have ruled out Korean individuals' damages claims for Japan's wrongful acts against humanity.[66] Following these decisions, Korean–Japanese relations considerably deteriorated, in addition to the failed diplomatic solutions for Korean comfort women since 2015.[67]

To bring an end to the impasse, on 6 March 2023 the conservative Yoon administration declared a compromise solution to establish a Korean foundation with Korean companies' donations to compensate the former forced workers,[68] while requesting Japan to reiterate and confirm its past war apology statements. After Korean steel giant POSCO contributed US$3 million,[69] it is now up to the Japanese government and enterprises to voluntarily compensate victims and cooperate with the Korean government and industry. This is critically important in view of the current geopolitical challenges and tensions in the region.

D. Reciprocity for Judgments Recognition

A last crucial conflict-of-laws question in the region relates to the recognition and enforcement of foreign judgments. Following the German model, both Japan and Mainland China require 'reciprocity', except in divorce cases.[70] Japanese case law takes a generous approach to assuming reciprocity, insofar as the foreign country is expected to recognise

Geppô 53-1, 1; Tokyo High Court, 23 June 2005, *Shômu Geppô* 52-2, 445; Tokyo High Court, 14 December 2017, *Shômu Geppô* 64-11, 1541. For Philippine comfort women, see Tokyo High Court, 6 December 2000, *Shômu Geppô* 47-11, 3301.

[63] 1965 Korea-Japan Reparation Agreement.

[64] 1972 Joint Communiqué (n 43).

[65] Supreme Court of Japan, 9 October 2003, LLI/DB05810115.

[66] Supreme Court of South Korea, 30 October 2018, http://justice.skr.jp/koreajudgements/12-5.pdf; see K Aoki, 'Chôyôkô Hanketsu to Kokusaishihô' [Korean Supreme Court Judgments for Korean Wartime Forced Laborers and Private International Law] (2022) 24 *Japanese Yearbook of Private International Law* 103.

[67] The Korean Park administration agreed with the Japanese government on 28 December 2015 that JPY 1 billion (about US$ 8 million) be paid to a foundation for comfort women without clearly stating Japan's war crimes. Following fierce criticism against this agreement, the subsequent Moon administration dissolved the foundation in 2019. Later, 12 former comfort women successfully sued the Japanese government for damages before the Seoul Central District Court on 8 January 2021. Yet, the same court dismissed the same kind of damages claims brought by 20 former comfort women against the Japanese government on 21 April 2021 on the grounds of sovereign immunity. See Asahi Shimbun, 25 April 2021, https://digital.asahi.com.

[68] See Report of the Asahi Shimbun, 6 March 2023, https://digital.asahi.com.

[69] See Report of the Asahi Shimbun, 16 March 2023, https://digital.asahi.com.

[70] For further details, see Y Nishitani, 'Coordination of Legal Systems by the Recognition of Foreign Judgments: Rethinking Reciprocity in Sino-Japanese Relationships' [2019] 14(2) *Frontiers of Law in China* 193 et seq; for China, see W Zhang, 'Recognition of Foreign Judgments in China: The Essentials and Strategies' (2013/14) *Yearbook of Private International Law* 321 et seq.

Japanese judgments under 'essentially equivalent' conditions ('legally based' reciprocity).[71] Reciprocity has therefore been granted with most jurisdictions, including Hong Kong SAR, South Korea, Singapore, Germany, France, Switzerland, the UK, the US and Australia.[72] Regrettably, however, this is not the case with Mainland China.

In the 1994 *Gomi Akira* case,[73] the Dalian Intermediate People's Court decided that Japanese judgments could not be enforced in Mainland China for lack of treaty or reciprocal relationships. This position was soon confirmed by the Supreme People's Court (SPC).[74] In response, in 2003 the Osaka High Court declined the recognition of Chinese judgments that confirmed the plaintiff as an investor, holding that Mainland China would not reciprocate to recognise Japanese judgments in view of its statutes, case law and practice.[75] Similarly, in 2015 the Tokyo High Court refused to render an exequatur for a Chinese judgment ordering damages payment for defamation in the absence of reciprocity.[76] Mainland China and Japan now find themselves in a deadlock, mutually denying recognition of judgments.

Historically, the concept of reciprocity stems from public international law presupposing the equality of sovereign states. It was also considered to promote the protection of citizens abroad.[77] However, unlike these conventional ideas grounded in state interests, today's judgments recognition system is geared towards the interests of private parties.[78] Although reciprocity is said to incentivise other states to recognise judgments, it may instead lead to a stalemate if the foreign state also requires reciprocity.[79] The existence of reciprocity cannot be ascertained for sure, as was the case between Germany and Japan.[80] Nor can reciprocity safeguard the quality of foreign judgments, for it cannot halt decisions originating from a state without the rule of law or an independent judiciary insofar as that state recognises Japanese judgments.[81] After all, negative reciprocity as a retaliation between states disregards private interests, compelling a time-consuming relitigation or causing conflicting

[71] For the precedent in Japan, see Supreme Court, 7 June 1983, *Minshû* 37-5, 611.

[72] For further details, see Nishitani (n 70) 210 et seq.

[73] Dalian Intermediate People's Court, 5 November 1994; see Zhang (n 70) 334 et seq.

[74] SPC, Reply of 26 June 1995 (Japanese translation: M Kiyokawa and M Awazu, 'Meiyo-kison de isharyô wo meijita Chûgoku hanketsu ni tsuite, sôgo-hoshô ga naikoto wo riyû ni Nihon de shikkô wo mitomenakatta case (No. 1)' [Refusal of the Enforcement of a Chinese Judgment in Japan, which Awarded Damages to the Victim of Defamation] [2015] 49 (1/2) *Sandai Law Review* 168 f.).

[75] Osaka High Court, 9 April 2003, *Hanrei Jihô* 1841, 111.

[76] Tokyo High Court, 25 November 2015, LEX/DB 25541803.

[77] S Nakano, 'Gaikoku Hanketsu no Shikkô' [Enforcement of Foreign Judgments] in K Shindô, H Takahashi and S Katô (eds), *Jitsumu Minji Soshôhô Kôza* [*Series on Civil Procedure Law Practice*], 3rd edn (Seirin Shoin, 2013) 450; A Takakuwa, 'Sôgo no Hoshô' [Reciprocity] in A Takakuwa and M Dogauchi (eds), *Kokusai Minji Soshô-hô: Zaisan-hô kankei* [*International Civil Procedure Law: Financial Disputes*] (Seirin Shoin, 2002) 378.

[78] B Elbalti, 'Reciprocity and the Recognition and Enforcement of Foreign Judgments: A Lot of Bark But Not Much Bite' (2017) 13 *Journal of Private International Law* 215 et seq.

[79] Takakuwa (n 77) 372 et seq.

[80] Although ex-art 200 Japanese Code of Civil Procedure (CCP) (now art 118 CCP) adopted almost literally the equivalent German rules (§ 328 ZPO [German Code of Civil Procedure]), Germany denied reciprocity with Japan in the absence of precedent (M Nagata, 'Nihon no saibansho ga kudashita zaisanhô-jô no arasoi ni taisuru hanketsu no Doitsu ni okeru shônin-shikkô: Doitsu minji soshôhô 328 jô 1kô 5gô no nihon ni taisuru kankei deno sôgohoshô no umu' [The Recognition and Enforcement of Japanese Judgments in Civil and Commercial Matters in Germany: The Existence of Reciprocity with Japan Pursuant to § 328 (1) No 5 ZPO] [1977] 42(2) *Nihon Hôgaku* 136 et seq). It was not until a Japanese court granted an exequatur for a German judgment in 1987 (Nagoya District Court, 6 February 1987, *Hanrei Jihô* 1236, 113) that reciprocity was confirmed.

[81] See Elbalti (n 78) 216; J Basedow, 'Gegenseitigkeit im Kollisionsrecht' in K Hilbig-Lugani et al (eds), *Zwischenbilanz. Festschrift für Dagmar Coester-Waltjen zum 70. Geburtstag* (Gieseking, 2015) 345 et seq.

judgments. Thus, calls have rightly been increasing *de lege ferenda* to abolish reciprocity[82] or restrict its scope[83] in Japan. This has also been the case among Chinese authors[84] and in other legal systems.[85]

Recently, Chinese case law has become more responsive and has started recognising foreign judgments based on 'de facto' reciprocity deriving from states other than its 35 bilateral treaty partners.[86] The 2016 Nanjing Intermediate People's Court allowed a Singaporean judgment to be executed, opining that Singapore had already recognised Chinese judgments.[87] 'De facto' reciprocity has gradually been extended to the US, South Korea, Australia, New Zealand, Germany and the UK.[88] Ultimately, the SPC's 2021 Judicial Policy[89] declared substituting 'de facto' reciprocity by 'legally based' (or 'presumed') reciprocity to enhance mutual commitment and cooperation. Mainland China is now expected to warrant the circulation of judgments emanating from most common law and civil law countries.[90] These developments can hopefully incentivise Japanese courts to grant reciprocity to Mainland China.

IV. 'Internationalisation': The Way Forward

In seeking a way forward, this chapter finally addresses the trends of 'internationalisation' towards joining international instruments and establishing cooperation in East Asia.

A. Recognition and Enforcement of Judgments

As mentioned above, the lack of reciprocity between Mainland China and Japan has led to a stalemate of litigation. Without treaty-based reciprocity, the recognition of judgments is also

[82] S Ikehara, 'Kokusai Torihiki' [International Business Transactions] in *Keieihôgaku Zenshû* (Diamond Sha 1967) 388; Y Okuda, 'Unconstitutionality of Reciprocity Requirement for Recognition and Enforcement of Foreign Judgments in Japan' (2018) 13 *Frontiers of Law in China* 168 et seq; Elbalti (n 78) 214; Nishitani (n 70) 219 et seq.

[83] For excluding reciprocity in status and family matters, see Y Honma, S Nakano and H Sakai, *Kokusai Minji Tetsuzuki-hô* [*International Civil Procedure Law*], 2nd edn (Yûhikaku, 2012) 196; for applying reciprocity only to foreign judgments requiring execution, see Takakuwa (n 77) 98.

[84] See Q He, 'The Recognition and Enforcement of Foreign Judgments between the United States and China: A Study of *Sanlian v. Robinson*' (2014) 6 *Tsinghua China Law Review* 37; W Zhang, 'Recognition and Enforcement of Foreign Judgments in China: A Call for Special Attention to Both the "Due Service Requirement" and the "Principle of Reciprocity"' (2013) 12 *Chinese Journal of International Law* 166; W Zhang, *Recognition and Enforcement of Foreign Judgments in China: Rules, Practice and Strategies* (Kluwer International, 2014) 94 et seq.

[85] Elbalti (n 78) 187 et seq.

[86] M Yu, 'List of China's Bilateral Treaties on Judicial Assistance in Civil and Commercial Matters (Enforcement of Foreign Judgments Included)', chinajusticeobserver.com/a/list-of-chinas-bilateral-treaties-on-judicial-assistance-in-civil-and-commercial-matters.

[87] Nanjing Intermediate People's Court, 9 December 2016, Case No (2016) Su 01 Xie Wai Ren No 3.

[88] See M Yu and G Du, 'August 2022 Update: List of China's Cases on Recognition of Foreign Judgments', conflictoflaws.net/2022/august-2022-update-list-of-chinas-cases-on-recognition-of-foreign-judgments.

[89] SPC, 'Conference Summary of the Symposium on Foreign-Related Commercial and Maritime Trials of Courts Nationwide' (31 December 2021); for further details, see M Yu and G Du, '2022 Breakthrough for Collecting Judgments in China', cjoglobal.com/wp-content/uploads/2022/06/2022-BREAKTHROUGH-FOR-COLLECTING-JUDGMENTS-IN-CHINA-CJO-GLOBAL.pdf.

[90] See M Yu and G Du, 'China's 2022 Landmark Judicial Policy Clears Final Hurdle for Enforcement of Foreign Judgments', conflictoflaws.net/2022/chinas-2022-landmark-judicial-policy-clears-final-hurdle-for-enforcement-of-foreign-judgments.

excluded in Indonesia and Thailand, and is considerably limited in Cambodia, Myanmar, the Philippines and Vietnam.[91] Abolishing the reciprocity requirement would be a desirable way forward, but is hard to achieve at the domestic law level.

To build bridges between East Asian jurisdictions, a more viable avenue would be to join the 2005 HCCH Choice of Court Convention[92] and the 2019 HCCH Judgments Convention.[93] The 2005 Convention is constructed as a double convention. It determines both the direct jurisdiction based on exclusive forum selection clauses and the recognition and enforcement of judgments emanating from the chosen court. While the contracting state, whose courts have been selected, is obliged to hear the case (Article 5), the other contracting states cooperate to dismiss the claim when unduly seised by one of the parties (Article 6), and to recognise and enforce the judgment rendered by the selected court (Articles 8 and 9). The 2019 Convention, on the other hand, is a single convention dealing solely with the recognition and enforcement of foreign judgments. It aims to facilitate the circulation of judgments without excluding the recognition of judgments via domestic law unless they run counter to the exclusive jurisdiction ground under Article 6 (Article 15), or via international or regional instruments (Article 23). The 2019 Convention has relatively restricted indirect jurisdiction grounds that were agreeable to various states (Article 5), while leaving the way open to recognise foreign judgments pursuant to national law.

The 2005 and 2019 Conventions have gained 33 and 29 contracting states respectively. In Asia, however, only Singapore has so far joined the 2005 Convention. It is hoped that other countries will follow suit, as regional law-making has hardly developed in Asia, unlike in Europe or Latin America.[94]

B. Alternative Dispute Resolution

Owing to the uncertainty surrounding litigation, business communities in East Asia have regularly turned to alternative dispute resolution (ADR) – ie, arbitration and mediation. ADR is an efficient, professional and confidential method of dispute resolution. Furthermore, the cross-border enforcement of arbitral awards, or settlement agreements resulting from mediation, is guaranteed worldwide by the 1958 New York Convention[95] and the 2018 Singapore Convention[96] respectively.

[91] See the relevant national reports in A Chong (ed), *Recognition and Enforcement of Foreign Judgments in Asia* (Asian Business Law Institute, 2017) and A Reyes (ed), *Recognition and Enforcement of Judgments in Civil and Commercial Matters* (Hart Publishing, 2019).

[92] See n 29 above.

[93] HCCH Convention of 2 July 2019 on the Recognition and Enforcement of Foreign Judgments in Civil or Commercial Matters.

[94] Y Nishitani, 'The HCCH's Development in the Asia-Pacific Region' in R Gulati, T John, and B Köhler (eds), *Elgar Companion to the Hague Conference on Private International Law* (Edward Elgar, 2020) 72 et seq.

[95] United Nations Convention on the Recognition and Enforcement of Foreign Arbitral Awards, done at New York on 10 June 1958. Its 172 contracting parties include the People's Republic of China (with Hong Kong SAR and Macao SAR), Japan, the Republic of Korea, Singapore, Thailand, Malaysia, Indonesia, the Philippines and India. Taiwan has not been permitted to join (uncitral.un.org/en/texts/arbitration/conventions/foreign_arbitral_awards/status2).

[96] United Nations Convention on International Settlement Agreements Resulting from Mediation, done at New York on 20 December 2018 (open for signature since 7 August 2019). The Convention has gained 12 states parties, including Japan, and 45 signatories. See uncitral.un.org/en/texts/mediation/conventions/international_settlement_agreements/status (as of 17 October 2023).

In Japan, international commercial arbitration and mediation are underdeveloped. The government has started to promote ADR only recently. Arbitration centres have newly been opened in Tokyo and Osaka,[97] along with a mediation centre in Kyoto.[98] On 28 April 2023, Japan's Diet approved amendments to the Arbitration Act[99] and the ADR Act,[100] and adopted the Implementation Act for the 2018 Singapore Convention to accede to it.[101] The amendments to the Arbitration Act primarily aim to introduce rules on provisional measures by the arbitral tribunal, along the lines of the 2006 amendment of the UNCITRAL Model Law.[102] The ADR Act now provides for a mechanism of rendering settlement agreements enforceable based on the parties' agreement in writing. This will be a leap forward for formalising ADR.

However, it is doubtful whether these measures will be sufficient in terms of providing competition with other established venues for ADR. In Asia, the hubs of ADR have been Singapore and Hong Kong. They have cutting-edge facilities, expertise and a long experience in case management. They also have the advantage of being common law systems, English-speaking and equipped with arbitration-friendly legislature and judiciary, as well as highly specialised arbitrators, lawyers and judges. Arguably, there is a long way to go before Japan catches up with these venues.

C. The 1980 HCCH Child Abduction Convention

A further important international setting in private international law is the 1980 HCCH Child Abduction Convention.[103] Once a child habitually resident in a contracting state has wrongfully been removed to or retained in another contracting state in breach of rights of custody, the 1980 Convention ensures that the child will be promptly returned to the state of origin without entering into custody issues on the merits, and that rights of access of the left-behind parent will be respected. By swiftly restoring the status quo, the 1980 Convention respects the best interests of the child and their right to maintain personal relations and direct contact with both parents.[104] As a global instrument, the 1980 Convention has gained 103 contracting states, including in Asia the People's Republic of China (limited to Hong Kong SAR (1997) and Macao SAR (1999)), Turkmenistan (1998), Uzbekistan (1999), Sri Lanka (2001), Thailand (2002), Singapore (2011), the Republic of Korea (2013), Kazakhstan (2013), Japan (2014), the Philippines (2016) and Pakistan (2017). Other countries like India, Indonesia and Vietnam are said to be envisioning accession. Yet, the implementation of the 1980 Convention remains a challenge for Asian countries that

[97] For 'Japan International Dispute Resolution Center', see idrc.jp.

[98] For 'Kyoto International Mediation Center', see jimc-kyoto.jp.

[99] Amendments to the Arbitration Act (Act No 15 of 28 April 2023).

[100] Amendments to the Act on Promotion of Use of Alternative Dispute Resolution ('ADR Act') (Art No 17 of 28 April 2023).

[101] Implementation Act for the 2018 Singapore Convention on International Settlement Agreements Resulting from Mediation (Art No 16 of 28 April 2023). Japan acceded to the Singapore Convention on 1 October 2023.

[102] See n 11 above.

[103] HCCH Convention of 25 October 1980 on the Civil Aspects of International Child Abduction.

[104] Articles 9(3) and 10(2) of the United Nations Convention on the Rights of the Child (CRC), done at New York on 20 November 1989.

frequently lack a clear concept of 'rights' and 'obligations' for child custody or favour the father as the natural custodian or guardian of the child, as is the case under traditional Hindu and Islamic law.[105]

Japan struggled to adapt to the 1980 Convention and qualify one parent's unilateral act of taking the child away from the other parent as illegal and to require the child's prompt return. This is because in Japan the mother typically takes the child and moves out of the house without the father's consent once a marital relationship breaks down. This act is not illegal under domestic law, even though the parents share parental authority, since the father is deemed not to have enforceable custody rights against the mother as a primary caregiver.[106] Moreover, 86.4 per cent of all divorces take the form of non-judicial consensual divorce.[107] The parents do not share parental authority after divorce ('clean break') and determine childcare and child support themselves. However, the parents' agreement remains unexamined by the authority and is usually difficult to enforce against the non-compliant parent.[108]

Nevertheless, upon joining the 1980 Convention on 1 April 2014, Japan established an efficient return mechanism for cross-border cases.[109] It is grounded in administrative cooperation through the Central Authority, which is the Minister of Foreign Affairs, and in return proceedings conducted by the Tokyo and Osaka Family Courts. Notably, amicable solutions through in-court conciliation or settlement agreements by out-of-court mediation constitute 62.0 per cent of the cases in Japan,[110] much higher than the average 30 per cent of all contracting states.[111] Case law has also developed,[112] addressing various issues to determine the child's habitual residence, grave risk exception, change of circumstances and habeas corpus orders. To strengthen the execution of return orders, the Implementation Act was amended in 2019, abolishing the 'simultaneous presence' of the taking parent and the child, and granting exceptions to the priority of money orders to proceed to coercive execution by substitute henceforth.[113]

Notably, on 1 February 2019, the UN Committee on the Rights of the Child adopted a periodic report for Japan in which it suggests that all necessary efforts be taken to ensure

[105] S Jolly and S Khanderia, *Indian Private International Law* (Hart Publishing, 2021) 157; see Y Nishitani, 'International Child Abduction in Asia' in M Freeman and N Taylor (eds), *Research Handbook on International Child Abduction* (Edward Elgar 2023) 200 et seq.

[106] T Hayashi, 'Kokugai Tenkyo ni kansuru Kadai to Tenbô' [Issues and Perspectives of International Relocation] (2020) 22 *Kokusaishiho Nenpo* 2.

[107] For 'Jinko Dôtai Chôsa 2021' [Population Census 2021], see www.mhlw.go.jp/toukei/list/81-1.html.

[108] For further details, see Y Nishitani, 'Kindschaftsrecht in Japan – Geschichte, Gegenwart und Zukunft' (2014) 37 *Zeitschrift für Japanisches Recht/Journal of Japanese Law* 77; Y Nishitani, 'Reformüberlegungen zum japanischen Familienrecht' in M Gebauer and S Huber (eds), *Gestaltungsfreiheit im Familienrecht* (Mohr Siebeck, 2017) 114; Y Nishitani, 'Access to the Child in Cross-Border Family Separation' (2021) 52 *Zeitschrift für Japanisches Recht/Journal of Japanese Law* 51.

[109] See the Implementation Act (Act No 48 of 19 June 2013).

[110] See the statistics at: www.mofa.go.jp/mofaj/files/100012143.pdf (as of 1 June 2023).

[111] N Lowe and V Stephens, 'Part 1 – A Statistical Analysis of Applications Made in 2015 under the Hague Convention of 25 October 1980 on the Civil Aspects of International Child Abduction – Global Report' (HCCH, No 11A of February 2018), para 62.

[112] See, inter alia, Supreme Court, 21 December 2017, *Saibansho Jihô* 1691, 10 (US) (INCADAT: HC/E/JP 1387); Supreme Court, 15 March 2018, *Minshû* 72-1, 17 (US) (INCADAT: HC/E/JP 1388); Supreme Court, 16 April 2020, *Minshû* 74-3, 737 (Russia) (to be reported in INCADAT).

[113] Act No 2 of 17 May 2019; for further details, see Nishitani (n 105) 203 et seq.

the return of and access to the child pursuant to the 1980 Convention.[114] Further, on 8 July 2020, the European Parliament adopted a resolution urging Japan to abide by the 1980 Convention and the UN Convention on the Rights of the Child to return children abducted from Germany, France and Italy, and ensure access to them by the left-behind parent. The European Parliament also suggested that Japan should introduce joint parental responsibility after divorce. This resolution reflects prior negotiations between the leaders of Germany, France, Italy and Japan.[115]

The establishment of joint parental authority is not directly linked to the implementation of the 1980 Convention. Yet, proper regulation of family matters after divorce is of crucial importance in Japan, considering that over 50 per cent of single mothers live below the poverty line.[116] Thus, Japan's Minister of Justice convened the Legislative Subcommittee on Family Law on 10 February 2021 to amend rules on divorce and related family matters, including parental authority, custody, access and child support.[117] The Legislative Subcommittee consulted on these issues, published an Interim Proposal on 15 November 2022 and obtained over 8,000 opinions from public consultation. A proposal will presumably be adopted soon to introduce the option of joint parental authority after divorce and to ensure measures in the best interests of the child to uphold contact with both parents and to combat domestic violence and child abuse.[118]

Although criticism by foreign countries of the practice in Japan has not always been accurate, Japan's acceptance of the 1980 Convention brought about positive developments in Japanese private international law and substantive family law. It is hoped that other Asian countries will follow suit, even though the Convention's implementation will require major reforms and adjustments in their domestic legal systems.

V. Conclusions

This chapter has sought to delineate latest developments of private international law in Japan and East Asia in view of the trends of nationalisation, regionalisation and internationalisation. While domestic legislation has largely advanced in the last two decades in accordance with the judicial reform and deregulation in Japan, enhancing an amicable relationship with the neighbouring countries and establishing international legal framework remain important tasks for Japan.

In the absence of overarching regional organisations in Asia, building bridges between states for cooperation faces major obstacles. In this respect, the HCCH will continue to play a crucial role through its Regional Office for Asia and the Pacific (ROAP) in Hong Kong.

[114] Committee on the Rights of the Child, "Concluding observations on the combined fourth and fifth periodic reports of Japan" adopted on 1 February 2019 (CRC/C/JPN/CO/4-5) (document dated 5 March 2019), tbinternet.ohchr.org/_layouts/15/TreatyBodyExternal/Countries.aspx.

[115] European Parliament Resolution, 8 July 2020, www.europarl.europa.eu/doceo/document/TA-9-2020-0182_EN.html.

[116] www.jil.go.jp/press/documents/20191017.pdf.

[117] The 189th Meeting of the Legislative Committee on 10 February 2021, Consultation No 113 on Amendments for Divorce and Related Family Matters, www.moj.go.jp/shingi1/shingi03500039.html.

[118] www.moj.go.jp/shingi1/housei02_003007.

Academics have also started to work together to mutually understand the existing conflict of laws rules in the region and to develop 'Asian Principles on Private International Law'. This is a stimulating task, given that Asian jurisdictions have divergent legal traditions grounded in the reception of Western legal systems and colonial history.[119] At present, a series of papers and books on Asian private international law continue to be published.[120] It is hoped that further cooperation can be enhanced in the region and can lead to the development of a common legal framework in East Asia.

[119] See N Takasugi and B Elbalti, 'Asian Principles of Private International Law' in D Girsberger, T Kadner Graziano and JL Neels (eds), *Choice of Law in International Commercial Contracts. Global Perspectives on the Hague Principles* (Oxford University Press, 2021) 399 et seq; W Chen and G Goldstein, 'The Asian Principles of Private International Law: Objectives, Contents, Structure and Selected Topics on Choice of Law' (2017) 13 *Journal of Private International Law* 411 et seq; M Uematsu, 'APPIL (Asian Principles of Private International Law) and its Perspective Regarding International Jurisdiction' (2019) 37 *Ritsumeikan Law Review* 35 et seq; see also CSA Okoli, 'The Recognition and Enforcement of Foreign Judgments in Civil and Commercial Matters in Asia' (2022) 18 *Journal of Private International Law* 522 et seq.

[120] See, eg, Studies in Private International Law – Asia by Hart Publishing.

8

Private International Law Developments in Hong Kong

WILSON LUI*

I. Introduction

Hong Kong is a Special Administrative Region of the People's Republic of China (PRC).[1] For some time prior to 1997, Hong Kong was a British colony with its legal system based on the common law. As the PRC has exercised its sovereignty over Hong Kong since 1 July 1997, the Basic Law of the Hong Kong Special Administrative Region (the 'Basic Law') now serves as the constitutional document for Hong Kong.[2] It provides for the 'One Country, Two Systems' arrangement by guaranteeing that the previous capitalist system and way of life shall remain unchanged for 50 years and that the socialist system and policies shall not be practised in Hong Kong.[3] Moreover, the Basic Law preserves the laws previously in force in Hong Kong, including the common law, rules of equity, ordinances, subordinate legislation and customary law.[4] The legal and judicial systems and principles previously practised in Hong Kong are also maintained.[5] The Hong Kong courts may adjudicate cases in accordance with the applicable laws and with reference to other common law precedents,[6] and the Court of Final Appeal in Hong Kong is vested with the power of final adjudication, which may invite judges from other common law jurisdictions to hear and decide cases.[7]

Considering this constitutional background and Hong Kong's status as an international legal and dispute resolution hub, Hong Kong has made frequent references to developments in other common law (and sometimes civil law) jurisdictions when deciding cases or when drafting or revising legislation. Hong Kong either *adopts* these foreign developments directly or *adapts* them to local needs. Moreover, it also *creates* new rules

* I thank Mr Kenneth Tsui for his helpful research assistance.

[1] The establishment of Special Administrative Regions is based on art 31 of the Constitution of the PRC.

[2] Basic Law, art 11. The power of interpretation of the Basic Law is vested in the Standing Committee of the National People's Congress: Basic Law, art 158.

[3] ibid art 5.

[4] ibid arts 8 and 18. Other laws in force in Hong Kong include national laws listed in Annex III to the Basic Law, and laws enacted by the legislature of Hong Kong.

[5] See, eg, Basic Law, arts 81, 86 and 87.

[6] ibid arts 19 and 84.

[7] ibid art 82.

and takes on new directions on its own. Such adoption, adaptation and creation processes are particularly important to Hong Kong because while Hong Kong is an inalienable part of the PRC, Hong Kong and Mainland China are considered as two jurisdictions for the purposes of private international law. This leads to a range of issues which can only be resolved by a skilful combination of these approaches.

Seen in this light, the rules of Hong Kong private international law have various sources. These include: (1) common law and statutory rules prior to 1997 that are maintained under Articles 8 and 18 of the Basic Law; (2) cases after 1997 decided by the Hong Kong courts; and (3) statutes or statutory amendments passed by the legislature of Hong Kong which have come into effect at any time since 1997. Within the last category, there is a further distinction between (a) those which originated from inter-regional and international conventions or instruments, which are subsequently incorporated as domestic law, and (b) those which are created to codify or amend pre-existing rules. Section II attempts to categorise private international law developments in Hong Kong with respect to the three main types of questions that arise in the discipline: jurisdiction, choice of law, and recognition and enforcement. Section III concludes with trends and future directions, as well as some predictions as to how Hong Kong will participate in or contribute to the harmonisation of rules. Harmonisation may well be considered as the fourth question of the modern discipline of private international law.[8]

II. Adoptions, Adaptations and Creations

A. Jurisdiction

Hong Kong courts have jurisdiction over all cases in Hong Kong, but have no jurisdiction over acts of state such as defence and foreign affairs.[9] The court's jurisdiction is invoked upon service.[10] If a party cannot be served in Hong Kong, the court may exercise 'long-arm jurisdiction' over that party by granting 'leave' (approval) for the plaintiff to serve the party 'out of jurisdiction'. The plaintiff must show: (1) a good arguable case under one of the 'gateways' in Order 11, rule 1(1) of the Rules of the High Court (Cap 4A) (RHC) or the Rules of the District Court (Cap 336H) (RDC); (2) a serious issue to be tried on the merits of the case; and (3) that Hong Kong is the appropriate forum for the trial of the action. When examining the appropriateness of the forum, the test of *forum non conveniens* laid out in the House of Lords case of *Spiliada*[11] was quickly adopted in Hong Kong[12] and has since been followed in multiple cases after the handover.[13] The principles for the grant of anti-suit injunctions are also similar.[14]

[8] W Lui and A Reyes, 'Introduction' in A Reyes and W Lui (eds), *Direct Jurisdiction: Asian Perspectives* (Hart Publishing, 2021) 1.
[9] Basic Law, art 19.
[10] Rules of the High Court (Cap 4A) (RHC), Ord 10; Rules of the District Court (Cap 336H) (RDC), Ord 10.
[11] *Spiliada Maritime Corporation v Cansulex Ltd, The Spiliada* [1987] AC 460.
[12] *The Adhiguna Meranti* [1987] HKLR 904.
[13] See, eg, *DGC v SLC (née C)* [2005] 3 HKC 293; *SPH v SA* (2014) 17 HKCFAR 364.
[14] See, eg, *Turner v Grovit* [2001] UKHL 65, [2002] 1 WLR 107; *Suen Kwai Kam v Central China Dragon Select Growth Fund* [2020] HKCFI 69 [25]; *Linde GmbH v Ruschemalliance Inc* [2023] HKCFI 2409.

Order 11 in the RHC and the RDC were substantially similar to Order 11 of the former English Rules of the Supreme Court. Both were modified over the years and they now differ in matters of detail: Hong Kong added several new grounds in 2008 in light of the Civil Justice Reform, while the revised rules in the UK are now contained in Practice Direction 6B of the Civil Procedure Rules. However, the Hong Kong courts have often interpreted these 'gateways' in alignment with English law. In *Fong Chak Kwan v Ascentic Ltd*, the Court of Final Appeal (CFA) considered the meaning of 'damage' under the tort gateway for jurisdiction over foreign defendants to serve out under Order 11, rule 1(1)(f).[15] The CFA accepted the majority view in the *Brownlie* cases[16] and adopted a wide and liberal interpretation founded on the 'natural and ordinary' meaning of the gateway. Lord Collins, writing as a non-permanent judge (NPJ) for the unanimous court, held that satisfying the gateways alone does not confer jurisdiction, as it must also be shown that the domestic forum is the proper place to bring the claim.[17] The court is entitled to consider the discretionary test of *forum non conveniens* and decide whether the case falls within both the 'letter' of the rule and the 'spirit' of the gateway.[18] This case shows the CFA's willingness to follow the common law footsteps while contributing further insights and developments to the common law world. Moreover, as a former judge of the UK Supreme Court, Lord Collins NPJ utilised his experience and knowledge when expanding on the majority's analysis and rejecting the minority's reasoning in the *Brownlie* cases. This is one of the occasions where the overseas non-permanent judges introduced different perspectives based on their past experiences accrued from other jurisdictions as 'globe-trotters'.[19] These efforts are invaluable contributions to the local jurisprudence as they facilitate the Hong Kong courts to actively consider the views of other jurisdictions and turn some of these into local practice through judgments which are binding under the stare decisis principle.

Although the determination of jurisdiction through long-arm jurisdictional gateways and the tests on *forum non conveniens* and anti-suit injunctions are largely similar, the concept of 'domicile' in the Hong Kong law and the English law differs significantly. Domicile is one of the personal connecting factors when determining jurisdiction. However, the common law rules have been described as a difficult concept 'dependent upon a refined, subtle, and frequently very expensive judicial investigation of the devious twists and turns of the mind of man'.[20] Indeed, 'it is frequently very difficult to determine a person's domicile, and the resulting uncertainty has given rise to criticism and to proposals for reform of the law'.[21] For example, the rule that the domicile of origin revives when a person abandons a domicile of choice has been much criticised 'since it may result in a

[15] *Fong Chak Kwan v Ascentic Ltd* (2022) 25 HKCFAR 135, [2022] HKCFA 12.

[16] *Brownlie v Four Seasons Holding Inc (Brownlie I)* [2017] UKSC 80, [2018] 1 WLR 192; *Brownlie v FS Cairo (Nile Plaza) LLC (Brownlie II)* [2021] UKSC 45, [2021] 3 WLR 1011.

[17] *Fong Chak Kwan* (n 15) [112].

[18] ibid [95], [117]–[119].

[19] Other examples include the judgment of Lord Millett NPJ in *Libertarian Investments Ltd v Hall* (2013) 16 HKCFAR 681 on the principles of equitable compensation, and the dissent of Gummow NPJ in *C v D* [2023] HKCFA 16 on the distinction between the 'jurisdiction' of the arbitral tribunal and the 'admissibility' of the claim.

[20] *R v Barnet LBC ex p Shah* [1983] 2 AC 309, 345.

[21] Lord Collins of Mapesbury et al (eds), *Dicey, Morris and Collins on the Conflict of Laws*, 16th edn (Sweet & Maxwell, 2022) para 6-052.

person's being domiciled in a country with which the connection is stale or tenuous and which, indeed, they may never even have visited'.[22]

In Hong Kong, the rules to determine a person's domicile (on or after 1 March 2009) have departed from the previous common law position and are now contained in the Domicile Ordinance (Cap 596).[23] While the general principles are retained, the specific rules have become substantially different. For instance, the place of domicile of children and incapacitated adults should be the territory where the person has his or her closest connection.[24] These reforms are to reflect modern realities, departing from the Victorian concept of domicile founded on the idea of the father being *paterfamilias*.[25] The Domicile Ordinance also abolishes the common law concepts of 'domicile of origin' and 'domicile of dependency'. These were the bedrock for deciding the domicile of a person under common law, but the actual applications and interactions between these two concepts have proven to be complex.[26] Under that premise, Hong Kong reforms and simplifies the common law rules by shaping it into laws that reflect the general modern practices in the jurisdiction. Such reform is not common in most other common law jurisdictions as they tend to maintain and work with the complicated set of rules, instead of codifying them into statutes.[27]

B. Choice of Law

It is impossible to describe in this short chapter all the choice-of-law rules in Hong Kong private international law. The following considers several areas that are deserving of attention.

A notable example in which Hong Kong follows a traditional common law concept is the double actionability rule, which provides that an act sued on in Hong Kong but committed in another jurisdiction can be tortious only if it is actionable under the law of both jurisdictions.[28] This has been abolished by statute in the UK[29] and New Zealand,[30] and has been discarded in Canada and Australia. While the CFA has confirmed the applicability of the rule, it also states that the rule might be reconsidered in the future.[31] This demonstrates that common law rules existing before 1997 are generally preserved in Hong Kong as a source of private international law rules. However, instead of blindly following other

[22] ibid para 6-079.

[23] Domicile Ordinance (Cap 596), ss 13 and 14.

[24] Domicile Ordinance (Cap 596), ss 4, 8 and 11.

[25] If a child's parents were married when he or she was born, it is assumed that his or her domicile is that of his or her father's: *Udny v Udny* (1869) LR 1 Sc & Div 441.

[26] G Johnston and P Harris, *The Conflict of Laws in Hong Kong*, 3rd edn (Sweet & Maxwell, 2017) para 7.009.

[27] Law Reform Commission of Hong Kong, *Report: Rules for Determining Domicile* (April 2005) ch 4.

[28] *Philips v Eyre* (1870) LR 6 QB 1; *Boys v Chaplin* [1971] AC 356. See also the exception in *Red Sea Insurance Co Ltd v Bouygues SA* [1995] 1 HKLR 224, which happens to be a Privy Council case on appeal from Hong Kong.

[29] Private International Law (Miscellaneous Provisions) Act 1995, which entered into force on 1 May 1996 (with one exception on defamation – see s 13).

[30] Private International Law (Choice of Law in Tort) Act 2017. Singapore is one other jurisdiction that adopts this rule: see, eg, A Chong and M Yip, *Singapore Private International Law: Commercial Issues and Practice* (Oxford University Press, 2023) ch 8.

[31] *Xiamen Xinjingdi Group Co Ltd v Eton Properties Ltd* (2020) 23 HKCFAR 348, [2020] HKCFA 32 [159].

common law jurisdictions, the Hong Kong courts will preserve, reconsider or discard common law rules according to the development of laws in the local context.[32]

One other striking feature of Hong Kong law is that it preserves the application of traditional Chinese laws, customs and usages.[33] As such, Chinese customary marriages and concubinages were possible until the reform of the marriage ordinances in 1971.[34] The application of Chinese law and custom might be characterised as a direct application of Hong Kong domestic law rather than as foreign law applied through the rules of private international law. These Chinese customary laws are applicable when all parties are Chinese persons of Hong Kong pre-nuptial domicile.[35] Therefore, the Hong Kong courts have often had to examine the validity of concubinage in family, land and probate cases. The Hong Kong courts will then be required to consider the customary law along with the normal rules on the validity of marriages and marital unions in private international law.

Another recent development relates to the methods to plead and prove foreign law. While Hong Kong follows the traditional common law position that expert evidence is required to prove foreign law, the UK has seen a relaxation of the requirements since the decision of *Brownlie II*.[36] It is further suggested that Hong Kong may see a similar relaxation, particularly due to time and costs concerns.[37]

In the area of cross-border insolvency, the laws of Hong Kong also differ from those of the neighbouring jurisdictions. In recent years, several Asian jurisdictions have incorporated the United Nations Commission on International Trade Law (UNCITRAL) Model Law on Cross-Border Insolvency (the 'Model Law'). For instance, Singapore adopted the Model Law (which prevails the Singapore domestic insolvency law) as a major strategy to position itself as a hub for insolvency and restructuring in the Asia-Pacific region.[38] The Model Law regime enables coordinated cross-border rescue and restructuring processes for companies while safeguarding the rights of foreign creditors. It focuses on four elements identified as key to the conduct of cross-border insolvency cases: access, recognition, relief (assistance) and cooperation.

Instead of adopting the Model Law, the Hong Kong courts have been utilising its common law framework to recognise foreign insolvency proceedings and foreign liquidators, and to provide assistance when issued with a formal letter of request from a foreign court.

[32] For example, when discussing whether *Patel v Mirza* [2016] UKSC 42, [2017] AC 467 (which overruled the reliance approach in *Tinsley v Milligan* [1994] 1 AC 340) should be followed despite the lack of Hong Kong authorities directly on point, the Court of Appeal remarked that '[a]dherence to an old [common law] rule … would only lead to a disconnect with other common law jurisdictions, and misunderstanding or confusion of parties engaged in commercial transactions': *Monat Investment Ltd v All Person(s) in Occupation of Part of the Remaining Portion of Lot No 591 in Mui Wo DD 4* [2023] 2 HKLRD 1311, [2023] HKCA 479 [52.5] (Yuen JA).

[33] Section 2 of the Marriage Reform Ordinance (Cap 179) defines 'Chinese law and custom' to mean 'such of the laws and customs of China as would immediately prior to 5 April 1843 have been applicable to Chinese inhabitants of Hong Kong'.

[34] For a detailed discussion, see W Lui, 'Hong Kong' in A Reyes, W Lui and K Nishioka (eds), *Choice of Law and Recognition in Asian Family Law* (Hart Publishing, 2023) 51–80.

[35] *Suen Toi Lee v Yau Yee Ping* (2001) 4 HKCFAR 474 [38].

[36] *Brownlie II* (n 16).

[37] For a detailed discussion, see W Lui, 'Hong Kong' in K Nishioka (ed), *Treatment of Foreign Law in Asia* (Hart Publishing, 2023) 25–50.

[38] Insolvency, Restructuring and Dissolution Act 2018 (Singapore), pt 11. Myanmar is another Asian jurisdiction which implemented the Model Law in 2020.

Earlier Hong Kong courts have recognised substantive and procedural limitations to such common law jurisdiction.[39] Departing from earlier decisions that Hong Kong courts cannot provide assistance to foreign liquidators unless the orders sought would be available under Hong Kong law,[40] the Hong Kong courts have recently shifted their focus in identifying the 'centre of main interest' (COMI). The applicant (liquidator) has to satisfy that: (1) the foreign insolvency proceedings are collective insolvency proceedings opened in the company's country of incorporation (including civil law jurisdictions);[41] (2) the foreign insolvency proceedings are conducted in the jurisdiction in which the company's COMI is located;[42] and (3) the assistance is necessary for the administration of a foreign winding-up.[43] This shows that the Hong Kong courts are developing their own set of rules on cross-border insolvency through court precedents, taking a different route from 'Model Law jurisdictions' such as Singapore.

Although Hong Kong does not adopt the Model Law, it is generally willing to incorporate interregional and international conventions or instruments as domestic law. For example, the UNCITRAL Model Law on International Commercial Arbitration 2006 is generally adopted in the Arbitration Ordinance (Cap 609).[44] Moreover, Hong Kong has adopted several Conventions of the Hague Conference on Private International Law (HCCH). These include the 1980 Hague Child Abduction Convention through the Child Abduction and Custody Ordinance (Cap 512), the 1985 Hague Trusts Convention through section 2 of the Recognition of Trusts Ordinance (Cap 76) and the 1961 Hague Form of Wills Convention through sections 24–29 of the Wills Ordinance (Cap 30). While these Hague Conventions are applicable to Hong Kong, the PRC did not enter into these Conventions.[45] Even for Conventions where both jurisdictions are parties, such as the 1965 Hague Service Convention, they are not applicable across the border as Hong Kong and Mainland China are within the same sovereign state. Separate arrangements are needed and there are practical difficulties in implementing these across the border.[46]

C. Recognition and Enforcement of Foreign Judgments and Arbitral Awards

The recognition and enforcement regime of Hong Kong is based on both the common law and statutes. Some foreign judgments can be recognised under the Foreign Judgments (Reciprocal Enforcement) Ordinance (Cap 319). Moreover, specific statutory regimes

[39] *Joint Official Liquidators of A Co v B & C* [2014] 4 HKLRD 374 [11]–[18].

[40] *Joint Administrators of African Minerals Ltd v Madison Pacific Trust Ltd* [2015] HKCFI 645 [12].

[41] *Re CEFC Shanghai International Group Ltd (in liquidation)* [2020] 1 HKLRD 676, [2020] HKCFI 167 [8]–[9].

[42] *Re Global Brands Group Holding Ltd (in liquidation)* [2022] 3 HKLRD 316, [2022] HKCFI 1789 [15]–[17], [31]–[42]; *Re Guangdong Overseas Construction Corporation* [2023] 3 HKLRD 262, [2023] HKCFI 1340.

[43] *Singularis Holdings Ltd v PricewaterhouseCoopers* [2014] UKPC 36, [2015] AC 1675 [25].

[44] For a detailed discussion, see, eg, S Wong, CK Kwong and W Lui, *Hong Kong Arbitration Judgments and Commentaries: Applications of the UNCITRAL Model Law and the provisions of the Hong Kong Arbitration Ordinance (Cap 609)* (Hong Kong Institute of Arbitrators, 2023).

[45] Hong Kong has never been a sovereign state and therefore cannot enter HCCH Conventions on its own. Such peculiar status is because the UK entered into these HCCH Conventions and extended their application to Hong Kong before 1997, and the PRC declared that they will continue to apply to Hong Kong after 1 July 1997.

[46] See section II.C below. See also Y Si, 'Some Thoughts on Improving the Service Mechanism of Judicial Documents in Hong Kong-Related Civil and Commercial Cases in China' (2023) 2 *China Journal of Applied*

have been introduced to tackle the cross-border issues between Hong Kong and Mainland China. As Hong Kong and Mainland China are considered as two jurisdictions for the purposes of private international law, this has at least two implications for Hong Kong in terms of recognition and enforcement. First, any judgment or order of Mainland China will be enforced or recognised in Hong Kong only if it fulfils the usual conditions for enforcement or recognition at common law or statute.[47] Second, this renders any international conventions and instruments inapplicable across the two jurisdictions, as Hong Kong is a territorial unit within the PRC.

The first attempt to facilitate recognition and enforcement of Mainland judgments is the Mainland Judgments (Reciprocal Enforcement) Ordinance (Cap 597) (MJREO), which entered into force on 1 August 2008. The MJREO follows the 2005 Hague Convention on Choice of Court Agreements closely in various respects, such as in terms of the 'exclusive choice of court agreement'. However, several challenges arise when applying the MJREO framework. One particular issue concerns whether the Mainland judgment is 'final and conclusive' as Mainland judgments or rulings may be reviewed under the trial supervision procedure (审判监督程序) under the PRC Civil Procedure Law, currently Chapter 16, Articles 209–24. Earlier cases have found this unacceptable as the Chinese court 'clearly … retains the power to alter its own decision',[48] but this was subsequently doubted in more recent cases.[49] Another hotly contested issue is whether the relevant jurisdiction clause is exclusive, with sometimes conflicting expert evidence.[50]

More recently, the Mainland Judgments in Civil and Commercial Matters (Reciprocal Enforcement) Ordinance (Cap 645) was passed and will enter into force in the near future. Cap 645 closely resembles the 2019 Hague Convention on the Recognition and Enforcement of Foreign Judgments in Civil or Commercial Matters. It provides for a broader basis for the recognition and enforcement of Mainland judgments in Hong Kong.

In relation to family matters, the lack of mutual arrangements between the Mainland and Hong Kong was highlighted in the Court of Appeal case of *Lai v Ling* in 2017, involving a child wrongfully removed by a parent to the Mainland.[51] The Mainland Judgments in Matrimonial and Family Cases (Reciprocal Recognition and Enforcement) Ordinance (Cap 639), which entered into force on 15 February 2022, provides for the reciprocal recognition and enforcement of specified orders and judgments given in respect of matrimonial or family cases between the Mainland and Hong Kong.

It should be noted that all three legislative frameworks have arisen based on mutual arrangements between the Supreme People's Court of the PRC and the Government of the Hong Kong SAR, signed in 2005 (for the MJREO), 2019 (for Cap 645) and 2017 (for Cap 639) respectively. The implementation of these arrangements in Hong Kong is by local legislation, thus resulting in a time gap of around three to five years. In the Mainland, these

Jurisprudence 115–126. [司艳丽，"完善我国涉港民商事案件司法文书送达机制的几点思考"，《中国应用法学》2023年第2期，第115–126頁].

[47] *First Laser Ltd v Fujian Enterprises (Holdings) Co Ltd* (2012) 15 HKCFAR 569 [43] (Lord Collins NPJ).

[48] *Chiyu Banking Corporation Ltd v Chan Tin Kwun* [1996] 2 HKLR 395; *Lam Chit Man v Lam Chi To* [2001–03] HKCLRT 141; *Lam Chit Man v Cheung Shun Lin* [2001–03] HKCLRT 243.

[49] *Lee Yau Wing v Lee Shui Kwan* [2007] 2 HKLRD 749 (Cheung JA); *Bank of China Ltd v Yang Fan* [2016] 3 HKLRD 7 (Anthony To J).

[50] *Bank of China Ltd v Yang Fan* (n 49); *Huang Shu Jian v Dai Wei* [2020] 1 HKC 309, [2019] HKCFI 1386.

[51] *Lai v Ling* [2017] 5 HKLRD 629.

arrangements are effected immediately by the promulgation of judicial interpretations by the Supreme People's Court of the PRC.

In relation to arbitral awards, the same question between Mainland China and Hong Kong arises – namely, the 1958 New York Convention does not apply between China and its Special Administrative Regions. As such, the Arrangement Concerning Mutual Enforcement of Arbitral Awards between the Mainland and the Hong Kong SAR in 1999 and the Supplemental Arrangement in 2020 provide for the framework which closely resembles the New York Convention. The current provisions on the recognition and enforcement of Mainland arbitral awards are contained in Part 10 Division 3 (sections 92–98) of the Arbitration Ordinance (Cap 609). These provisions mirror those for Convention awards (Part 10 Division 2, sections 87–91), as well as those for Macao awards (Part 10 Division 4, sections 98A–98D) (which were added in 2017). The grounds for refusal (sections 89, 95 and 98D) largely follow Article 36 of the UNCITRAL Model Law on International Commercial Arbitration 2006.

To bolster the attractiveness of Hong Kong as an arbitration venue, the Arrangement Concerning Mutual Assistance in Court-Ordered Interim Measures in Aid of Arbitral Proceedings by the Courts of the Mainland and of the Hong Kong SAR was introduced in 2019. This provides for a set of procedures for Hong Kong parties to apply for interim measures in the Mainland courts and vice versa.[52] These interim measures include the preservation of assets, evidence and conduct in the Mainland, and injunctions and other interim measures to maintain or restore the status quo pending determination of the dispute in Hong Kong. There have been over 90 applications since the implementation of the Arrangement.

III. Trends and Future Directions

Hong Kong is certainly an interesting case study on how private international law rules have developed and transformed over time, particularly in the post-handover period. In order to maintain its role as an international legal and dispute resolution hub, Hong Kong must keep an international outlook by referring to developments in other jurisdictions within the Asian region and globally, while adapting them to the local contexts in a myriad of areas such as commercial law and family law.

With the close interactions with Mainland China, there is potential to further develop inter-regional private international law within the Greater Bay Area (GBA) and in light of the One Belt One Road Initiative (OBOR). The development plans of Hong Kong are centred on the cornerstone that Hong Kong continues to practise the common law system under the 'One Country, Two Systems' arrangement. The common law expertise of Hong Kong will likely be 'exported' to the GBA and other OBOR jurisdictions and play an important role in national development plans. Future issues may include a potential uniform commercial code within the GBA and an international commercial court in

[52] See www.hkiac.org/arbitration/arrangement-interim-measures.

Hong Kong skilled at dealing with cross-border disputes.[53] These may be possible directions of development.

Recently, there has also been discussion regarding the formulation of a set of principles on Asian private international law.[54] While Hong Kong's position might be seen as one that inclines favourably towards the traditional common law position, there is plenty of space where Hong Kong's legal system and rules can take a pioneering and leading role in formulating the Asian private international law principles.

Last but not least, it is argued that soft law instruments will play an increasingly significant role in future harmonisation efforts.[55] Given an increasing scepticism (whether justified or not) towards the HCCH instruments, there is an urgent need to consider how non-binding forms of guidance can be devised to further promote the overarching goal. In particular, Asia comprises a plurality of legal systems, cultures and traditions that may require a different direction and thinking when compared with Europe or the West. The focus for Asian jurisdictions is perhaps not on uniformity, but on harmonised diversity. Moreover, there is indeed much benefit in Ralf Michaels' idea of seeing Asia 'as a method': 'Asia is no longer object or subject but method, no longer one but many parts that are in dialogue with each other, no longer recipient or opponent of Western law and instead co-producer of modernity and of modern law'.[56]

As has been shown in this chapter, Hong Kong has been adopting multiple developments in Asia and abroad, while adapting them to the local context. With its geographical, historical, legal and cultural background, it is in an excellent position to blend legal cultures and ideas and to experiment with new directions of development. There is certainly promising room for Hong Kong to position itself at the forefront of the development of Asian private international law.[57]

[53] The development of the Qianhai Shenzhen–Hong Kong Intellectual Property and Innovation Hub is one example of cross-boundary cooperation: see https://www.cedb.gov.hk/en/policies/intellectual-property-protection-main-text-of-document.html.

[54] See, eg, W Chen and G Goldstein, 'The Asian Principles of Private International Law: Objectives, Contents, Structure and Selected Topics on Choice of Law' (2017) 13(2) *Journal of Private International Law* 411–34; W Lui, 'Researching and Teaching Private International Law in Asia' (2023) 20(2) *Indonesian Journal of International Law*, Article 2.

[55] W Lui, 'The Need for Finality and Certainty in International Commercial Dispute Resolution' in S Menon and A Reyes (eds), *Transnational Commercial Disputes in an Age of Anti-globalism and Pandemic* (Hart Publishing, 2022) 183–208.

[56] R Michaels, 'How Asian Should Asian Law Be?' in G Low (ed), *Convergence and Divergence of Private Law in Asia* (Cambridge University Press, 2022) 227–51; Lui (n 55).

[57] For a detailed exposition of Hong Kong private international law and its relationship with Asian private international law, see W Lui and A Reyes, *Hong Kong Private International Law* (Hart Publishing, 2024).

9

New Developments in Korean Private International Law

JONG HYEOK LEE*

I. Introduction

Private international law was first introduced to Korea as part of the Eurocentric international legal order known as *Mangukgongbeob* [萬國公法] in the late nineteenth century. Since 1905, the subject has been an integral part of the curriculum at the Judicial Officer Training School (*Beopgwanyangseongso* [法官養成所]). In 1908, Yu Mun-Hwan [劉文煥], a professor at the School, published the first Korean textbook on private international law. However, the development of Korea's independent code and jurisprudence in this field was interrupted from 1910 to 1945 due to the imposition of Japanese colonial rule.[1]

Progress resumed in 1962 with the enactment and enforcement of Korea's Extra-National Private Law (*Seoboesabeop* [涉外私法], hereinafter the 'KENL'). Modelled after Japan's Law Concerning the Application of Laws in General (*Horei* [法例]), the KENL reflected the significant influence of Gebhard's draft (*Gebhardsche Entwürfe*) of 1887 on both Korea and Japan. This influence continued until 2001 when Korea, preceding Japan and China, became the first country in East Asia to enact legislation on private international law (*Gukjesabeop* [國際私法], hereinafter the '2001 KPIL') that deviated from Gebhard's draft and incorporated provisions on international jurisdiction and applicable law within the same code. During the process of independently legislating from 1999 to 2001,[2] Korea prioritised international consistency and drew inspiration from various sources, including the regimes of the Hague Conference on Private International Law and the EU, notably the Rome Convention on the Law Applicable to Contractual Obligations (hereinafter the 'Rome Convention'), as well as domestic legislations of European countries, with a particular emphasis on Switzerland. Inspired by Switzerland's comprehensive model, the 2001 KPIL stipulated provisions on international jurisdiction and applicable law together, and, within its Chapter of General

* This chapter was funded by the 2023 Research Fund of the Seoul National University Asia-Pacific Law Institute, donated by the Seoul National University Foundation.

[1] For details, see JH Lee, 'Hanguk gukjesabeop chogisa sango' ['A Preliminary History of Korean Private International Law'] (2018) 24(2) *Gukjesabeobyeongu* [*Korean Journal of Private International Law*] 241, 246 et seq.

[2] For details, see KH Suk, 'The New Conflict of Laws Act of the Republic of Korea' (2003) V *Yearbook of Private International Law* 99, 101 et seq.

Principles, included the provision on the application of overriding mandatory rules (Article 7) and the general exception clause (Article 8).

In 2014, Korea re-initiated a revision process to establish a more comprehensive framework on international jurisdiction. The revision goes beyond the previous legislation with only three provisions concerning international jurisdiction: one provision declares the general principle of a substantial relationship between Korea and the parties or the dispute (Article 2); and two others cover the special rules for consumer contracts and employment contracts (Articles 27 and 28). The introduction of a new law consisting of 36 new articles that cover the entirety of private legal relationships officially came into effect on 5 July 2022 (hereinafter the '2022 KPIL') and marks a significant milestone in the Korean legal system.[3]

The following description examines the recent advancements in Korean private international law, focusing on the 'challenges and responses' to foreign legislation, precedents and jurisprudence.

II. Jurisdictional Immunity

A. Restrictive State Immunity

Traditionally, international law has upheld the principle of sovereign equality, whereby no state can be sued as a defendant in the courts of another state. It is generally understood in Korea that the determination of jurisdictional immunity logically takes precedence over the determination of international jurisdiction. Initially, the Supreme Court of Korea (SCK) recognised absolute sovereign immunity without distinguishing between *acta jure imperii* and *acta jure gestionis*, as evident in its ruling on 23 May 1975 (Docket No 74Ma281). However, the SCK reversed its stance in the *en banc* ruling on 17 December 1998 (Docket No 97Da39216) and subsequent ruling on 13 December 2011 (Docket No 2009Da16766), limiting sovereign immunity to *acta jure imperii* and excluding *acta jure gestionis*. In a recent ruling on 27 April 2023 (Docket No 2019Da247903) concerning the Mongolian embassy's encroachment on land owned by a Korean company, the SCK recognised state immunity for claims of demolition and eviction, but rejected state immunity for the claim of return of unjust enrichment arising from the embassy's occupation of the land.

In the 'comfort women' lawsuits against the Japanese government,[4] the Seoul Central District Court's ruling on 8 January 2021 (Docket No 2016Gahap505092) recognised the Japanese government's responsibility for premeditated, organised and widespread crimes against humanity committed during the forced mobilisation and exploitation of 'comfort

[3] For an overview, see E-K Cho, 'Sur la contribution coréenne à l'unification du droit international privé: l'achèvement de la réforme de la LDIP coréenne' (2022) *Rev Crit DIP* 169. The Korea Legislation Research Institute's unofficial English translation of the 2022 KPIL is available at: http://elaw.klri.re.kr.

[4] For a comprehensive analysis on the conflict-of-laws issues, see JH Lee, '"Comfort Women" Lawsuits against Japan before the Korean Courts: Legal Issues from the Perspective of Private International Law' (2019) 7 *Korean Yearbook of International Law* 197.

women' in the Japanese colonial period. The Court concluded that state immunity cannot be applied in such cases, as these acts fall outside the protection of sovereign immunity. Conversely, in another division of the same court's ruling on 21 April 2021 (Docket No 2016 Gahap580239), the lawsuit was dismissed on the basis of recognising state immunity for sovereign acts of the Japanese government, taking into account the prevailing practices of the international community, including the ruling of the International Court of Justice (ICJ) in the *Jurisdictional Immunities of the State* case.[5]

B. North Korea: A Special Situation

Should the North Korean government be granted state immunity by South Korean courts? According to the Preamble to the South-North Agreements on Reconciliation, Non-aggression and Exchanges and Cooperation, known as the South-North Basic Agreements, signed on 13 December 1991, the relationship between South Korea and North Korea is characterised as 'not being a relationship between states, a special interim relationship stemming from the process towards reunification'. In a series of compensation lawsuits filed by individuals abducted to North Korea during the Korean War or their descendants, South Korean courts did not recognise jurisdictional immunity for the North Korean government and its supreme leader, Kim Jong Un. However, in certain cases, South Korean courts could have exercised discretion and applied North Korean law *ex officio* based on the principle of quasi-international private law to address specific civil law issues. For claims against Kim Jong Un, the descendant of the direct tortfeasors, Kim Il Sung and Kim Jong Il, the issue of whether the claims could have been inherited might need to be determined according to North Korean law, which serves as the *lex patriae* for Kim Il Sung and Kim Jong Il according to South Korea's choice-of-law rules for succession.

Additionally, the recent lawsuit filed by the South Korean government on 14 June 2023 (Docket No 2023Gahap69051), seeking 47.7 billion KRW (approximately US$36.7 million) in damages for the explosion and demolition of the South Korean government's liaison office in the Kaesong Industrial Complex by the North Korean government, raises considerations regarding the statute of limitations. While the South Korean government has invoked the three-year statute of limitations under South Korean civil law, an argument can be made for the application of the two-year or even shorter statute of limitations under Article 261 of North Korean civil law as *lex loci delicti commissi*, as the tort took place in Kaesong, which falls within the jurisdiction of North Korea. This is because South Korea's private international law may designate North Korean law as the applicable law. Article 31 of North Korea's private international law mandates the cumulative application of the law of the place where the tort occurred and the law of the court's jurisdiction. This provides a basis for arguing the cumulative application of South Korean law through *renvoi*. However, if North Korean law prescribes a shorter statute of limitations compared to South Korean law, the right to assert the claim would be considered as extinguished.

[5] *Jurisdictional Immunities of the State (Germany v Italy: Greece Intervening)* [2012] ICJ Reports 99.

III. International Jurisdiction

A. General Principles

Before 2001, in the absence of provisions on international jurisdiction in the KENL, it appears that the SCK, as evidenced by the rulings of 28 July 1992 (Docket No 91Da41897) and 21 November 1995 (Docket No 93Da39607), employed the approach of double functionality (*Doppelfunktion*). This approach involved applying the domestic territorial jurisdictional rules of Korea's Civil Procedure Law (KCPL) to determine whether a Korean court had international jurisdiction over the case with foreign element(s). However, if an exceptional circumstance was found in a particular case, indicating that a Korean court's exercise of international jurisdiction was incongruous with the nature of the things (*Natur der Sache*), the lawsuit would be dismissed because the Korean court lacked international jurisdiction.[6]

However, both the 2001 and the 2022 KPIL establish the principle that a Korean court has international jurisdiction when there is a substantial relationship between the parties or the dispute and Korea (Article 2(1)), and also state that the determination of whether a Korean court has international jurisdiction should fully consider the special characteristics of international jurisdiction, taking into account the domestic jurisdictional rules (Article 2(2)). The SCK further elaborates on this principle in various rulings, including the decision on 27 January 2005 (Docket No 2002Da59788) concerning a domain name dispute, the decision on 25 March 2021 (Docket No 2018Da230588) regarding a sales price dispute and the decision on 28 October 2021 (Docket No 2019Meu15425) concerning a case on divorce and the designation of a foster parent. The SCK emphasises that when determining international jurisdiction, the court should prioritise ensuring fairness between the parties and the appropriateness, speediness and cost-effectiveness of the trial. The SCK also highlights that in doing so, it is necessary to consider both: (i) the interests of individuals, such as fairness, convenience and predictability; and (ii) the interests of the court and the state, such as the appropriateness, speediness and efficiency of the trial, as well as the effectiveness of the judgment.

B. *Forum Non Conveniens* and *Lis Pendens*

From the perspective of *forum non conveniens*, the aforementioned 2002Da59788 decision encapsulated the essence of this doctrine. The SCK acknowledged that Korea's international jurisdiction may overlap with that of many other countries and, after considering the contents and other relevant circumstances of the dispute at hand, it concluded that Korea was not deemed an inappropriate forum for exercising international jurisdiction over the case. Through this decision, the SCK conceptually distinguished between the existence of international jurisdiction and its exercise.[7] Upon this basis, Article 12 of the 2022 KPIL codified

[6] See Suk (n 2) 112–13; JH Lee, 'International Jurisdiction to Adjudicate under the Korean Private International Law: Analysis of Recent Leading Cases of the Supreme Court of Korea' (2012) 53 *Seoul Law Journal* 639, 641–45. *cf* art 3-9 of Japan's Civil Procedure Law of 2011.

[7] For details on this decision, see Lee (n 6) 645 et seq.

the doctrine of *forum non conveniens* as follows: even if a Korean court has international jurisdiction under the 2022 KPIL, if there is a clear exceptional circumstance where it is deemed inappropriate for a Korean court to exercise such jurisdiction and a foreign court having international jurisdiction would be more appropriate to resolve the dispute, the Korean court may, upon the defendant's request, suspend the proceedings or dismiss the lawsuit. Prior to suspending the proceedings or dismissing the lawsuit, the Korean court must provide the plaintiff with an opportunity to present its argument. However, this is not the case when the parties have mutually agreed upon the international jurisdiction of a Korean court.

The 2022 KPIL incorporates various jurisdictional bases, which may give the impression of exorbitant jurisdiction in certain cases. For instance, Article 3(3) provides that a Korean court has international jurisdiction over the case against a corporation or organisation whose principal place of business, statutory seat under the articles of association or centre of business administration is located in Korea or which was established in accordance with Korean law. Moreover, personal sovereignty of the state over individuals with its nationality allows for international jurisdiction based on nationality in the following cases: marriage and divorce cases where both spouses hold Korean nationality (Article 56(1)(c) and 56(2)(d)); cases relating to the establishment or dissolution of a natural parent–child relationship and the confirmation or cancellation of adoption, where the child and at least one of the defendant parents hold Korean nationality (Articles 57(b) and 58(2)); cases concerning parental authority, custody and visitation rights involving a minor child, where the child and at least one of the parents hold Korean nationality (Article 59(b)); and cases concerning guardianship of an adult, where the ward holds Korean nationality (Article 61(1)(b)). Despite potential criticism surrounding the expansive jurisdictional grounds established by the 2022 KPIL, Article 12 empowers the Korean courts to actively suspend the proceedings or dismiss the lawsuits upon the plaintiff's request, with the overarching goal of achieving a balance between legal certainty and flexibility.

Another noteworthy issue is that the 2022 KPIL stipulates the principle of *forum non conveniens* as a ground for not allowing the suspension of proceedings in the case of *lis pendens*. According to Article 11(1), when the same case involving the same parties is pending in a foreign court and subsequently filed in a Korean court, the Korean court may, at its discretion or upon the request of a party, suspend the proceedings if it is expected that the foreign court's judgment will be recognised in Korea. However, an exception is allowed when it is evident that adjudicating the case in a Korean court is more appropriate than in a foreign court (Article 11(1)(b)). In this context, the doctrine of *forum non conveniens* plays an important role as it allows the continuation of the later-filed lawsuit in Korea, despite the prior filing of a lawsuit in a foreign jurisdiction.

C. Targeted Activity Criterion

The 2022 KPIL establishes that activities directed towards Korea serve as jurisdictional bases for Korean courts in the following cases. First, concerning the special jurisdiction of a place of business, if there is an intention to file a lawsuit against an individual, corporation or organisation engaging in continuous and organised business activities in Korea or directed towards Korea, and the lawsuit is related to those activities, Korean courts have jurisdiction (Article 4(2)). Moving forward, Korean courts are expected to specify the nature and frequency of business activities in order to determine whether the criteria under Article 4(2) are met.[8]

Second, with respect to the special jurisdiction of a place of tort, if a tortious act is committed in Korea or directed towards Korea, or if its result arises in Korea, Korean courts have jurisdiction. However, if the emergence of the result in Korea was not foreseeable, then Korean courts do not have special jurisdiction for the tort (Article 44). The foreseeability test included in the proviso of Article 44 serves the function of restricting the excessive recognition of jurisdiction in cases where a tortious act is committed through the internet, specifically in situations where mere access to a website is feasible.[9] In cases where a tortious act is directed towards Korea, it can be anticipated that its result will emerge in Korea. Therefore, it is essential to specify the meaning of 'directed towards Korea'. Even though the cases were rendered before 2022, it remains significant to refer to the principle derived from the concept of 'purposeful availment' established by precedents in the US.[10] Korean [illegible] applied this principle in a series of product liability cases, encompassing both [illegible] recognition jurisdictions. In the SCK's rulings of 21 November 1995 [illegible]07) and 12 February 2015 (Docket No 2012Da21737), as well as the Se[illegible]ing on 26 January 2006 (Docket No 2002Na32662), it was declared that the determination of international jurisdiction in cases where a manufacturer, producing and selling goods, is sued in a court where damage to a consumer occurred depends on whether the manufacturer could reasonably foresee the lawsuit being filed in that particular co[illegible]the occurrence of the damage and whether there is a substantial relationship with the place where the damage occurred. When assessing the substantial relationship, factors such as whether the manufacturer intentionally took actions to benefit from the transaction profits in the area where the damage occurred can be considered. Examples of such actions include product design tailored for the market in that area, advertising the product in that area, regular consultations with customers from that place, or establishing a sales agency in that area.

Third, regarding the special jurisdiction of intellectual property infringement, Korean courts have jurisdiction in the following situations: (i) if an incidental act of infringement occurs in Korea; (ii) if the act of infringement is directed towards Korea; or (iii) if the result of the infringement arises in Korea. In such cases, Korean courts have jurisdiction over the quantifiable results that have occurred within Korea (Article 39(1)). However, if a principal act of infringement is committed in Korea, Korean courts have jurisdiction over all the results stemming from the act, including those that have occurred in foreign countries (Article 39(3)). These provisions have generated controversy due to their reliance on the Mosaic approach originating from the European Court of Justice (ECJ)'s *Shevill* judgment,[11]

[8] See KH Suk, *Gukjejaepangwanhalbeop* [*International Adjudicatory Jurisdiction Law*] (Parkyoungsa, 2022) 77–80.

[9] ibid 240–42.

[10] The origin is *Hanson v Denckla*, 357 US 235 (1958) at 253: 'it is essential in each case that there be some act by which the defendant purposefully avails itself of the privilege of conducting activities within the forum State, thus invoking the benefits and protections of its laws'. A recent ruling in *Admar Int'l, Inc. v Eastrock*, LLC, 18 F 4th 783 (5th Cir 2021) states that 'the defendant must take the additional step of targeting the forum state in a manner that reflects "purposeful availment" of the opportunity to do business in that state' (at 785).

[11] Case C-68/93 *Shevill v Presse Alliance SA* [1995] ECR I-415.

differentiation of the quantitative scope of jurisdiction by distinguishing between the principal act and incidental act of intellectual property infringement, and deviation from the foreseeability criterion established in Article 44. From the perspective of the juxtaposition of jurisdictional rules and choice-of-law rules, the debate has been provoked by the distinction between the place where the act of infringement occurs and the place where its result arises, as well as the differentiation between the place where the principal act of infringement occurs and the place where the incidental act of infringement occurs. This debate raises the question of whether the traditional territorial approach in intellectual property infringement should be re-examined.

IV. Governing Law

A. Contracts

i. Contracts in General

Like the KENL under Article 9 and the 2001 KPIL under Article 25(1), [illegible] 5(1) of the 2022 KPIL also stipulates party autonomy in contracts. The SCK has adopted an interpretive stance that respects the explicit choice of law made by the parties as much as possible. For instance, the SCK's ruling on 25 October 2012 (Docket No 2009Da77754) de[illegible] even if the governing law is agreed upon only as 'US law' without specifyi[illegible]lar state in the US, the agreement remains valid to the extent that admiralty law, [illegible]ich applies nationwide, is applied.

While the KENL did not explicitly mention the implied choice of law by the parties, both the 2001 and the 2022 KPIL explicitly allow an implicit choice of law when it can be reasonably inferred from the contract's contents and all relevant circumstances. Recently, the SCK has elaborated several criteria to reduce legal uncertainty in this regard. To recognise the implied choice of law, the court should carefully and comprehensively consider the contract's contents and objective factors, such as each party's nationality, address, place of establishment and principal place of business, as well as backgrounds and details of the contract's formation.[12] It is important to note that simply because the parties did not dispute the governing law during the proceedings, it does not automatically affirm an implicit choice of law.[13] Furthermore, even if the parties express unanimous agreement on the applicable law during the proceedings, it does not automatically constitute an agreement on the governing law. For such an agreement, the attorney representing the client in the proceedings must possess separate legitimate authority in addition to the powers of attorney.[14] The above-mentioned approach by the SCK should also be applied in cases where there is an agreement to exclude the application of the United Nations Convention on Contracts for the International Sale of Goods (CISG) in accordance with Article 6 of

[12] The SCK's ruling on 28 July 2022, Docket No 2019Da201662.
[13] The SCK's ruling on 13 January 2022, Docket No 2021Da269388.
[14] The SCK's ruling on 24 March 2016, Docket No 2013Da81514.

the CISG. The intention of the parties to exclude the application of the CISG can be made implicitly, but it must be obvious and genuine.[15]

In cases where the parties have not explicitly or implicitly chosen the governing law for their contract, Article 46 of the 2022 KPIL states that the law of the country with the closest connection to the contract shall govern. It is presumed that if the contract was entered into as part of a business activity, the country where the party conducting the characteristic performance of the contract has its relevant place of business is considered to be the country most closely related to the contract. This presumption can be challenged and overcome only through careful examination and scrutiny. It is important to note that although Article 46(2) specifically mentions (i) transfer contracts, (ii) utilisation contracts and (iii) service provision contracts, including mandate contracts and work contracts, the same approach of analysing the characteristic performance of the contract should be applied to unlisted types of contracts.[16] For example, the SCK's ruling on 27 January 2011 (Docket No 2009Da10249) decided that the legal relationship between an issuing bank and an acquiring bank concerning the payment of a letter of credit is presumed to be governed by the law of the jurisdiction where the issuing bank is located. This presumption, rooted in the analysis of characteristic performance, entails the expectation that the issuing bank will fulfil its obligation to repay the letter of credit by authorising the purchase of relevant documents, such as bills of exchange, and agreeing to reimburse the specific amount stated in the letter of credit.

ii. Consumer Contracts

Since the enactment of the 2001 KPIL, passive consumers who enter into contracts with business entities have been protected through the application of special choice-of-law rules. In particular, the targeted activity criterion mentioned in (ii) in the list below was introduced in consideration of the ongoing expansion of e-commerce during that period in 2001. Article 42(1)(a) of the 2022 KPIL sets out specific requirements for a passive consumer to be protected. These requirements include: (i) the contract being entered into by a consumer for a purpose other than business activity; (ii) the business entity engaging in or directing its activities towards the country where the consumer has a habitual residence prior to the conclusion of contract; and (iii) the contract falling within the scope of the business activities of the business entity. According to Article 47(1), even if the parties have made a choice of law in a consumer contract, the protection granted to the consumer by the mandatory rules of the law of the consumer's habitual residence cannot be waived. These mandatory rules are understood to be applicable to the terms and conditions of consumer contracts and do not extend to indirect protections imposed on the business entity through relevant laws.[17]

In a lawsuit filed by Korean users against Google LLC and Google Korea LLC seeking the disclosure of their personal data provided to the US government in relation to the Edward Snowden case, the SCK issued a significant ruling. According to the SCK's decision

[15] JH Lee, 'Some Private International Law Issues in CISG Cases at Korean Courts' (2020) 8 *Korean Yearbook of International Law* 173, 175–78.
[16] KH Suk, *Gukjesabeop haeseol* [*Commentary on Private International Law*] (Parkyoungsa, 2013) 311.
[17] ibid 325.

on 13 April 2023 (Docket No 2017Da219232), Article 27 of the 2001 KPIL, subsequently split into Articles 42 and 47 of the 2022 KPIL, protects consumers in their habitual residence who were attracted by advertisements from foreign business entities. Its purpose is to ensure a reasonable expectation of the application of mandatory rules for consumer protection and to substantially guarantee access to justice for consumers facing difficulties in filing a lawsuit in a foreign court. The SCK stressed the importance of interpreting this clause cautiously and in a manner favourable to consumers. The SCK concluded that the contract between Google LLC and its users, which states that it is governed by Californian law, cannot be excluded from the scope of a consumer contract under Article 27(1)(a) of the 2001 KPIL, the equivalent of Article 42(1)(a) of the 2022 KPIL. This is because Google LLC generates revenue by utilising user data such as age, gender, location and behaviour patterns, even if the user does not directly pay Google LLC under the contract. The SCK also ruled that, to a certain extent, data regarding whether user data had been provided to the US government for purposes such as national security and criminal investigation should be disclosed.

In the absence of a choice of law, the law of the consumer's habitual residence governs the consumer contract (Article 47(2)). The 2001 and the 2022 KPIL do not impose any limitations on the scope of consumer contracts. Nevertheless, attempts have been made to interpret it in a manner similar to Article 5(4) of the Rome Convention, which served as a reference for the enactment of the 2001 KPIL. The Seoul Central District Court's ruling on 5 December 2012 (Docket No 2012Na24544) applied teleological reduction and concluded that Article 27 of the 2001 KPIL does not apply to (i) contracts of carriage or (ii) contracts for the supply of services where the services are exclusively provided to consumers in a country other than their habitual residence. However, the SCK's ruling on 28 August 2014 (Docket No 2013Da8410) overturned the court of appeal's decision and determined that such an interpretation was not possible due to the absence of restrictions in the wording of the law.

iii. Employment Contracts

As Korean companies expand their international business activities and foreign companies establish operations in Korea, the nature of employment contracts has indeed become more cross-border. In the past, when there were no specific rules on employment contracts in the KENL, the SCK's ruling on 26 May 1970 (Docket No 70Da523, 524) denied the foreign elements in the employment contracts between a Korean company and Korean nationals who provided labour in Vietnam, and determined not to apply the KENL itself and to apply Korean law directly. Nowadays, there are numerous cases where foreigners or Koreans working at the Korean branch of a foreign company enter into employment contracts governed by foreign law, and foreigners or Koreans working at foreign construction sites of Korean companies enter into employment contracts governed by foreign law due to regulatory requirements. In these situations, the application of mandatory rules under Korean law becomes a crucial consideration.

Article 48 of the 2022 KPIL addresses the issue. It states that even if the parties choose the law governing an employment contract, the protection provided to the employee by mandatory rules in the law of the country where the employee regularly works cannot be waived (Article 48(1)). If the parties have not chosen a governing law, the general rule is that the employment contract is governed by the law of the country where the employee regularly provides labour (Article 48(2)). Regarding seafarers' employment contracts without a choice of law, the SCK's rulings on 12 July 2007 (Docket No 2005Da39617, 47939) determined that the country where the employee regularly provides labour is the country of the ship's registry. For registered ships, it refers to the country of registration, and for unregistered ships, it refers to the country whose flag the ship is entitled to fly. In such cases, one can argue that the law of the jurisdiction where the entity actually controlling the ship is located should be applied through the general exception clause in Article 21(1) of the 2022 KPIL.[18] Alternatively, the law of the jurisdiction where the place of business that concluded the employment contract with the employee is located should be applied based on the supplementary provision in Article 48(2) of the 2022 KPIL.

B. Torts

The principle of *lex loci delicti commissi*, which states that the law governing a tort is determined by the place where the tort was committed, has been consistently upheld in both the KENL and the 2001 and the 2022 KPIL.[19] Since the SCK's rulings on 22 March 1983 (Docket No 82Daka1533), it has been established that the concept of the place where a tort was committed encompasses both the place where a tortious act occurred (*Handlungsort*) and the place where its result arose (*Erfolgsort*). Article 52(1) of the 2022 KPIL clarified this point by slightly revising Article 32(1) of the 2001 KPIL. It explicitly provides that a tort shall be governed by the law of the place where a tortious act occurred or the law of the place where its result arose. However, the lack of a clear hierarchical relationship between the two places poses difficulties in determining which one should be applied when they are situated in different countries. In such cases, notable rulings such as the Seoul High Court's decision on 26 January 2006 (Docket No 2002Na32662) in a product liability case and the SCK's decision on 24 May 2012 (Docket No 2009Da22549) in a wartime forced labour case have declared that the victim is entitled to choose the law that is most advantageous to him or her as the law governing the tort.[20] Regarding the rationale behind this, the 2002Na32662 ruling stated that the protection of the victim's infringed legal interests can be further enhanced, and this should not be considered as causing unexpected harm to the defendant during the course of the lawsuit.

[18] The SCK's ruling on 24 July 2014 (Docket No 2013Da4839) involved a case where the captain and seafarers of a vessel registered in Panama claimed priority for their wages against a bank, the maritime lienholder. Considering factors such as the nationality and principal place of business of the actual owner or operating company of the vessel, the vessel's main voyage and base, the nationality of the seafarers, the governing law of their employment contracts, the place where the act establishing the maritime lien took place and the applicable law for the act, and the location of the court or parties involved in the vessel's auction procedure, the SCK recognised the priority of the captain and seafarers' wages in accordance with the Korean Commercial Code, designated by the general exception clause of art 8 of the 2001 KPIL.

[19] The 2001 KPIL has deviated from the principle of cumulative application of Korean law regarding the establishment and effects of a tort, which was previously stipulated in art 13(2) and (3) of the KENL, influenced by the English double actionability rule. *cf* art 22(1) and (2) of Japan's Law on General Rules for Application of Laws of 2007.

[20] *cf* art 17 of Japan's Law on General Rules for Application of Laws of 2007, which prioritises the place where the result arose over the place where a tortious act occurred and applies the latter only when the former could not have been foreseen.

In addition, as adopted in the 2001 KPIL, Articles 52(2), (3) and 53 of the 2022 KPIL sequentially mitigate the principle of *lex loci delicti commissi* by introducing principles that take precedence over Article 52(1). Notwithstanding Article 52(1), Article 52(2) provides that if both the tortfeasor and the victim had their habitual residences in the same country at the time the tort occurred, the law of that country shall govern the tort (the principle of the place of common habitual residence). Overriding Article 52(1) and (2), Article 52(3) specifies an exception that states if the tort violated a legal relationship between the tortfeasor and the victim, the law applicable to that legal relationship shall govern the tort (the principle of accessory connection). Furthermore, Article 53 allows the parties to agree that the tort shall be subject to Korean law even after the tort has occurred, thereby granting party autonomy in the choice of governing law regardless of Article 52.

However, the 2022 KPIL does not include choice-of-law rules specifically addressing special tort liabilities, such as defamation, product liability, prospectus liability, unfair competition and environmental damage, except for Article 40, which pertains to the infringement of intellectual property.[21] Due to the lack of specific rules, it has been suggested that Article 21(1) should be utilised for the dynamic interpretation and application of Articles 52 and 53. This approach aims to ensure that the most appropriate law is applied to special tort liabilities by allowing flexibility in determining the governing law. Article 21 of the 2022 KPIL, equivalent to Article 8 of the 2001 KPIL, which is modelled after Article 15 of Switzerland's Private International Law, states that if the designated governing law under the KPIL is only marginally related to the legal relationship in question and there obviously exists another country's law that is most closely related, the law of that other country shall govern, unless the parties have agreed upon the applicable law. The following specifically addresses product liability and prospectus liability as examples.

i. Product Liability

In the lawsuit against US defoliant manufacturers filed by Korean Vietnam War veterans who were harmed by and suffered from Agent Orange sprayed during the Vietnam War by US military forces, the Seoul High Court determined the governing law for product liability as follows:

> [I]n a product liability case, the place where the tort was committed includes not only the place where the product was produced, the place where the product was acquired, and the place where the product was distributed to the market, but also the place where the product was finally used. Therefore, the governing law can be (i) the US law as the law of the place where the product was produced, (ii) the Vietnamese law as the law of the place where the product was finally used, and (iii) the Korean law as the law of the place where the result arose. Based on the fact that the veterans' exposure to Agent Orange is included in the result, (iv) the Vietnamese law can be included in the law of the place where the result arose, but there is no difference as the Vietnamese law can be designated as the law of the place where the tortious act occurred.[22]

[21] Article 40 states that the protection of intellectual property shall be governed by the law of the place where the infringement occurs.

[22] Seoul High Court's ruling on 26 January 2006, Docket No 2002Na32662.

The Court concluded that the plaintiff had selected Korean law as the governing law among these options because the plaintiff consistently argued based on Korean law. However, in this case, the Court did not explicitly specify the country that could be regarded as the place where the product was acquired or where the product was distributed to the market. If the multiple connecting points presented by the Court result in reduced predictability for the tortfeasor and an excessive number of options for the victim, it becomes necessary to appropriately adjust the available options by using the general exception clause of Article 21(1).

ii. Prospectus Liability

If a foreign company intends to conduct a public offering in the Korean capital market, or if a Korean or foreign company plans to conduct a public offering in foreign capital market(s) with the expectation that the securities will be resold to 50 or more Korean investors,[23] the issuer, whether a Korean or a foreign company, is required to submit a prospectus to Korea's Financial Services Commission. In such cases, Korean investors have the right to claim damages against the issuer, underwriters and so on, regardless of whether they are domestic or foreign. This right stems from the prospectus liability provision of Article 125 of Korea's Financial Investment Services and Capital Markets Law (KCML). This provision does not have an automatic extra-territorial application, despite the extra-territorial application clause of Article 2 of the KCML, which provides that 'the Act shall apply to any act conducted in a foreign country as well if such act has an effect on Korea'.[24] While the application of Article 125 of the KCML could be supported by Article 2 of the KCML, which makes it an overriding mandatory rule, as specified in Article 20 of the 2022 KPIL,[25] it should be noted that Article 125 of the KCML is applicable only when Korean law is designated as the governing law for the prospectus liability in question according to the rules of private international law. Since prospectus liability is considered a tort, Articles 52 and 53 of the 2022 KPIL could be invoked for the determination of the applicable law.

[23] In this context, a Korean investor refers to an investor participating in trading activities within the Korean capital market, independent of factors such as an individual's nationality, address or habitual residence and a company's place of establishment, statutory seat or centre of administration.

[24] The predecessor was art 2-2 of Korea's Monopoly Regulation and Fair Trade Law of 2005, which states that 'the Act shall apply to any act conducted in a foreign country as well if such act affects the Korean market', which is equivalent to art 3 of the current version of the law. Similar provisions have been introduced increasingly in the Korean legal system. For instance, art 6(2) of Korea's Law on the Report and Use of Specified Financial Transactions Information of 2021 provides that 'the Act shall apply to any financial transaction of virtual asset service providers conducted in a foreign country as well if such transaction has an effect on Korea'. In addition, art 2-2 of Korea's Telecommunication Business Law of 2021 and art 5-2 of Korea's Law on the Promotion of Utilisation of Information and Communications Network and the Protection of Data of 2020 provide respectively that 'the Act shall apply to any act conducted in a foreign country as well if such act affects the Korean market or the users in Korea'. It is worth noting that these two laws refer to not only 'the Korean market' but also 'the users in Korea'.

[25] Article 2 of the KCML holds different meanings for each regulatory means, including administrative regulation, criminal punishment and civil liability. These means vary in terms of their legal character and effects, necessitating the establishment of their own normative structure to ensure a well-balanced legal system for regulating cross-border capital market torts within the regulatory tripod framework. See JH Lee, 'Extraterritorial Application Clause in the Korean Capital Markets Law and its Implications to the Choice-of-Law Rules for Prospectus Liability: Focusing on the Comparison with the Extraterritorial Application of Administrative Regulation and Criminal Punishment' (2023) 22(1) *Journal of Korean Law* 43, 51 et seq.

For the application of Article 125 of KCML in cross-border prospectus liability cases, the application of Articles 52(2), (3) and 53 should be avoided by invoking the general exception clause of Article 21(1).[26] Investors should not be permitted to agree with an issuer, underwriter or intermediary on the applicable law of prospectus liability in order to uphold the objectives of prospectus regulation, despite Article 53. Furthermore, investors alleging misrepresentation in a prospectus should have an equal right to pursue claims, regardless of their direct contractual relationship with the potential party responsible for prospectus liability, despite Article 52(3). Given the potential diversification and fragmentation of governing law in cases involving multiple investors residing in different countries or the presence of an issuer, underwriter and intermediary established or located in multiple countries, it is justifiable to exclude the application of Article 52(2) in such situations. When interpreting Article 52(1) in cases involving pure economic loss, such as prospectus liability, determining the hypothetical location of the result among the investor's bank account, habitual residence or centre of financial interests poses challenges. Therefore, only the place where the tortious act occurred should be considered, and the location of the market should be deemed its place of occurrence.

V. Recognition and Enforcement of Foreign Judgments

Article 27(1) of Korea's Civil Execution Law states that a judgment of execution shall be rendered without examining the merits of the foreign judgment, whether it is right or wrong (denial of *révision au fond*). Article 217(1) of the KCPL establishes the conditions for the recognition of foreign judgments as follows: (i) the foreign judgment must be deemed final and conclusive or recognised with equivalent effects; (ii) the foreign court must have international jurisdiction in accordance with the rules on international jurisdiction in Korean law; (iii) the losing defendant must have been served with the written complaint or any relevant documents in a lawful manner, allowing sufficient time for response, and if the defendant was not served, it must have still provided a response to the lawsuit; (iv) the foreign judgment must not be contrary to Korea's public policy (*ordre public*), both in terms of substance and procedure; and (v) reciprocity must exist between Korea and the foreign country, and if reciprocity does not exist, the foreign country's criteria for recognising foreign judgments must be substantially the same as or similar to those stipulated in the KCPL. Article 217-2 of the KCPL further stipulates that the court may recognise only a portion of the foreign judgment, and in assessing this, the court should consider whether the costs and expenses related to the lawsuit, including attorney fees, are included in the amount of damages determined by the foreign court.

The public policy requirement mentioned in (iv) in the list above, particularly in relation to the recognition of foreign judgments ordering treble, quintuple or punitive damages, has been a contentious issue. Previously, the SCK ruled that such foreign judgments should not be recognised for the portion exceeding the actual damages caused, as these types of damages are considered non-compensatory and contrary to Korea's public policy.[27] However, with

[26] For details, see Lee (n 25) 63 et seq.

[27] See KH Suk, *Gukjeminsasosongbeop* [*International Civil Procedure Law*] (Parkyoungsa, 2012) 379–83.

the introduction of treble or quintuple damages in certain areas of Korea's legal system, starting from the Law on Fair Transactions in Subcontracting in 2011, the SCK's stance had to change to accommodate this shift towards pursuing substantial damages beyond traditional compensatory damages. On 11 March 2022 (Docket No 2018Da231550), the SCK made a significant ruling regarding a Hawaii judgment related to unfair trade practices. The SCK stated that a foreign judgment applying foreign law and ordering threefold or fivefold damages should be recognised and enforced as such, as long as the foreign law applied in the foreign court belongs to the same legal area in Korea's legal system that allows for threefold or fivefold damages.

The SCK's ruling of 2022 also carries significant implications for the application of foreign law by Korean courts. Article 52(4) of the 2022 KPIL, which corresponds to Article 32(4) of the 2001 KPIL, states that when a foreign law is designated by the choice-of-law rules for torts, the right to claim compensation for tortious damage will not be recognised: (i) if it is not evidently intended for the purpose of duly compensating the injured party; or (ii) if it is exercised beyond the scope that is essentially necessary for paying due compensation to the injured party. In light of the SCK's criterion of identicality or similarity of legal areas between Korean and foreign laws, Korean courts cannot deny the application of foreign law solely because it orders threefold or fivefold damages.

In reviewing the public policy criterion, Korea does not require that the foreign court applied the same governing law as would have been designated under the KPIL or resulted in the same or similar results as if the hypothetical governing law had been applied. In a previous ruling by the Seoul High Court on 12 May 1971 (Docket No 70Na1561), the recognition of a divorce judgment from the State of Nevada was denied because the Nevada judgment applied Nevada law as *lex fori* according to the hidden conflicts rule, instead of applying Korean law, which would have been determined according to the KENL. However, the ruling of 1971, which appeared to have been influenced by the now-abandoned French doctrine,[28] was considered as an exceptional case. It is generally understood that the requirement to apply the same governing law as in Korea is not obligatory.[29]

VI. Recognition of Legal Situations Established Abroad

In the EU, extensive discussions have taken place regarding the recognition of legal situations established in another Member State. These discussions were initiated by the ECJ's *Überseering* judgment,[30] which addressed the recognition of the legal capacity and the capacity to be a party to legal proceedings of a company established abroad. The judgment was based on the freedom of establishment guaranteed by Articles 43 and 48 of the Treaty Establishing the European Community. Similarly, the ECJ's *Grunkin and Paul* judgment[31] focused on recognising a child's surname registered abroad, which combined the father's and mother's surnames. This judgment relied on the freedom of movement and residence

[28] See D Bureau and H Muir Watt, *Droit international privé*, vol I, 4th edn (PUF, 2018) 543 et seq.
[29] See Suk (n 27) 407–08.
[30] Case C-208/00 *Überseering BV v Nordic Construction Company Baumanagement GmbH* [2002] ECR I-9919.
[31] Case C-353/06 *Stefan Grunkin and Dorothee Regina Paul* [2008] ECR I-7639.

of EU citizens, as provided by Article 18(1) of the Treaty. Furthermore, through Regulation (EU) 2016/1191,[32] the EU has facilitated the free movement of foreign public documents related to civil status and family matters stated in Article 2(1) of the Regulation.

It is important to note that these legal developments within the EU are influenced by the specific legal framework of the EU. Therefore, these discussions and judgments cannot be universally accepted in Korea, except in specific situations, such as the circulation of the Asia Region Fund Passport.[33] Consequently, the legal situations established in foreign countries are subject to scrutiny under Korean choice-of-law rules. They will only have effect in Korea as far as they comply with the applicable law designated by Korea's private international law.[34] Even if the principles of the EU are accepted to a certain extent, if a legal status established abroad (such as same-sex marriage or surrogate motherhood, or a legal status established in North Korea) contradicts Korea's public policy, recognition shall be denied.[35]

However, the situation changes when a multilateral or bilateral treaty that specifically regulates the recognition of a legal situation established abroad is in effect in Korea. An example of such a treaty is the Hague Convention on Protection of Children and Co-operation in Respect of Intercountry Adoption. Korea has successfully completed the legislative process in its National Assembly for the Law on Intercountry Adoption, which implements the Convention, on 30 June 2023. The country is currently in the process of acceding to the Convention. If Korea becomes a Contracting State to the Convention, as stipulated in Article 23(1) of the Convention and Article 22(1) of Korea's Law on Intercountry Adoption, any adoption certified by the competent authority of another Contracting State shall be automatically recognised by operation of law in Korea.

Another example is the Treaty of Friendship, Commerce and Navigation between Korea and the US (hereinafter the 'KORUS Treaty'), which became effective in 1957. While it may not have garnered much attention previously, the initial public offering of Coupang Inc, a Delaware company with its principal executive office in Seoul, and the sole owner of Coupang Corp, a Korean e-commerce company,[36] drew significant interest when it was conducted on the New York Stock Exchange in 2021. According to Article 16 of the 2001 KPIL, the equivalent of Article 30 of the 2022 KPIL, the following principles apply: (i) a corporation or organisation is governed by the laws of the jurisdiction where it was established; and (ii) if a corporation or organisation established in a foreign country has its principal place of business or conducts its primary business in Korea, it becomes subject to Korean law. Given that

[32] Regulation (EU) 2016/1191 of the European Parliament and of the Council of 6 July 2016 on promoting the free movement of citizens by simplifying the requirements for presenting certain public documents in the European Union and amending Regulation (EU) No 1024/2012.

[33] The Asia Region Fund Passport, adopted by the Memorandum of Cooperation between Korea, Japan, Australia, New Zealand and Thailand, is modelled after the EU's Undertakings for Collective Investment in Transferable Securities. Its aim is to promote the cross-selling of collective investment securities, specifically those of public offering funds. It is subject to prospectus liability under art 125 of the KCML, as well as joint responsibility under art 186 of the KCML.

[34] KH Suk, 'Gukjesabeobeseo jungeobeobui jijeonge gareumhaneun seungin: Yureobyeonhabeseoui nonuiwa uri beobeui sisajeom' ['Recognition in Lieu of Designation of Applicable Law in Private International Law: Discussion in the European Union and Implications for Korean Law'] (2021) 35 *Gukjegeoraewa beop* [*Dong-A Journal of International Business Transactions Law*] 1, 5–6.

[35] ibid 46–47.

[36] See Coupang Inc's registration statement (Form S-1) under the Securities Act of 1933, available at: https://www.sec.gov/Archives/edgar/data/1834584/000162828021001984/coupang-sx1.htm.

Coupang Inc falls within the scope of (ii) above, yet was not (re-)established under Korean law, the question arises regarding its legal capacity in Korea. However, this issue is resolved by Article 22(3) of the KORUS Treaty, which deems a US company a Korean company and recognises its legal status within Korea, and vice versa.[37]

Another significant issue arises concerning the recognition of Coupang Inc's Class B shares, which possess 29 times the voting power of its Class A shares. This issue stems from the absence of dual-class shares in Korea. Coupang Inc's Class B shares, despite holding substantial voting rights in the US, are not recognised as such in Korea. Instead, they are treated as equivalent to Class A shares, in accordance with the limitations set by Korean law.[38] This discrepancy is a result of applying the principle of adaptation in private international law, which acknowledges the differences in legal systems across countries. This situation could potentially create an arbitrage opportunity for companies seeking to conduct an initial public offering in a jurisdiction with different regulations. The situation is expected to undergo some changes with the upcoming revision of the Law on Special Measures for the Promotion of Venture Company, which will be effective from 17 November 2023. This revision will allow unlisted venture companies to issue shares with multiple voting rights ranging from two to ten times. Under this new framework, if a foreign unlisted venture company has its principal place of business or conducts its primary business in Korea, the differentiated voting rights associated with shares may be recognised to the extent permitted by Korean law. However, Coupang Inc, being a listed company, falls outside the scope of application of this forthcoming law.

VII. Conclusion

This chapter offers a brief overview of the current developments in certain aspects of Korean private international law. In its pursuit to be recognised as a civilised nation from a European standpoint, Korea embraced private international law in the late nineteenth century. As Korea progressed through the twentieth century, experiencing increased internationalisation through an open economy and the influx of foreigners, the demand for private international law grew exponentially. Consequently, in 2001, Korea transitioned from an outdated system rooted in nineteenth-century regimes from Germany and Japan to a comprehensive framework that encompasses international jurisdiction and applicable law within a unified code. Additionally, detailed provisions pertaining to international jurisdiction were incorporated in 2022. Currently, Korea is seeking further revisions to its choice-of-law rules. Driven by both their interests in comparative law research and the necessity of addressing pressing legal issues involving Korean individuals or companies, private international lawyers in the global community need to pay more attention to the evolving landscape within this domain in Korea.

[37] Article 22(3) of the KORUS Treaty states as follows: 'As used in the present Treaty, the term "companies" means corporations, partnerships, companies and other associations, whether or not with limited liability and whether or not for pecuniary profit. *Companies constituted under the applicable laws and regulations within the territories of either Party shall be deemed companies thereof and shall have their juridical status recognized within the territories of the other Party*' (emphasis added).

[38] *cf* art 25(3) of Italy's Private International Law of 1995.

PART 3

Relations of Courts

10

Choice-of-Court Agreements in Japanese Conflict of Laws

DAI YOKOMIZO*

I. Introduction

A choice-of-court agreement is often used in international transactions. It serves to enhance the predictability of the parties with regard to the forum of disputes which may occur in the future. However, the extent to which party autonomy is respected in the determination of the international adjudicatory jurisdiction varies from jurisdiction to jurisdiction. This chapter will discuss the treatment of Japanese conflict of laws (or private international law) on this issue. First, it will briefly describe the situation before the jurisdictional provisions were introduced into the Code of Civil Procedure in 2012 by referring to a famous 1975 Supreme Court decision and later lower court decisions (section II). Then, after clarifying the features of the legislation relating to international adjudicatory jurisdiction (section III), it will touch on some issues which remain to be solved (section IV). It should be noted that Japan has not yet ratified the Convention of 30 June 2005 on Choice of Court Agreements (the Hague Choice of Court Convention).

II. The *Chisadane* Case and the Following Lower Court Decisions

Before 2012, there were no explicit provisions with regard to international adjudicatory jurisdiction in Japan.[1] As regards choice-of-court agreements, the Supreme Court rendered an important decision in 1975 in the *Chisadane* case.[2] This concerned the transportation of

* This chapter is an outcome of the Grants-in-Aid for Scientific Research (the Japanese Society for the Promotion of Science, for Scientists (A): 2019–2023) project: 'Analysis on Multi-layered Structure of Global, National, and Local Legal Orders and the Principles of Their Coordination' (Principal Researcher: Professor Hiroki Harada).

[1] For the tendency of decisions and academic opinions before 2012, see generally D Yokomizo, 'The New Act on International Jurisdiction in Japan: Significance and Remaining Problems' (2012) 34 *Zeitschrift für Japanisches Recht* [*Journal of Japanese Law*] 95, 97–99.

[2] Supreme Court, Judgment, 28 November 1975, 29 *Minshu* [Report of the Supreme Court Decisions on Civil Cases] 1554. The English text can be found in (1976) 20 *Japanese Annual of International Law* 106.

crude sugar from Brazil to Japan by a Dutch shipping company. Since a portion of the crude sugar was damaged by sea water during transportation, a Japanese insurance company, which had made an insurance payout to the Japanese importer of the crude sugar, brought an action against the Dutch company before the Kobe District Court. In the bill of lading, there was a choice-of-court clause which designated the court of Amsterdam as the court having exclusive jurisdiction on all disputes arising out of the bill of lading. Based on this clause, the defendant sought dismissal of the case.

The Supreme Court declared the choice-of-court clause valid and dismissed the case. It established three conditions for the validity of a choice-of-court agreement: (a) the dispute in question is not subject to the exclusive jurisdiction of the Japanese courts; (b) the foreign court designated by the choice-of-court clause has international adjudicatory jurisdiction over the case; and (c) the clause in question is not 'excessively unreasonable and against the rules of public policy'. The Court held that the choice-of-court clause in question satisfied all the conditions. This case is considered to show the Supreme Court's preference on respect for the party autonomy.[3]

However, in cases following this decision, the lower courts considered a variety of elements in order to examine the above-mentioned third condition (which will be referred to as the 'public policy condition'): the relation between the dispute in question and Japan or the country designated by the clause, the location of the evidence, the plaintiff's burden of taking an action abroad, the circumstances in which the choice-of-court clause was drafted and inequality between the parties.[4] For example, the Tokyo District Court denied the validity of a choice-of-court clause, considering that the designated country was not the place in which the defendant had its principal office and that the case in question had a close connection to Japan.[5] There are also other cases in which the court declared a choice-of-court clause invalid from the viewpoint of the inequality between the parties when one of the parties was a consumer, an employee, an individual or a small and medium-sized enterprise, emphasising the protection of the weaker party, or the close connection between the dispute in question and Japan.[6] Thus, interpreting the public policy condition in an

[3] K Ishiguro, *Kokusai Minji Sosho Ho [International Civil Procedure]* (Shinseisha, 1996) 177–80 (however, the author is against the decision).

[4] Tokyo District Court, Judgment, 28 February 1994, 876 *Hanrei Taimuzu* [*Law Times Reports*] 268; Tokyo District Court, Preliminary Judgment, 13 September 1999, 154 *Kaijiho Kenkyu Kaishi* [*Maritime Law Review*] 89; Tokyo District Court, Judgment, 28 April 2000, 1743 *Hanrei Jiho* [*Judicial Reports*] 137; Tokyo High Court, Judgment, 28 November 2000, 1743 *Hanrei Jiho* 137; Tokyo District Court, Judgment, 19 June 2006, unpublished (Case No Hei 17 (Wa) 8909, available at Westlaw Japan: 2006WLJPCA06190004); Tokyo District Court, Judgment, 16 June 2010, unpublished (Case No Hei 21 (Wa) 44086, available at Westlaw Japan: 2010WLJPCA06168003); Tokyo District Court, Judgment, 30 November 2010, 2104 *Hanrei Jiho* 62; Tokyo District Court, Judgment, 14 February 2012, unpublished (Case No Hei 22 (Wa) 7042, available at Westlaw Japan: 2012WLJPCA02148003); Tokyo High Court, Judgment, 28 June 2012, unpublished (Case No Hei 24 (Ne) 2216, available at LLI/DB: L06721017); Tokyo District Court, Judgment, 14 November 2012, 1066 *Rodo Hanrei* [*Labour Cases*] 5; Tokyo District Court, Judgment, 19 April 2013, unpublished (Case No Hei 23 (Wa) 17514, available at Westlaw Japan: 2013WLJPCA04198001); Tokyo High Court, Judgment, 18 September 2013, unpublished (Case No Hei 25 (Ne) 3187, available at LLI/DB: L06820705); Tokyo District Court, Judgment, 14 January 2014, 2217 *Hanrei Jiho* 68; Tokyo High Court, Judgment, 17 November 2014, 2243 *Hanrei Jiho* 28; Osaka High Court, 20 February 2014, 225 *Hanrei Jiho* 77; Tokyo District Court, Judgment, 8 September 2015, unpublished (Case No Hei 26 (Wa) 1590, available at Westlaw Japan: 2015WLJPCA09088006).

[5] Tokyo District Court, Preliminary Judgment, 13 September 1999 (n 4).

[6] Tokyo High Court, Judgment, 28 June 2012 (n 4); Tokyo District Court, Judgment, 14 November 2012 (n 4); Osaka High Court, 20 February 2014 (n 4); Tokyo High Court, Judgment, 17 November 2014 (n 4).

extensive way, the lower courts took into consideration the concrete circumstances of the case in order to decide on the validity of the choice-of-court clause in question, instead of respecting for the party autonomy as much as possible.[7] This tendency of lower court decisions was generally supported by academic opinion.[8]

III. Legislation in 2012

In the above-mentioned situation, the new legislation on international adjudicatory jurisdiction came into force in 2012.[9] As regards choice-of-court agreements, Article 3-7 (1) of the Code of Civil Procedure provides that the parties may determine by agreement the state with whose court an action between them may be filed.[10] A choice-of-court agreement is valid if it is made with regard to certain legal relationships and the agreement was made in writing (Article 3-7 (2)).[11] Also, a choice-of-court agreement cannot be invoked if the designated court is unable to exercise its jurisdiction by law or in fact (Article 3-7 (4)).[12] These provisions were drafted, inspired by European instruments such as Council Regulation (EC) No 44/2001 of 22 December 2000 on jurisdiction and the recognition and enforcement of judgments in civil and commercial matters (the Brussels I Regulation), the Brussels Convention on jurisdiction and the enforcement of judgments in civil and commercial matters, and the Lugano Convention on jurisdiction and the recognition and enforcement of judgments in civil and commercial matters.

The new legislation manifestly shows an attitude favourable to party autonomy, whereas it introduced special rules for the protection of the weaker party.

A. Protection of the Weaker Party

Under the new legislation, the effect of choice-of-court clauses inserted into consumer contracts or labour contracts is limited. Its purpose is to prevent the stronger party from

[7] S Kato, 'Case Note' (2015) 1484 *Juristo* [*Jurist*] 143.

[8] See, for example, M Mitsuki, 'Choice-of-Court Agreement' in T Sawaki and J Akiba (eds), *Kokusai Shiho no Soten: Shinpan* [*Controversial Issues on Private International Law: New Edition*] (Yuhikaku, 1996) 232 (claiming that the validity of a choice-of-court agreement should be determined on a case-by-case basis, taking entirely into consideration elements such as the parties of the case, the relation between the case and Japan or the country of the designated court, difficulty of proof, effectiveness of the decision, the process which led to the conclusion of the choice-of-court agreement and the reasonableness of its purpose).

[9] The English translation is found in (2011) 54 *Japanese Yearbook of International Law* 723 and (2010) 12 *Kokusaishiho Nenpo* [*Japanese Yearbook of Private International Law*] 228. With regard to this new Act, see generally Yokomizo (n 1); M Dogauchi, 'Forthcoming Rules on International Jurisdiction' (2010) 12 *Kokusaishiho Nenpo* 212; M Dogauchi, 'New Japanese Rules on International Jurisdiction: General Observation' (2011) 54 *Japanese Yearbook of International Law* 260; K Takahashi, 'Japan's Enacted Rules on International Jurisdiction: With a Reflection on Some Issues of Interpretation' (2011) 13 *Kokusaishiho Nenpo* 146.

[10] Article 3-7 (1) of the Code of Civil Procedure: 'The parties may determine by agreement the state with whose court or courts an action between them may be filed.'

[11] Article 3-7 (2): 'The agreement set forth in the preceding paragraph shall not become effective unless it is made with respect to an action based on certain legal relationships and made in writing.' If a choice-of-court agreement is made by means of an electromagnetic record, such an agreement is deemed to have been made in writing; Article 3-7 (3).

[12] Article 3-7 (4): 'An agreement to the effect that an action can be exclusively filed with a court or courts of a foreign state may not be invoked, if such a Court or courts are unable to exercise their Jurisdiction by law or in fact.'

circumventing protecting rules by forcing the weaker party to accept the unfavourable clause which designates an inconvenient court.[13] In the field of conflict of laws, special choice-of-law rules relating to consumer contracts and labour contracts were introduced in the amendment in 2006 (Articles 11 and 12 of the Act on General Rules on Application of Laws [*Ho no Tekiyo ni kansuru Tsusokuho*]). The introduction of these special rules followed this direction.

First, in cases in which a choice-of-court clause is invoked against the weaker party, with regard to consumer contracts, Article 3-7 (5) (i) of the Code of Civil Procedure gives effect only to the agreement designating the court of the consumer's domicile at the moment of the conclusion of the contract.[14] Also, as regards individual labour-related civil disputes, a choice-of-court agreement concluded for disputes arising in the future is valid under two conditions: it is agreed that an action can be filed with a court of a state where the place of performance of his or her labour at that time is located and that it is agreed at the time of termination of a labour contract (Article 3-7 (6) (i)).[15] In both cases, the choice-of-court agreement is deemed to be non-exclusive.[16]

Second, a choice-of-court agreement is effective in favour of the weaker party, that is, in cases where the weaker party takes an action before the agreed court, or where he or she invokes the agreement in order to dismiss an action taken by the stronger party before the court other than the one agreed by the parties.[17] Thus, the stronger party cannot invoke the choice-of-court agreement in order to detach the weaker party from its forum of protection, whereas the weaker party always has the option to make use of the choice-of-court agreement in his or her favour.

[13] Y Nakanishi, A Kitazawa, D Yokomizo and T Hayashi, *Kokusai Shiho Dai 3 Han* [*Private International Law: 3rd Edition*] (Yuhikaku, 2022) 166.

[14] Article 3-7 (5): 'The agreement set forth in paragraph (1) with respect to a dispute arising in the future from a consumer contract shall be effective only in the cases specified in the following items:

> (i) In cases where it is agreed that action can be filed with a court or courts of the state where the consumer had his/her domicile at the time or conclusion of the consumer contract.'

[15] Article 3-7 (6): 'An agreement set forth in paragraph (1) with respect to an individual labour-related civil dispute arising in the future shall be effective only in the cases specified in the following items:

> (i) In cases where it is agreed at the time of termination of a labour contract and it is agreed that an action can be filed with a court or courts of a state where the place of performance of his/her labour at that time is located.'

[16] Article 3-7 (5) (i) and (6) (i): '(an agreement to the effect that such action can be filed only with the court or courts of such state shall be deemed not to disturb the filing of actions with the courts of other states, excluding the cases listed in the following Item)'.

[17] Article 3-7 (5): 'The agreement set forth in paragraph (1) with respect to a dispute arising in the future from a consumer contract shall be effective only in the cases specified in the following items:

> …
>
> (ii) In cases where a consumer files an action with a court of the state agreed in the agreement or in cases where a business operator files an action in Japan or a foreign state and a consumer invokes the agreement in the proceedings in his/her favour.'

Article 3-7 (6): 'An agreement set forth in paragraph (1) with respect to an individual labour-related civil dispute arising in the future shall be effective only in the cases specified in the following items:

> …
>
> (ii) In cases where an employee files an action with a court of the state agreed in the agreement, or in cases where an employer files an action in Japan or a foreign state and an employee invokes the agreement in the proceedings in his/her favour.'

B. Respect for the Party Autonomy in International Commerce

Whereas reinforcing the protection of consumers and employees, the new legislation shows its preference on respect for the party autonomy in other contracts. Article 3-9 relating to special circumstances,[18] the existence of which denies the international adjudicatory jurisdiction of the Japanese courts even if a jurisdictional ground exists in Japan, is not to apply to cases where the action is filed on the ground of choice-of-court agreement designating the courts of Japan exclusively.[19] This solution is justified by the need to guarantee predictability in dispute resolution to actors in international commerce.[20]

As regards the public policy condition that the Supreme Court established in the *Chisadane* case, there is no indication about this condition in the jurisdictional provisions. This results from the legislative process in which it was considered unnecessary to specify non-contradiction with public policy as a condition for the validity of the agreement, since this condition is evident.[21] It follows that this condition is always to be satisfied under the new legislation.[22] However, academic opinion claims that this condition should be interpreted in a more restricted way in order to enhance the predictability of the parties in the case of derogative or jurisdiction-depriving effects of a choice-of-court agreement, considering that the legislator showed its preference on respect for party autonomy in the case of prorogation by the exclusion of the application of Article 3-9 relating to exceptional circumstances, as has been mentioned earlier.[23]

Thus, on the one hand, the new legislation protects consumers and employees as the weaker parties, but on the other hand, it is more oriented than before towards respect for party autonomy in other contracts.

[18] This provision was introduced based on the previous case decisions, in particular, a judgment of the Supreme Court (Supreme Court, Judgment, 11 November 1997, 51 *Minshu* 4055; an English translation can be found in (1998) 41 *Japanese Annual of International Law* 117). For the criticism of this provision from the viewpoint of legal certainty and parties' foreseeability, see Yokomizo (n 1) 109.

[19] Article 3-9 of the Code of Civil Procedure: 'Even where the courts of Japan have jurisdiction over an action (*excluding cases where the action is filed on the ground of choice of court agreement designating the courts of Japan exclusively*), the court may dismiss the whole or a part of such action when it finds special circumstances under which a trial and judicial decision by the courts of Japan would undermine equity between the parties or disturb realisation of a proper and prompt trial, taking into consideration the nature of the case, the degree of the defendant's burden of submitting defense, the location of the evidence and any other circumstances' (emphasis added).

[20] T Sawaki and M Dogauchi, *Kokusai Shiho Nyumon Dai 8 Han* [*Introduction to Private International Law: 8th Edition*] (Yuhikaku, 2018) 309. It was discussed whether this exception should be allowed for choice-of-court agreements until the last meeting of the drafting committee. See M Dogauchi, 'Nihon no Atarashii Kokusai Saiban Kankatsu Rippo ni tsuite' [On the New Legislation on International Adjudicatory Jurisdiction in Japan] (2011) 12 *Kokusaishiho Nenpo* 186, 203.

[21] T Sato and Y Kobayashi (eds), *Ichimon Itto Heisei 23 Nen Minji Soshoho To Kaisei* [Q&A *Reform of the Code of Civil Procedure etc. in 2011*] (Shojihomu, 2012) 140–41.

[22] Y Sakurada, *Kokusai Shiho Dai 6 Han* [*Private International Law: 6th Edition*] (Yuhikaku, 2012) 370; Sawaki and Dogauchi (n 20) 306; Y Nakanishi, 'Kokusai Saiban Kankatsuki: Zaisan Jiken' [International Adjudicatory Jurisdiction: Patrimonial Matters] in H Takahashi and S Kato (eds) *Jitsumu Minji Sosho Koza [Dai 3 Ki] Dai 6 Kan* [*Lecture on Practice of Civil Procedure: The 3rd Period, Volume 6*] (Nihon Hyoron Sha, 2013) 327.

[23] K Takahashi, 'Case Note' (2012) 210 *Bessatsu Jurisuto* [*Jurist, Special Issue*] 200, 201. See also Sawaki and Dogauchi (n 20) 306 (pointing out that this general principle should be cautiously applied due to the fact that special rules relating to choice-of-courts agreements in consumer contracts and labour contracts were introduced, and that the predictability should be given importance when considering international transactions).

IV. Current Issues

In spite of the new legislation in 2012, there still exist certain cases in which the validity of a choice-of-court agreement is not clear. Among them, this section will focus on three cases.

A. Cases in which an Overriding Mandatory Rule of the Forum should Apply

First, is a choice-of-court agreement designating a foreign court valid if an overriding mandatory rule of the forum should apply to the case? The answer to this question is extremely varied from jurisdiction to jurisdiction.[24]

The Tokyo District Court and the Tokyo High Court rendered decisions on this issue recently.[25] In this case, a Japanese company which concluded long-term contracts for the supply of products with American companies took an action before the Tokyo District Court seeking the abolition of unfavourable clauses, the suspension of the claim from the American companies for the purchase of the products in question, and damages on the ground of the abuse of the dominant position in violation of Japanese competition law. In each contract, there existed a choice-of-court clause which exclusively designated the Michigan court as the competent court to resolve any disputes arising directly or indirectly out of the contract in question.

The Tokyo District Court and the Tokyo High Court dismissed the case, holding that the choice-of-court agreement was valid. They dealt with this issue as a question relating to the public policy condition established by the Supreme Court in the *Chisadane* case. Their reasoning was as follows: a choice-of-court agreement which would lead to the consequence of excluding the application of an overriding mandatory rule of Japan is invalid only in cases in which the result of the application of all the relevant applicable rules by the agreed court would be different from the result of the application of all the relevant applicable rules in Japan to an unacceptable degree from the viewpoint of the maintenance of the general interests concerning competition law. However, it did not seem appropriate to make such a difficult comparison about the application of the applicable rules at the stage of the determination of the international adjudicative jurisdiction.[26]

[24] See M Weller, 'Choice of Court Agreement under Brussels Ia and under the Hague Convention: Coherences and Clashes' (2017) 13 *Journal of Private International Law* 91, 105–07; BGH v 5. 9. 2012, VII ZR 25/12 (Germany); Cass. civ. 1er, 22 October 2008, 2/2009 *Journal du Droit International* 599 (France). For the US, see H Muir Watt, 'L'affaire Lloyd's: globalisation des marchés et contentieux contractuel' (2002) 91 *Revue critique de droit international privé* 509; H Buxbaum, 'The Role of Public Policy in International Contracts: Reflections on the U.S. Litigation Concerning Lloyd's of London' (2002) *Praxis des Internationalen Privat- und Verfahrensrechts* 232. See generally D Yokomizo, 'Gaikoku Saibansho wo Shitei suru Senzokuteki Kankatsu Goi to Kyokoteki Tekiyo Hoki' [Exclusive Choice-of-Court Agreement Designating a Foreign Court and Overriding Mandatory Rules] (2018) 70 *Hoso Jiho* [*Lawyers Association Journal*] 2975.

[25] Tokyo District Court, Judgment, 6 October 2016, 1515 *Kinyu Shoji Hanrei* [*Financial and Business Law Precedents*] 42 and Tokyo High Court, Judgment, 25 October 2017, unpublished (Case No Hei 28 (Ne) 5514, available at Westlaw Japan: 2017WLJPCA10256010).

[26] D Yokomizo, 'Case Note' (2018) 56 *Shiho Hanrei Rimakusu* [*Private Law Precedents*] 142.

Some authors allow room for denying the validity of a choice-of-court agreement by the public policy condition in cases where the application of Japanese overriding mandatory rules may be circumvented as the result of the choice-of-court agreement in question.[27] However, considering the fact that the new legislation is oriented towards the respect for party autonomy as has been mentioned above, the cases where the derogative effect of a choice-of-court agreement is denied due to the overriding mandatory rules of the forum should be limited. In this author's opinion, they should be limited to the cases in which: a) the application of an overriding mandatory rule concretising the general interest is as important as the rules relating to matters referred to in the provision relating to exclusive jurisdiction; or b) it is evident that the parties had the intention of avoiding an overriding mandatory rule of Japan.[28]

B. Cases in which Only One Party can Choose the Forum in the Dispute

Second, if a choice-of-court agreement allows only one party to choose the forum at the time of the dispute, is it valid in Japan? The Tokyo District Court gave an affirmative reply to this question.[29] In the case of a dispute arising out of maritime transportation, the validity of the following clause was examined: 'claims or disputes arising out of the present bill of lading will be resolved by the law and the court of the country in which the transporter have its principal office, the country of the place of the expedition or of the disembarkation, according to the choice of the transporter'. The court found the places reasonable since they had a sufficiently close connection with the bill of lading and held that the clause in question would not disturb the legal security, since the holder of the bill of lading could confirm the transporter's choice prior to the litigation. One commentator opposed the decision, pointing out that the said clause is contrary to the International Convention for the Unification of Certain Rules Relating to Bills of Lading and the Japanese law based on this convention, which forbids the change of liability of the transporter in a way unfavourable to the owner.[30]

Considering the Supreme Court decision in favour of the transporter and the attitude of the new legislation favourable to party autonomy, such an agreement should be considered valid, except in exceptional cases in which the predictability of a party is hampered in the concrete case – for example, by the fact that the transporter exercises its right to choose too late.[31]

[27] M Dogauchi, 'Kokusai Saiban Kankatsu Goi no Yukosei: Tokyo Chisai Heisei 28 Nen 2 Gatsu 15 Nichi Chukan Hanketsu wo Megutte' [Validity of Choice-of-Court Agreements in International Adjudicatory Jurisdiction: Concerning Preliminary Judgment on the Tokyo District Court on 15 February 2016] (2016) 1077 *New Business Law* 25, 33–34; Sawaki and Dogauchi (n 20) 307; H Tezuka, 'Kankatsuken ni kansuru Goi [Oso Kankatsu Fukumu]' [Choice-of-Court Agreements (including Jurisdiction by Appearance)] (2012) 138 *Bessatsu NBL* [*New Business Law, Special Issue*] 74.

[28] Yokomizo (n 24) 35.

[29] Tokyo District Court, Judgment, 24 September 2008, unpublished (Case No Hei 19 (Wa) 30011, available at Westlaw Japan: 2008WLJPCA09248005).

[30] F Masuda, 'Case Note' (2012) 1442 *Jurisuto* [*Jurist*] 120.

[31] S Kato, 'Ippo Tojisha ni Sentakuken wo Fuyo suru Kokusaiteki Kankatsu Goi no Yukosei' [Validity of an International Choice-of-Court Agreement Granting the Right to Choose the Forum to One Party] in Y Asano, H Harada, T Fujitani and D Yokomizo (eds) *Seisaku Jitsugen Katei no Gurobaruka* [*Globalisation of Policy-Implementing Process*] (Kobundo, 2019) 177, 191–92.

C. Cases in which the Inequality Exists in Other Contracts than Consumer or Labour Contracts

Finally, in cases in which the inequality of bargaining power between the parties manifestly exists in contracts other than consumer and labour contracts, is a choice-of-court agreement valid? This is especially significant in the case of contracts between a small and medium-sized enterprise and a large company. As has been briefly mentioned earlier, before the new legislation, the lower courts took into account the imbalance in such cases in order to evaluate if the said clause was excessively unreasonable and contrary to the rules of public policy. How then should it be considered under the new legislation?

In a case concerning a contract between a Japanese small and medium-sized enterprise and a large Californian company, the Tokyo District Court rendered an interesting decision.[32] It declared a choice-of-court agreement designating the Californian court invalid. However, instead of holding that the clause was excessively unreasonable and contrary to the rules of public policy, it held that the clause in question was not made with respect to an action based on certain legal relationships. In fact, in this case, the clause was drafted to the effect that it applies to any dispute between the parties regardless of whether it arises out of the present contract or not. One commentator pointed out, probably rightly, that the court may have hesitated to rely on the public policy condition in that case to deny the validity of the said choice-of-court agreement.[33] The risk then remains that, under the new legislation, the courts will not consider the imbalance between the parties in contracts other than consumer and labour contracts. In fact, on appeal of the above-mentioned case, the Tokyo High Court held that the choice-of-court clause in question was valid, since it could be interpreted to sufficiently specify the disputes covered by the clause.[34] However, there may be cases in which the inequality of bargaining power between the parties manifestly exists (such as cases of contracts between a small and medium-sized enterprise and a large company). Thus, it is desirable to amend the relevant provisions so that the court could deny the validity of a choice-of-court agreement in these cases.

V. Are Japanese Choice-of-Court Agreements Good Models for Other East Asian Jurisdictions?

Finally, we reflect on how these Japanese rules relating to choice-of-court agreements can be good models for the entire East Asian region.

Striking a balance between the predictability of the parties in international transactions and the protection of public interests or state policies depends on the social and economic context of each jurisdiction. Thus, determining how to do so will also have to be context-specific. Therefore, the solution to this problem in Japan may not be desirable in other jurisdictions. The above-mentioned new legislation, which is oriented towards respect for

[32] Tokyo District Court, Intermediary Judgment, 15 February 2016, unpublished (Case No Hei 26 (Wa) 19860, available at Westlaw Japan: 2016WLJPCA02156001).

[33] Y Hayakawa, 'Case Note' (2017) 20 *Shin Hanrei Kaisetsu Watch* [*New Commentary on Precedents Watch*] 329.

[34] Tokyo High Court, Judgment, 22 July 2021, unpublished (Case No Rei Gan (Ne) 5049, available at D-1Law: 28283185).

party autonomy clarifying the scope of the protection for the weaker parties, resulted from the strong request from enterprises (through lawyers in the legislative committee) which conduct their activities in a cross-border way. In jurisdictions in which there are no such big companies, the solution would be different.

Apart from this fact, the Japanese rules seem to have some problems to be improved. First, under the current rules, it is not clear in which cases a choice-of-court agreement designating a foreign court should be denied in order to guarantee the application of Japanese overriding mandatory rules, as has been discussed earlier. To clarify these cases, it seems appropriate to add matters relating to which the relevant overriding mandatory rules should apply regardless of the existence of a choice-of-court agreement to the provision relating to exclusive jurisdiction (Article 3-5 of the Code of Civil Procedure).[35]

Second, it should be re-examined whether it is appropriate to focus on consumer contracts and labour contracts for special treatment in terms of the protection of the weaker party. On the one hand, there may be consumer contracts or labour contracts in which the bargaining power between the parties is not unequal, such as electronic transactions between individuals on digital platforms and labour contracts with regard to famous athletes.[36] On the other hand, there may exist contracts other than consumer contracts and labour contracts in which the weaker party should be protected, such as those between an individual or a small and medium-sized company and a large company. In order to respond to these problems while keeping the predictability of the parties to a certain extent, it is desirable to adjust the relevant rules. First, as for rules relating to consumer contracts and labour contracts, it is desirable to introduce an exceptional treatment to exclude from the scope of the provision those in which a consumer or an employee cannot be considered as a weaker party to be protected.[37] Second, as regards contracts other than consumer contracts and labour contracts, it is appropriate to make it possible that the public policy condition can invalidate those in which the bargaining power between the parties is extremely

[35] Article 3-5: '(1) Actions provided for in Part VII, Chapter II (excluding those provided for in sections 4 and 6 of the same Chapter) of Companies Act, in Chapter VI, Section 2 of Act on General Incorporated Associations and General Incorporated Foundations (Act No 48 of 2006) or any other similar actions in relation to association or foundation incorporated under other laws and regulations of Japan shall be exclusively subject to the jurisdiction of the courts of Japan.

(2) Actions relating to a registration shall be exclusively subject to the jurisdiction of the courts of Japan, if the place where the registration should be made is located in Japan.

(3) Actions relating to the existence or non-existence or the validity of intellectual property rights (meaning 'intellectual property rights' provided for in Article 2, Paragraph (2) of Intellectual Property Basic Act (Act No 122 of 2002)) which become effective by registration for their establishment shall be exclusively subject to the jurisdiction of the courts of Japan, if the registration is done in Japan.'

It is true that exclusive jurisdiction in the international context is sometimes criticised in that it restricts private interests from the viewpoint of state policies. See D Yokomizo, 'Kokusai Senzoku Kankatsu'[International Exclusive Jurisdiction] (2012) 245 *Nagoya Daigaku Hosei Ronshu* [*Nagoya University Journal of Law and Politics*] 123, 127–28. However, it is possible to re-evaluate its significance in this context as the one contributing to the predictability of the parties. See Yokomizo (n 24) 3012.

[36] For the former example, see D Yokomizo, 'Digital Platform and Conflict of Laws' (2021) 64 *Japanese Yearbook of International Law* 202, 225.

[37] See, for example, A Sarntikasem, 'Regulatory Framework for the International Choice of Court Agreements in Thailand: Revisiting the Validity and Jurisdictional Protection of Weak Parties' (doctoral thesis, Nagoya University, 2022, available at https://nagoya.repo.nii.ac.jp/records/2004279) 234–35 (suggesting that Thai laws may restrict the scope of jurisdictional protection for certain consumers in choice-of-court agreements by using the amount of the claim for a pecuniary remedy as a threshold for assuming that consumers in transactions who exceed a certain amount would be in a relatively strong bargaining position). The other possibility is the introduction of an exceptional rule in a general way. Which of these would be more appropriate should be further examined in the future.

different by erasing the exception of the exclusive choice-of-court agreement from Article 3-9 of the Code of Civil Procedure relating to special circumstances.[38]

These possible improvements may give some impulses to other Asian jurisdictions which intend to develop rules relating to choice-of-court agreements in international adjudicatory jurisdiction.

VI. Conclusion

This chapter has dealt with the development of Japanese conflict of laws with regard to the treatment of choice-of-court agreements. Although choice-of-court agreements are particularly important in international transactions, there are considerable differences in issues concerning their validity. In this sense, it seems useful to introduce the development of the treatment on this issue in Japan, in particular the change of orientation between the respect for the party autonomy and other interests. It is particularly useful to consider the new rules as giving an impulse to other Asian jurisdictions that are developing their own courts' approaches to choice-of-court agreements.

[38] See n 19 (the emphasised part).

11

The 1965 Basic Treaty

An Obstacle to 'Normal' Relations between South Korea and Japan?

SAMUEL GUEX

On 30 October 2018, South Korea's Supreme Court ordered Nippon Steel & Sumitomo Metal Corporation (hereinafter 'Nippon Steel') to compensate four South Koreans for wartime forced labour and unpaid work. It upheld a lower court ruling in 2013, which had ordered the Japanese firm to pay each plaintiff 100 million won ($87,720) in compensation. The four men had lodged the damages suit against the firm in Korea in 2005 after losing similar litigation in Japan.[1] The Korean Supreme Court's landmark ruling sparked a strong reaction from the Japanese side, which responded with measures of 'economic retaliation' such as reinforced export control and regulation, and the removing of South Korea from the 'white list' for preferential trading (2019). South Korea, in turn, removed Japan from its own 'white list' and threatened to dissolve the General Security of Military Information Agreement (GSOMIA) signed with Japan in 2016. For months, Korean people boycotted Japanese goods and refrained from travelling to Japan, an example of the many areas into which this historical dispute spilled.

The crisis, which caused bilateral relations to hit an all-time low, once again highlighted differences in interpretations of two treaties signed in 1965 to establish diplomatic relations between the two states and resolve claims for reparations due to Korea from Japan's occupation of its territory: the Treaty on Basic Relations between Japan and the Republic of Korea (hereinafter the 'Treaty') and the Agreement between Japan and the Republic of Korea Concerning the Settlement of Problems in Regard to Property and Claims and Economic Cooperation (hereinafter the '1965 Agreement' or 'Claims Agreement'). It is the latter agreement that was at the centre of these diplomatic rows, especially its Article II, paragraph 1:

> The High Contracting Parties confirm that the problems concerning property, rights, and interests of the two High Contracting Parties and their peoples (including juridical persons) and the claims between the High Contracting Parties and between their peoples,

[1] 'Supreme Court Orders Japanese Firm to Provide Compensation for Wartime Forced Labor' *Yonhap News Agency*, 30 October 2018, en.yna.co.kr/view/AEN20181030006753315.

> including those stipulated in Article IV(a) of the Peace Treaty with Japan signed at the city of San Francisco on September 8, 1951, have been settled completely and finally.[2]

Citing the above article, the Abe Shinzō administration repeated that problems concerning claims had been 'settled completely and finally' by the 1965 Agreement.[3] The Moon Jae-in administration, for its part, stated that it respected its judiciary's decision, which ruled that 'the right of an individual to claim damages against unlawful acts had never been waived' by the Agreement.[4]

The same stances[5] were reiterated one month later in relation to a similar case, when South Korea's Supreme Court ordered Mitsubishi Heavy Industries to compensate victims of forced labour.[6] They were then repeated in other court decisions, such as the verdict of the Seoul Central District Court, which in January 2021 ordered the Japanese government to pay 100 million won in damages to a group of former 'comfort women' who suffered under Japan's military brothel system during the Second World War.[7] Motegi Toshimitsu, Japan's Foreign Minister, declared that the 1965 Agreement 'stipulated that the issue concerning property and claims between Japan and the Republic of Korea, including the issue of comfort women, was "settled completely and finally" and no contention shall be made (Article II)'.[8] The South Korean Ministry of Foreign Affairs released a commentary in which it stated that: 'The Korean government respects the court's ruling, and will make every possible effort to restore the honor and dignity of the "comfort women" victims.'[9]

Based upon these court rulings and official statements, one might conclude that both sides hold diametrically opposed views on the 1965 Agreement and its scope regarding the problem of individual claims. One might even wonder whether the Treaty, which provided the basic framework for the normalisation of relations between Japan and South Korea, has not become the main obstacle to 'normal' – or peaceful – relations between the two countries. After all, the Treaty was not meant to settle the colonial past and it left out many important issues, such as the 'comfort women'. But are the Treaty and the Agreement the real problem? Does the Japanese government really hold that the Agreement precludes any

[2] 'Agreement on the Settlement of Problems Concerning Property and Claims and on Economic Co-operation between Japan and the Republic of Korea. Signed at Tokyo, on 22 June 1965' *United Nations – Treaty Series* (1966) 258.

[3] 'Regarding the Decision by the Supreme Court of the Republic of Korea, Confirming the Existing Judgments on the Japanese Company (Statement by Foreign Minister Taro Kono)', 30 October 2018, www.mofa.go.jp/press/release/press4e_002204.html.

[4] 'Address by President Moon Jae-in on Korea's 75th Liberation Day', 15 August 2020, www.korea.net/Government/Briefing-Room/Presidential-Speeches/view?articleId=188823.

[5] 'Regarding the Decision by the Supreme Court of the Republic of Korea, Confirming the Existing Judgments on the Japanese Company (Statement by Foreign Minister Taro Kono)', 29 November 2018, www.mofa.go.jp/press/release/press4e_002242.html.

[6] 'Supreme Court Orders' (n 1).

[7] '"Comfort Women" Win First Legal Victory against Tokyo in Wartime Sex Slavery Case', 8 January 2021, en.yna.co.kr/view/AEN20210108003353315.

[8] 'Regarding the Confirmation of the Judgment of the Seoul Central District Court of the Republic of Korea in the Lawsuit Filed by Former Comfort Women and Others (Statement by Foreign Minister MOTEGI Toshimitsu)', 23 January 2021, www.mofa.go.jp/press/danwa/press6e_000269.html.

[9] 'MOFA Spokesperson's Commentary on the Ruling on the Civil Action Filed by "Comfort Women" Victims against the Japanese Government', 19 January 2021, www.mofa.go.kr/eng/brd/m_5674/view.do?seq=320545&srchFr=&amp%3BsrchTo=&amp%3BsrchWord=&amp%3BsrchTp=&amp%3Bmulti_itm_seq=0&amp%3Bitm_seq_1=0&amp%3Bitm_seq_2=0&amp%3Bcompany_cd=&amp%3Bcompany_nm=&page=10&titleNm=.

individual claim? Does the South Korean government really endorse the conclusions drawn by the Supreme Court? And what about the stances adopted by former administrations? To answer these questions, this chapter will first present the case and the characteristics of South Korea's Supreme Court ruling, as well as the main problems it poses. It will then examine how official narratives evolved in both countries to suit particular needs and will contend that political will – or lack of it – and not the Treaty and the Agreement in themselves is the real key to the solving of bilateral disputes and the achievement of real 'normalisation' of the relations between Japan and South Korea.

I. The Nippon Steel Case

The four plaintiffs were born in the 1920s in Korea and worked at steel mills in Japan during the last years of the Second World War. They were four of many Korean workers who were recruited to alleviate Japan's severe labour shortage, which was particularly acute after the outbreak of the Pacific War. The legal basis for these recruitments was provided by the National Mobilisation Law (Kokka sōdōinhō), passed in 1938, and the National Conscription Ordinance (Kokumin chōyōrei), which was passed in 1939 in Japan and enacted three years later in Korea. The plaintiffs were recruited by the predecessor of Nippon Steel Corporation (Old Nippon Steel) and worked under arduous and dangerous conditions. They resided in dormitories under strict surveillance from police and military police, had very few opportunities to go outside, were occasionally beaten by the superintendents or the police and were not paid for their labour.[10] In 1997, two of the plaintiffs brought a lawsuit against Japan for compensation in a Japanese court, which ruled against them, arguing that the legal personality of Nippon Steel Corporation was different from its predecessor, Old Nippon Steel. The judgment was upheld by Japan's Supreme Court in 2003, bringing the case to an end in Japan.[11]

II. South Korean Cases

In 2005, having exhausted the Japanese judiciary, the two plaintiffs, joined by two others, brought their case to the Seoul District Court in South Korea. The Court dismissed the case on the grounds that Old Nippon Steel and (New) Nippon Steel, the defendant, did not have the same legal personality and that the statute of limitations had expired. The plaintiffs appealed to the Seoul High Court, but the Court found no error in the decision of the District Court and dismissed the case. The first turning point came when the Supreme Court decided in 2012 to overturn the decision of the lower court and to remand the case

[10] On the difference between 'conscription' and 'forced labour', see J Ju, 'A Positive International Law Approach to the South Korea-Japan Conflicts Concerning South Korean Tort Claims: Breaking the Vicious Circle' (2023), 30 – an updated version of 'A Positive International Law Approach to the Ongoing South Korea–Japan Conflicts: Breaking the Vicious Circle' (2022) 10 *Korean Journal of International & Comparative Law* 161, Available at: ssrn.com/abstract=4392743 or dx.doi.org/10.2139/ssrn.4392743.

[11] D Tamadai, 'The Japan-South Korea Claims Agreement: Identification of Subsequent Agreement and Practice' (2020) 22 *International Community Law Review* 107, 124.

to the Seoul High Court. The Supreme Court considered that the decision of the Japanese courts had been premised on the legality of Japan's colonial rule, which was contrary to the spirit of the South Korean Constitution. Therefore, compensation claims based on the illegality of colonial rule were not subject to the Claims Agreement.[12]

On remand, the Seoul High Court revoked the original ruling in line with the decision of the Supreme Court and ordered the Japanese company to pay compensation for damages. Regarding the key issue of whether the compensation claims were subject or not to the 1965 Claims Agreement, the Seoul High Court held that the Agreement was meant to resolve the financial and civil debts problem between both countries and that it did not cover compensation for Japan's colonial rule. Consequently, the plaintiff's individual right to make a claim was not extinguished by the Agreement.[13] The defendant appealed to the Supreme Court, which upheld the Seoul High Court's ruling, thus putting a final end to a 21-year process initiated in 1997.

III. The 2018 Supreme Court Judgment

The Supreme Court particularly examined three legal questions: the recognition or not of prior Japanese judgments, the statute of limitations and, above all, the interpretation of the 1965 Claims Agreement. First, the Court held that South Korea cannot recognise the judgments in Japan as they were 'contrary to good morals and other social order of Korea', as they were premised on the recognition that Japan's colonial rule over Korea was lawful so that it was valid to apply Japan's National Mobilisation Law and National Conscription Ordinance to the plaintiffs.[14] Second, faced with the three-year prescription period of Korean tort law, the Court took into consideration the importance of the disclosure in 2005 by the Roh Moo-hyun administration of classified documents relating to the Korea–Japan negotiations, which brought a new understanding on the meaning of the Claims Agreement. The release of these documents challenged the common understanding in South Korea that the Agreement comprehensively settled the individual right of Korean nationals to make claims against Japan or its nationals. The Court concluded that only after the release of those documents could the plaintiffs have reasonably brought their case. Since prescription must be applied in good faith, the defendant's refusal to perform its obligation toward the plaintiffs would be an abuse of this right, contrary to the principle of good faith.[15]

The third legal question, and arguably the most controversial, was the interpretation of the Claims Agreement. Specifically, the question was whether the Agreement foreclosed individual Korean forced labourers from raising compensation claims against Japanese private actors. The Supreme Court gave a negative answer, holding that the plaintiffs' claim for compensation should not be considered as included within the scope of application of the Claims Agreement. The Court stressed that the plaintiffs' claim for compensation was

[12] S Lee and S Lee, 'Yeo Woon Taek v. New Nippon Steel Corporation. 2013 Da 61381. Compensation for Damages (Others)' (2019) 113 *American Journal of International Law* 592, 595.

[13] Seoul High Court, 2012 Da 44947 (10 July 2013).

[14] South Korea Supreme Court, 2013 Da 61381 (30 July 2018), 12.

[15] Lee and Lee (n 12) 597.

premised on the inhumane and wrongful acts of Nippon Steel (engagement of the plaintiffs without informing them of the severe working conditions, exposition to life threatening danger or physical harm, withholding of their wages) directly related to Japan's unlawful colonial rule.

Examining the Treaty negotiations between Japan and South Korea, the Supreme Court pointed out that the Claims Agreement was not intended to settle compensation claims against Japan's unlawful colonial rule, but rather was merely a political agreement to resolve financial and civil debts issues between both countries. As a matter of fact, it was also the position of Japan that the money provided according to Article 1 of the Claims Agreement was basically in the nature of economic cooperation and not compensation for Japan's colonial occupation:

> During the course of negotiations over the Claims Agreement, the Japanese government fundamentally denied legal compensation for the harm caused by forced labor while also failing to acknowledge the illegality of its colonial rule. The two governments of Korea and Japan, consequently did not reach a consensus on the nature of Japan's control over the Korean Peninsula. In such a situation, it is difficult to conclude that the ability to make a claim for compensation was included within the scope of application of the Claims Agreement.[16]

Though the judgment basically resorted to the same arguments of the 2012 decision, it clarified the legal nature of the plaintiffs' claims. These were not related to unpaid wages or compensation, but moral damages arising from the illegal Japanese colonial rule. As such, they were not included within the scope of the Claims Agreement, which was limited to the settlement of claims arising from lawful acts characterised by the Supreme Court as 'financial and civil debts relation'.[17] Most importantly, the 2018 decision of the Supreme Court was historical in that it represented the first final and binding civil judgment ordering a corporation to pay damages for war crimes committed during the Second World War, thus seemingly negating the very basis of the South Korea–Japan relationship. It explains the fierceness of the Japanese government's reaction and the sweeping Korea-bashing among Japanese media outlets.[18]

Specialists of international law were prompt to examine the Supreme Court's decision. Some supported the decision from the perspective of international customary rules, arguing that the Claims Agreement, which failed to define the meaning of 'claim', was meant to solve civil matters of property and debts rather than addressing the state's wrongdoings during Japanese colonisation.[19] Others viewed the decision as a proof of the independence of the judiciary, underlining the appropriateness (*t'adang*) and the necessity of such a judgment in order to relieve anti-humanitarian acts.[20] Some others expressed doubts about using the South Korean Constitution to legitimate the right of victims of forced labour to raise

[16] South Korea Supreme Court, 2013 Da 61381 (30 July 2018), 16. Translation by S Lee and S Lee, 'Decision of the Korean Court on Japanese Forced Labor re New Nippon Steel Corporation (Supreme Court, Case 2013 Da 61381, Final Judgment)' (2019) 7 *Korean Journal of International and Comparative Law* 104.

[17] Dai (n 11) 129.

[18] M Uchida, *Moto chōyōkō wakai e no michi: senji higai to kojin seikyūken* (Chikuma shobō, 2020) 54.

[19] KJ Lee, 'The Supreme Court Decision on the Liability of Japanese Company for Forced Labor during the Japanese Colonial Era and its Implications' (2019) 18 *Journal of Korean Law* 350.

[20] T Kong, 'Kangje tongwŏn sonhae paesang p'angyŏl: yŏksajŏk pujŏngŭi wa sijŏngjŏk chŏngŭi' (2019) 22 *Pŏpch'ŏlhak yŏngu* 313.

claims, or about the Korean refusal to establish an arbitral commission to settle the dispute in compliance with Article III (2)[21] of the Claims Agreement.[22]

To be sure, many points at issue with the 2018 judgment were already raised by the 2012 Supreme Court decision and were thoroughly discussed at the time. Yet, it should be noted that although, by and large, a majority of South Korean scholars have been supportive of the Supreme Court's decision, some have voiced doubts and criticisms, showing that the dividing lines of the debate are not necessarily drawn according to nationality.[23] While legal issues relating to the judgment have been examined thoroughly, the position of the South Korean and Japanese governments, by contrast, has received less attention.

A. Strategic Ambiguity

From a layperson's perspective, one would probably be tempted to side with Japan's current official position and consider that claims between both countries, including individual claims, were indeed settled once and for all. The 1965 Agreement clearly stated that claims between Japan and South Korea 'and between their peoples' had been 'settled completely and finally'. As a matter of fact, the issues of unpaid wages to mobilised Koreans as well as compensation to victims of wartime mobilisation were included in the general list of demands presented by the Korean side to Japan during the first round of negotiations in February 1952.[24] In 1961, during the last stages of this long process, as both sides discussed the details of these issues, the South Korean negotiators demanded that Korean victims, including individuals who had been mobilised during the war, be compensated. The Japanese side agreed and even proposed that the victims be compensated individually, but the Korean side dismissed this offer, preferring instead a lump-sum payment from Japan. It assured that the South Korean government would then make sure to pay compensation to the victims individually.[25] Since it is on this premise that the Agreement was based, it would then follow that the responsibility for paying compensation to Korean victims rests with the South Korean government.[26]

[21] 'Any dispute which cannot be settled under the provision of paragraph 1 above shall be submitted for decision to an arbitral commission of three arbitrators; one to be appointed by the Government of each High Contracting Party within a period of thirty days from the date of receipt by the Government of either High Contracting Party from that of the other High Contracting Party of a note requesting arbitration of the dispute; and the third to be agreed upon by the two arbitrators so chosen or to be nominated by the Government of a third power as agreed upon by the two arbitrators within a further period of thirty days. However, the third arbitrator must not be a national of either High Contracting Party.'

[22] T Yamada, '"Chōyōkō" hanketsu no kokusaihō jō no ronten' (2020) 66 *Ajia kenkyū* 88.

[23] For an overview of South Korean international law scholars' opinions, see S Lee, 'The Views of Korean International Law Scholars Regarding the 2012 Supreme Court Decisions on Compensation for Forced Labor' (2014) 2 *Korean Journal of International and Comparative Law* 193.

[24] 'Outline of Agreement between South Korea and Japan Concerning Property and Claims' (Han-Il gan chaesan mit ch'ŏnggukwŏn hyŏpchŏng yogang), commonly referred to as 'Eight Items'.

[25] S Takasaki, *Kenshō Nik-Kan kaidan* (Iwanami shoten, 1996) 108. Takasaki considers it doubtful that the Japanese government was sincere in its offer for individual compensation. He contends that Japanese negotiators knew that individual compensation would require from the victims the exhibition of various proofs to estimate the amount of compensation, and that such a process would take so much time that the South Korean side preferred a more rapid political settlement.

[26] J Ju, 'The Japan-Korea Dispute Over the 1965 Agreement' *The Diplomat*, 23 October 2020, thediplomat.com/2020/10/the-japan-korea-dispute-over-the-1965-agreement.

The lump-sum payment, which eventually amounted to $300 million, was the product of a 'strategic ambiguity' that avoided labelling the categories of the claims payment.[27] From the Korean standpoint, Japan's payment should be considered reparations. Japan, however, rejected this perspective. To resolve the difference, terms like 'compensation' or 'reparations' were purposely avoided and do not appear in the Claims Agreement. This strategy, which left room for different interpretations, greatly contributed to the success of the negotiations and the signing of the Agreement, but it also sowed the seeds of recent disputes. The Park Chung-hee government, for its part, proceeded as if the payment included reparations from Japan.[28] In July 1965, it published a document called 'Comments on the Treaty and the Agreements between the Republic of Korea and Japan', in which it clearly explained its stance regarding the issue of forced labour:

> When examining the contents of our property and right to claims to be eliminated pursuant to the provision on settlement of problems concerning property and right to claim, which were among the 8 items requested from Japan, which was initially suggested by our delegation, those rights were to be completely extinguished. Therefore, unpaid wages and compensation for those subject to forced labor as well as the various claims of Korean nationals against the Japanese government and Japanese nationals were to be completely and financially extinguished.[29]

In line with its view that all individual claims had been settled by the Agreement and that it bore the responsibility to compensate Korean victims, the South Korean government enacted a series of acts in order to define the terms and conditions of this compensation. In 1966, the Act on the Administration and Management of Claims Funds settled the basic matters on use of the funds, establishing that civil claims of South Korean citizens against Japan until 15 August 1945 must be compensated with the claims funds settled according to the present law.[30] It was followed in 1971 by the 'Act on the Registration of Civil Claims against Japan', which defined the conditions for collecting accurate evidence and documents for civil claims against Japan.[31] For instance, the registration was limited to those who had been conscripted or drafted as soldiers, civilian employees or labourers and those who died before 15 August 1945. Finally, in 1974, the 'Act on Compensation for Civil Claims against Japan' provided the final details regarding the compensation, in particular the amount of 300,000 won to be given to the victims of Japanese mobilisation.[32] By 1977, more than 80,000 claims were compensated for a total amount of some 9 billion won (representing approximately 10 per cent of the $300 million provided by Japan under the Claims Agreement).[33]

[27] T Webster, 'South Korea Shatters the Paradigm: Corporate Liability, Historical Accountability, and the Second World War' (2022) 26 *UCLA Journal of International Law and Foreign Affairs*, 123, 141.

[28] N Park, 'Resolution of Korean Forced Labor Claims Must Put Victims at the Center' *United States Institute of Peace*, 30 August 2022, www.usip.org/publications/2022/08/resolution-korean-forced-labor-claims-must-put-victims-center.

[29] South Korea Supreme Court, 2013 Da 61381 (30 July 2018), 32. Translation by Lee and Lee (n 16) 117.

[30] 'Chŏnggukwŏn chagŭm ŭi unyong mit kwalli e kwan han pŏmnyul' (Law 1741), www.law.go.kr/%EB%B2%95%EB%A0%B9/%EC%B2%AD%EA%B5%AC%EA%B6%8C%EC%9E%90%EA%B8%88%EC%9D%98%EC%9A%B4%EC%9A%A9%EB%B0%8F%EA%B4%80%EB%A6%AC%EC%97%90%EA%B4%80%ED%95%9C%EB%B2%95%EB%A5%A0/(01741,19660219).

[31] 'Tae-Il mingan chŏnggukwŏn shingo e kwan han pŏmnyul' (Law 2287), www.law.go.kr/LSW/lsInfoP.do?lsiSeq=3450#0000.

[32] 'Tae-Il mingan chŏnggukwŏn posang e kwan han pŏmnyul' (Law 2685), www.law.go.kr/LSW/lsInfoP.do?lsiSeq=3452#0000.

[33] South Korea Supreme Court, 2013 Da 61381 (30 July 2018), 8.

Until the 2000s, one dozen claims for compensation were brought to South Korean courts, but they were all rejected on various grounds, particularly legal prescription. More importantly, no judgment questioned the validity of the Treaty or asserted that individual rights to claim damages had never been waived by the 1965 Agreement.[34]

As shown by the above, the 1965 Treaty and the Claims Agreement were not the object of serious criticisms in South Korea, at least from the political and judicial authorities. The idea that individual claims had not been settled did not come up in South Korea until the 1990s. Does this mean that the diplomatic dispute sparked by the South Korean Supreme Court in 2018 is the result of South Korea's inconsistency and unilateral change of mind or, in short, its failure to meet the commitments made in 1965 when it agreed to sign the Claims Agreement? In other words, are the grievances and criticisms of the Japanese government, which sees the judgment as a 'breach of international law' that 'violates Article II of the Agreement' and 'completely overthrows the legal foundation of the friendly and cooperative relationship that Japan and the Republic of Korea have developed since the normalization of diplomatic relations in 1965',[35] perfectly legitimate?

B. Diplomatic Protection

Surprisingly, it was not South Korea that first came up with the idea that the 1965 Agreement had not waived individual rights to claim damages. Here is what Japan's Foreign Minister Shiina Etsusaburō had to say on that matter in November 1965, facing questions at the House of Representatives from a special parliamentary committee on the Treaty and the agreements recently signed with South Korea:

> Ishibashi Masatsugu: Are you saying that Japan has wrongfully waived the right of claim guaranteed to all individuals by international law, without the consent of these individuals?
>
> Shiina Etsusaburō: We have only renounced diplomatic protection.[36]

While the South Korean government was preparing the legal framework to compensate individual claims, thereby acknowledging that the Agreement had settled the issue, the Japanese government was defending the opposite view, namely that the Agreement had not waived the individual right of claim. The trick was to argue that what Japan had renounced was diplomatic protection, not the right of an individual to raise a legal claim in national court. What is diplomatic protection and what advantage did it bring to the Japanese government? According to the *Parry & Grant Encyclopaedic Dictionary of International Law*, 'it is an elementary principle of international law that a State is entitled to protect its subjects, when injured by acts contrary to international law committed by another State, from whom they have been unable to obtain satisfaction through the ordinary channels'.[37]

[34] 'Hanguk chŏnhu posang chaep'an illam', justice.skr.jp/souran/ksouran-kr-web.htm.

[35] 'Regarding the Decision by the Supreme Court of the Republic of Korea, Confirming the Existing Judgments on the Japanese Company (Statement by Foreign Minister Taro Kono)', 30 October 2018.

[36] House of Representatives (50th Session), Special Committee on the Treaty and Agreements between Japan and the Republic of Korea (10th Meeting), 5 November 1965.

[37] JP Grant and JC Barker, *Parry & Grant Encyclopaedic Dictionary of International Law* (Oxford University Press, 2009) 156.

Does it mean that back then, Japan acknowledged the possibility that a South Korean citizen could use an individual right to claim damages? As the continuation of the above exchange clearly shows, the concern of the Japanese government was elsewhere:

> Ishibashi Masatsugu: In that case, does it mean that all individuals have a right of claim against South Korea? …
>
> Fujisaki Mari:[38] Even if Japanese citizens would lay claim to their rights against South Korea, these rights would be dealt with according to South Korean domestic law, and in practice, they would probably be rejected by South Korea.[39]

At the time, compensation to South Korea was not the only problem faced by the Japanese government. Compensation for the Japanese goods and properties left in Korea after the end of the colonial rule was another concern, which was equally important if not more so. During the negotiations, Japan played a two-pronged game. On the one side, it brought up the issue of compensation for Japanese losses as a counterweight, or as bargaining material, to mitigate South Korean demands. On the other side, it succeeded in settling both issues – compensation to South Korean and Japanese citizens – in one deal. In renouncing to diplomatic protection, the government waived its right to take up the cases of its nationals and resort to diplomatic action or international judicial proceedings on their behalf.[40] In other words, it 'conveniently' discarded its right to protect its citizens. In order to get away with this and ensure that the Treaty would be accepted domestically, Japanese authorities had to convince their citizens that they had not waived their individual right to seek redress from South Korea, hence the efforts made by Shiina Etsusaburō to avoid admitting having renounced the right of individual claim, even though he knew perfectly well that these individual claims would be turned down by South Korea. In settling the issue of claims, Japan not only got off lightly on the compensation paid to South Koreans, but also avoided facing potentially more expensive claims from its own citizens.[41] This stance was subsequently repeated several times, such as in 1991 by the director of the Treaties Bureau in front of the House of Councillors.[42]

It was not the first time that Japan resorted to this notion of diplomatic protection to suit its interests. In the wake of the Treaty of San Francisco, which ended the state of war between Japan and the Allied powers, the Japanese government faced claims for damages from victims of the atomic bombings of Hiroshima and Nagasaki. They considered these bombings to be in violation of international law and wanted to file damage suits against the US. The problem was that Japan, with the signing of the Treaty of San Francisco, had waived 'all claims of Japan and its nationals against the Allied Powers and their nationals arising out of the war or out of actions taken because of the existence of a state of war'.[43] Unable to sue the US, these Japanese victims directed their demands to the Japanese government, which they held responsible for the situation. In order to escape its responsibility and avoid litigation from its citizens, the government came up with the idea that, at San Francisco, it had

[38] Director of Treaties Bureau (*jōyakukyoku-chō*), Ministry of Foreign Affairs.
[39] House of Representatives (50th Session), Special Committee on the Treaty and Agreements between Japan and the Republic of Korea (10th Meeting), 5 November 1965.
[40] ibid.
[41] F Yoshizawa, *Nik-Kan kaidan 1965* (Kōbunken, 2015) 97.
[42] House of Councillors (121st Session), Budget Committee (3rd Meeting), 27 August 1991.
[43] Treaty of San Francisco, art 19.

merely renounced diplomatic protection and not the right of victims of the atomic bombings to file damage suits against the US.[44]

The same interpretation was used in relation to the Joint Declaration signed in 1956 between the USSR and Japan, which provided that: 'The USSR and Japan agree to renounce all claims by either State, its institutions or citizens, against the other State, its institutions or citizens, which have arisen as a result of the war since 9 August 1945'.[45] Faced with demands from former Japanese prisoners of war in the USSR, the Japanese government explained that the renouncement of claims mentioned in the Joint Declaration meant the renouncement of diplomatic protection and that the government had not renounced the individual right of Japanese nationals to bring claims. If they wished to exercise this right, they should do so according to Soviet national laws.[46]

Even though this interpretation was originally meant to avoid its responsibility towards Japanese nationals, the Japanese government stuck to it when faced with South Korean individual demands. During the 1990s, the Japanese government faced dozens of trials for compensation. While the Japanese courts rejected these civil actions, the Japanese state, as defendant, never asserted that South Koreans' individual rights of claim had been waived by the 1965 Agreement.[47]

Another element suggests that at the time of the signing of the Claims Agreement, the Japanese government did not consider individual claims as extinguished. Shortly after concluding the Claims Agreement, Japan enacted the Property Rights Measure Law,[48] which extinguished the property rights of South Korean nationals against Japan or its nationals. If the Agreement between Japan and the Republic of Korea Concerning the Settlement of Problems in Regard to Property and Claims and Economic Cooperation – which stipulated that these problems had been settled completely and finally – had extinguished all property rights of South Korean nationals, why would Japan need a domestic law to extinguish these property rights? For some experts, it proves that the Japanese government did not view 'settled completely and finally' as equivalent to 'extinguished'. Furthermore, as its name shows, the Property Rights Measure Law extinguished the 'property rights' of South Korean nationals, but it did not extinguish their 'claims'. In the absence of a hypothetical 'Claims Rights Measure Law', South Korean individual claims may well have been 'settled completely and finally' by the Claims Agreement, but they were by no means 'extinguished'.[49] In 2018, among the 13 justices of the South Korean Supreme Court, three justices co-signed a separate opinion in which they pointed out this Japanese domestic law. They argued that if the Claims Agreement had indeed extinguished the individual right of South Korean nationals to make a claim, such a law would have been unnecessary. For them, it was yet more evidence that Japan did not consider the Agreement to have extinguished individual claims.[50]

[44] Uchida (n 18) 39.

[45] Joint Declaration by the Union of Soviet Socialist Republics and Japan (19 October 1956), *United Nations – Treaty Series* (1957), 114.

[46] House of Councillors (120th Session), Committee of the Cabinet (3rd Meeting), 26 March 1991.

[47] S Yamamoto et al, *Chōyōkō saiban to Nik-Kan seikyūken kyōtei: Kankoku daihōin hanketsu o yomitoku* (Gendai jinbunsha, 2019) 110.

[48] Daikan minkoku tō no zaisanken ni kan suru sochihō.

[49] Yamamoto et al (n 47) 105.

[50] Lee and Lee (n 16) 117.

C. Individual Claims

With South Korea's democratisation and the birth of the first civilian government in 1993, various cases of human rights violations were revealed to the South Korean public. These revelations strengthened calls for transitional justice to rectify past wrongs. Leaders of the 1979 military coup, former Presidents Chun Doo-hwan and Roh Tae-woo, and military leaders closely linked to the authoritarian regime of Chun were the first targets of these demands. With the establishment in 1996 of the first truth commission to investigate the Kŏch'ang massacre (1951), where hundreds of civilians in South Kyŏngsang Province were slaughtered by the South Korean army, the past wrongs to be addressed were extended to the rights violations that took place during the Korean War.[51]

Issues relating to the Japanese colonial period also drew renewed attention, which led to an increase in the number of trials held in which individuals sought compensation. Compared to the 1970s and 1980s, which only saw nine trials in Japan for wartime reparations, of which only one was filed by a South Korean national, the 1990s saw more than 50 trials, of which roughly half were filed by South Korean former 'comfort women' or victims of forced labour.[52] In the end, Japanese courts dismissed all the cases on the grounds of prescription, waiver by international treaty or sovereign immunity.[53]

This resurging of the colonial past forced both governments to re-assess their stance on the 1965 Treaty and the Agreement, particularly regarding the issue of individual claims. In South Korea, amid growing pressure from former 'comfort women' and victims of forced labour, the first signs of change in the interpretation of the Agreement emerged under the administration of Kim Young-sam. In 1995, Foreign Minister Kong Ro-myŏng declared that the South Korean government recognised individual rights of claim and that it did not instruct such victims of Japanese colonisation to relinquish the exercise of these rights.[54] In 2000, Kim Dae-jung's Foreign Minister Lee Jung-bin went one step further in response to Kim Wŏn-ung, a member of the National Assembly, who urged the South Korean government to take action to force Japan to recognise its responsibility and offer compensation to former 'comfort women' and victims of forced draft, conscription and labour. Kim Wŏn-ung asked specifically whether the South Korean government, like the Japanese government, considered that all compensation had been settled by the 1965 Agreement. If so, did it mean that only compensation between both states had been settled or that 'individual compensation' (*kaein ŭi paesang*) too had been settled? In a written response, Lee Jung-bin acknowledged that with the 1965 Agreement, the issue of claims between both governments had reached a first conclusion (*iltallak*). However, he added that the South Korean government considered that the Agreement had no influence on the right to file suits for individual claims (*kaein ŭi chŏnggukwŏn*).[55] With this response, Kim Dae-jung's administration radically departed from the stance adopted by Park Chung-hee at the time of the signing of the Agreement.

[51] A Wolman, 'Looking Back While Moving Forward: The Evolution of Truth Commissions in Korea' (2013) 14 *Asian-Pacific Law & Policy Journal* 27, 37.

[52] 'Nihon sengo hoshō saiban sōran', justice.skr.jp/souran/souran-jp-web.htm.

[53] Webster (n 27) 131.

[54] National Assembly (177th Session), Committee on Unification and Foreign Affairs (3rd Meeting), 20 September 1995.

[55] 'Sŏmyŏn chilmun ŭi tappyŏnsŏ t'ongji', www.justice.skr.jp/2000reply.pdf.

This evolution was further strengthened a few years later when Kim Dae-jung's successor, Roh Moo-hyun, declassified diplomatic documents relating to the negotiations for the Basic Treaty. The decision was the result of continuing disclosure requests for documents relating to these negotiations, which led to a judgment of the Seoul Administrative Court that ruled in favour of disclosure in 2004.[56] The following year, a Joint Private and Public Committee on Follow-up Measures upon the Release of the Documents of the Korea-Japan Negotiations (Han-Il hoedam munsŏ konggae husok taech'aek kwallyŏn mingan kongdong wiwŏnhoe) was set up to discuss the limits of the legal validity of the Treaty. Its conclusions provided the basis for the official stance of South Korean governments since then, as well as legal theories that were subsequently adopted by South Korean courts in their judgments. The Committee made two important observations regarding the general understanding of the 1965 Agreement:

> The Claims Agreement was not intended to make a claim for compensation for Japan's colonial rule over Korea, but rather to resolve financial, civil debts and credit relations between Korea and Japan pursuant to Article 4 of the San Francisco Treaty;[57] that the inhumane and wrongful acts, including the Japanese military comfort women issue, committed by Japanese state authorities should not be deemed to be settled by the Claims Agreement so that responsibility of the Japanese government remains; and that the issues regarding ethnic Koreans who were forced to work on Sakhalin Island and the victims of the atomic bombings were not included in the Claims Agreement.[58]

In other words, the Claims Agreement did not provide an unconditional exoneration of the Japanese government, which remained legally liable in the case of anti-humanitarian acts (*panindojŏk haengwi*). This conclusion paved the way to South Korean courts, which, in the 2000s, began to rule in favour of the victims.

The Committee also acknowledged the responsibility of former South Korean governments. Since the Claims Agreement did not determine the amount for each item, but was concluded as a lump-sum settlement, the South Korean government had a moral responsibility to use part of the funds received from Japan to compensate the victims of forced labour. The South Korean government also bore responsibility for excluding the victims of forced labours as recipients of the compensation distributed in 1975 following the enactment of the 'Act on Compensation for Civil Claims Against Japan'.[59]

The first rulings that reflected these observations appeared a few years later, specifically in the *Nippon Steel* case. In its 2008 judgment, the Seoul District Court dismissed the case on the grounds that Old Nippon Steel and New Nippon Steel, the defendant, did

[56] Lee and Lee (n 12) 594.

[57] Treaty of Peace with Japan (1951), art 4(a): 'Subject to the provisions of paragraph (b) of this Article, the disposition of property of Japan and of its nationals in the areas referred to in Article 2, and their claims, including debts, against the authorities presently administering such areas and the residents (including juridical persons) thereof, and the disposition in Japan of property of such authorities and residents, and of claims, including debts, of such authorities and residents against Japan and its nationals, shall be the subject of special arrangements between Japan and such authorities. The property of any of the Allied Powers or its nationals in the areas referred to in Article 2 shall, insofar as this has not already been done, be returned by the administering authority in the condition in which it now exists. (The term nationals whenever used in the present Treaty includes juridical persons)', treaties.un.org/doc/Publication/UNTS/Volume%20136/volume-136-I-1832-English.pdf.

[58] South Korea Supreme Court, 2013 Da 61381 (30 July 2018), 10. Translation by Lee and Lee (n 16) 98.

[59] 'Han-Il hoedam munsŏ konggae husok taech'aek kwallyŏn mingwan kongdong wiwŏnhoe kaech'oe' (2005), www.opm.go.kr/flexer/view.do?ftype=hwp&attachNo=73036.

not have the same legal personality, and that the statute of limitations had expired, but it did acknowledge that while the 1965 Agreement resulted in the waiving of diplomatic protection, it did not waive the individual's claim to compensation.[60]

D. Claims Settled/Waived

Faced with dozens of lawsuits from Asian victims who exploited the Japanese government's own argument that individual claims remained valid, Japan tried to reverse course. From 2000, it started to argue that all claims had been settled by the Treaty of San Francisco and the 1965 Claims Agreement.[61] This remains the official stance held by Japan today.[62] To a certain extent, South Korea and Japan almost literally switched their positions in the 2000s. To mitigate criticisms against this turnaround, Japanese officials at times had to resort to further 'interpretative acrobatics',[63] like the following remark made in 2001 by Ebihara Shin, director of the Treaties Bureau. In response to a member of the House of Councillors who asked about the government's position in relation to the lawsuit filed by former Dutch prisoners of war against Japan, Shin explained:[64]

> Concerning our statement that it was extinguished, it does not mean that claims [*seikyūken*] held by individuals have been extinguished, but that pursuant to Article 14 (b) [of the Treaty of San Francisco] the legal obligation [of Japan] to answer claims [*seikyū*] based on these claims [*seikyūken*] and debts was extinguished, and accordingly relief is denied.[65]

Such an interpretation, devised to prove that there was no discrepancy between Japan's position on individual claims before and after 2000, does not change the fact that the Japanese government discarded the 'diplomatic protection' argument – which had previously allowed it to argue that (Japanese) individual claims *were not* extinguished – in favour of an argument that, in the end, was tantamount to saying that claims held by individuals *were* extinguished. The new interpretation was based on Article 14 (b) of the Treaty of San Francisco:

> Except as otherwise provided in the present Treaty, the Allied Powers waive all reparations claims of the Allied Powers, other claims of the Allied Powers and their nationals arising out of any actions taken by Japan and its nationals in the course of the prosecution of the war, and claims of the Allied Powers for direct military costs of occupation.

[60] Seoul District Court, Case 2005 Gahap 16473 (6 March 2008).

[61] According to some authors, this shift was motivated by the desire of the Japanese government, faced with American prisoners of war seeking compensation in American courts, to consolidate its position by aligning itself with the US government's position holding that the San Francisco Peace Treaty waived all claims of American and Allied nationals against Japan and Japanese nationals. See K Tokudome and A Tokudome, 'Individual Claims: Are the Positions of the US and Japanese Governments in Agreement in the American POW Forced Labor Cases?' (2003) 21 *UCLA Pacific Basin Law Journal* 1, 18.

[62] 'Background and Position of the Government of Japan Concerning the Issue of Former Civilian Workers from the Korean Peninsula (FACT SHEET)', www.mofa.go.jp/mofaj/files/000499948.pdf.

[63] Park (n 28).

[64] In 1994, former Dutch prisoners of war and civilian internees filed a lawsuit against Japan for compensation for damages during the Second World War. In 2001, the Tokyo High Court dismissed the case. See 'Nihon sengo hoshō saiban sōran' (General Survey of Compensation Lawsuits in Postwar Japan).

[65] House of Councillors (151st session), Foreign Relations and Defense Committee (4th meeting), 22 March 2001.

The central point here is that the Allied powers explicitly 'waive all reparations claims', allowing the Japanese government to come up with the idea that its legal obligation to meet claims was extinguished. As seen above, Japan's courts dismissed the great majority of cases on various grounds, but after the Japanese government's about-turn, some judgments reflected that position, including cases relating to Korea's colonial period. In the second *Fujikoshi* lawsuit, where former 'comfort women' demanded an official apology and compensation, the Toyama District Court dismissed the case in 2007, arguing that even if the plaintiffs would exercise their right to claim, Japan and its nationals had no legal obligation to respond to these demands.[66]

It remains to be seen whether this interpretation can apply to South Korea, which did not sign the Treaty of San Francisco. More importantly, and somewhat ironically, this interpretation put forward by the Japanese government was later used by the South Korean Supreme Court against Nippon Steel in its landmark ruling. A second separate opinion was co-signed by Justices Kim So-young, Lee Dong-won and Roh Jeong-ho agreeing with the majority opinion that the plaintiffs could exercise their right to make a claim for compensation against Nippon Steel for forced labour despite the Claims Agreement. However, the three Justices applied different reasoning from the majority opinion, observing that the principle of modern law, where a state is a separate legal entity from an individual, extends to international law. Therefore, if a state waives a right on behalf of an individual, it is necessary to provide explicit grounds in the concerned treaty:

> However, the provisions on waiver or the elimination of an individual's right to make a claim are found nowhere within the text of the Claims Agreement. In this respect, there is a notable expression of the term waiving claims in Article 14 (b) of the San Francisco Treaty, signed between Japan and the Allied Nations on September 8, 1951, which reads that 'the Allied Powers waive all reparations claims of the Allied Powers, other claims of the Allied Powers and their nationals … and claims of the Allied Powers for direct military costs of occupation'. While the expression such as 'the problems concerning claims is settled completely and finally' was used, it [is] highly unlikely that such an expression has the same meaning as a waiver or extinguishment of an individual's right to make a claim in light of the necessity for a strict interpretation discussed earlier.[67]

IV. Conclusion

As the first final and binding civil judgment ordering a corporation to pay damages for war crimes committed during the Second World War, the 2018 Korean Supreme Court decision was groundbreaking. While highly controversial, the decision has set a precedent likely to influence other cases involving corporate legal liability and colonial compensation. The legal reasoning is debatable and has prompted many reactions among specialists of international law.

It is particularly worth noting that the Supreme Court relied heavily on the idea of 'colonial illegality' to reach its conclusion. For instance, the 'Eight Items' presented by the South Korean delegation during the first Korea–Japan talks in 1952 included requests for

[66] 'Nihon sengo hoshō saiban sōran'.
[67] South Korea Supreme Court, 2013 Da 61381 (30 July 2018), 30. Translation by Lee and Lee (n 16) 116.

payment of unpaid wages, compensation and other rights to claim of the forced Korean draftees. However, according to the Supreme Court, these requests were not premised upon the illegality of Japan's colonial rule. Therefore, the Supreme Court found it difficult to conclude that unpaid wages, compensation and other rights to claim of conscripted Koreans were covered by the 1965 Agreement.[68]

Since the 1990s, 'colonial illegality' has become the common understanding of Japanese colonial rule in South Korea – a view that is reflected in the term 'Period of forced occupation by the Japanese empire' (*Ilche kangjŏmgi*), commonly used to designate the colonial period in Korean. This idea itself is another hot topic between the two countries and is also probably one of the most divisive among scholars. Unlike other controversial issues such as the 'comfort women', where the majority of South Korean and Japanese historians agree on the basic historical facts and, by and large, share the same appraisal of this issue, the same historians find it difficult to reduce their differences on this topic of illegality. Even Japanese progressive scholars and politicians, who acknowledge Japan's moral responsibility and advocate apologies and compensation to the victims of Japanese colonisation, consider the annexation of Korea to be perfectly legal.[69] Thus, relying on this controversial narrative of 'colonial illegality' is not likely to contribute to the acceptance of the Supreme Court's decision on the Japanese side.

On the other hand, the debate about the legality of the annexation may also provide a hint to resolving the fallout of *Nippon Steel* and similar cases. Instead of resorting to 'colonial illegality' to shore up demands of compensation, it might be more productive to put the issue of compensation into the larger context of colonialism and the moral responsibility of former colonial powers. For, if only 'illegally colonised' victims were entitled to apologies and compensation, it would suggest that former colonies like Taiwan, where colonisation was carried out 'legally', would not qualify to make such demands.[70]

The above reminder and analysis of former official positions from both the South Korean and Japanese governments on the issue of claims show the limits of a purely legal approach to forced labour. The simple fact that different administrations have adopted radically opposed positions to the point that South Korea and Japan swapped their positions around in the 2000s is a case in point. The Basic Treaty and the Claims Agreement may well have left many problems unresolved, but they are not in themselves an obstacle to transitional justice. On the contrary, they were the product of many compromises and devised precisely to leave room for divergent interpretations. In other words, the Treaty and the Agreement neither preclude nor impose the payment of individual compensation. The real question is the political will, especially on the Japanese side, to face the legacy of the colonial period.

Political leaders of both countries seem to be aware of this, as they have left the door open for negotiations. A closer look behind the harsh rhetoric reveals that both governments have been keen to avoid the use of specific terms like 'diplomatic protection' or 'extinguished claims'. The official position of the Japanese government merely rehashes the wording of the 1965 Agreement, 'settled completely and finally', without going into detail about legal

[68] South Korea Supreme Court, 2013 Da 61381 (30 July 2018), 15.

[69] On this topic, see for instance the special issue of *Seoul Journal of Korean Studies* 18 (2005).

[70] F Unno, 'Professor Yi's Article "Annexation of Korea Failed to Come into Being" Reexamined' (2005) 18 *Seoul Journal of Korean Studies* 107, 110.

interpretation on individual claims. The Moon Jae-in administration, for its part, was even more cautious, avoiding any declaration on the legal liability of the Japanese corporation and simply expressing the basic principle of separation of powers between the executive and the judiciary. Moon Jae-in's successor, Yoon Suk-yeol, went a step further and, together with his Japanese counterpart, Prime Minister Fukuda Kishio, conveyed his commitment to resolving the forced labour issue.[71] In doing so, both sides will hopefully keep in mind the importance of consulting the victims and obtaining their approval. The consequences of failing to do so should be obvious by now, as shown by the failure of the 2015 Japan-South Korea Comfort Women Agreement, which fell apart due to its dismissal by the victims and lack of public support.

[71] H Lee, 'Yoon, Japan's Kishida Agreed to Seek Quick Settlement of Forced Labor Issue: Official', en.yna.co.kr/view/AEN20221116008500315.

PART 4

Family and Succession Law

12

New Developments in Chinese Private International Law in the Area of International Family Law

12 Years after the Entry into Force of the Chinese PIL Act

WEIZUO CHEN

On 1 April 2011, the Law of the People's Republic of China (PRC) on the Application of Laws to Civil Relationships Involving a Foreign Element (hereinafter the 'PIL Act'),[1] which was adopted at the 17th Meeting of the Standing Committee of the 11th National People's Congress on 28 October 2010, entered into force. As this was the very first piece of legislation on PIL in the 74-year history of the PRC, it would be of practical importance to have a closer look at the new development of Chinese PIL in the area of international family law from the perspectives of international jurisdiction, choice of law, and the recognition and enforcement of foreign court decisions.

I. Chinese Courts' International Jurisdiction Over Family Law Matters on the Basis of the Rules on General Territorial Jurisdiction

Chinese international civil procedural law contains no special jurisdictional rules on the international jurisdiction of Chinese courts over family law matters. In order to exercise international jurisdiction over family law matters, Chinese courts apply the rules on general territorial jurisdiction under the PRC Civil Procedure Law by analogy.[2]

[1] Unofficial English translation by W Chen in J Basedow, G Rühl, F Ferrari and P de Miguel Asensio (eds), *Encyclopedia of Private International Law* (Edward Elgar, 2017) 3069–72; unofficial French translation by W Chen, N Nord and L Bertrand in (2011) 1 *Revue critique de droit international privé* 189.

[2] The PRC Civil Procedure Law is the Chinese code of civil procedure which was adopted at the 4th Session of the 7th National People's Congress on 9 April 1991, amended for the first time in accordance with the Decision on Amending the PRC Civil Procedure Law adopted at the 30th Meeting of the Standing Committee of the

Pursuant to Article 22 (1) of the PRC Civil Procedure Law,[3] Chinese courts are granted general territorial jurisdiction, which is not exclusive, if the defendant is domiciled in China, or if the defendant is habitually resident in China in cases where the place of the defendant's domicile differs from the place of his or her habitual residence.

However, pursuant to Article 23, Item (1) of the PRC Civil Procedure Law,[4] a civil lawsuit concerning personal status (eg, a divorce suit) brought against a person not residing in Chinese territory shall be under the jurisdiction of the Chinese court at the place of the plaintiff's domicile or, if the place of the plaintiff's domicile differs from the place of his or her habitual residence, at the place of the plaintiff's habitual residence.[5]

II. Choice-of-Law Rules in Family Law Matters

As far as the Chinese choice-of-law rules in family law matters are concerned, habitual residence plays a prominent role.

With regard to the conditions of a marriage, Article 21 of the PIL Act provides for the following connecting factors:[6] the place of the parties' common habitual residence, the parties' common nationality and (provided there exists no common nationality and the marriage is to be entered into at the place of either party's habitual residence or in the

10th National People's Congress on 28 October 2007 (effective as of 1 April 2008), for the second time in accordance with the Decision on Amending the PRC Civil Procedure Law adopted at the 28th Meeting of the Standing Committee of the 11th National People's Congress on 31 August 2012 (effective as of 1 January 2013), for the third time in accordance with the Decision on Amending the PRC Civil Procedure Law and the PRC Administrative Litigation Law adopted at the 28th Meeting of the Standing Committee of the 12th National People's Congress on 27 June 2017 (effective as of 1 July 2017), and for the fourth time in accordance with the Decision on Amending the PRC Civil Procedure Law adopted at the 32th Meeting of the Standing Committee of the 13th National People's Congress on 24 December 2021 (effective as of 1 January 2022).

[3] Article 22 (1) of the PRC Civil Procedure Law provides: 'A civil lawsuit brought against a citizen shall be under the jurisdiction of the people's court at the place where the defendant has his/her domicile; if the place of the defendant's domicile is different from that of his/her habitual residence, the lawsuit shall be under the jurisdiction of the people's court at the place of his/her habitual residence.' Article 22 (2) of the PRC Civil Procedure Law provides: 'A civil lawsuit brought against a legal person or any other organisation shall be under the jurisdiction of the people's court at the place where the defendant has his/her domicile.' Article 22 (3) of the PRC Civil Procedure Law provides: 'Where the domiciles or habitual residences of several co-defendants in the same lawsuit are in the areas under the jurisdiction of two or more people's courts, all of those people's courts shall have jurisdiction over the lawsuit.'

[4] Article 23 of the PRC Civil Procedure Law provides: 'The civil lawsuits described below shall be under the jurisdiction of the people's court at the place where the plaintiff has his/her domicile; if the place of the plaintiff's domicile is different from that of his/her habitual residence, the lawsuit shall be under the jurisdiction of the people's court at the place of the plaintiff's habitual residence:

(1) those concerning personal status brought against persons not residing within the territory of the PRC;
(2) those concerning the personal status of persons whose whereabouts are unknown or who have been declared as missing.
(3) those brought against persons who are undergoing mandatory education measures; and
(4) those brought against persons who are in imprisonment.'

[5] W Chen, *Chinese Civil Procedure and the Conflict of Laws* (Tsinghua University Press, 2011) 31–34.

[6] Article 21 of the Chinese PIL Act provides: 'The conditions of a marriage are governed by the law of the place of the parties' common habitual residence; in the absence of a place of common habitual residence, the conditions of a marriage are governed by the law of the country of the common nationality; if there exists no common nationality and the marriage is to be entered into at the place of either party's habitual residence or in the country of either party's nationality, the conditions of a marriage are governed by the *lex loci celebrationis*.'

country of either party's nationality) the place of celebration of the marriage. However, the formalities of a marriage are valid if they satisfy the *lex loci celebrationis*, the law of the place of either party's habitual residence or the law of the country of either party's nationality (Article 22 of the PIL Act).[7]

With regard to personal relationships between spouses, Article 23 of the PIL Act provides for their common habitual residence and their common nationality as the connecting factors.[8] Nevertheless, the connecting factor 'their common nationality' shall be employed subsidiarily in the absence of the connecting factor 'their common residence'. With regard to property relationships between spouses, sentence 1 of Article 24 of the PIL Act allows the choice of one of the following legal systems by the parties: the law of the place of either party's habitual residence, the law of the country of either party's nationality or the law of the place where the principal property is located. Absent a choice of law by the parties, sentence 2 of Article 24 of the PIL Act provides for their common habitual residence and their common nationality as the connecting factors.[9] Nevertheless, the connecting factor 'their common nationality' shall be employed subsidiarily in the absence of the connecting factor 'their common habitual residence'.

With regard to divorce by mutual consent, sentence 1 of Article 26 of the PIL Act allows the parties to choose by agreement the law of the place of either party's habitual residence or the law of the country of either party's nationality as applicable. Absent a choice of law by the parties, sentence 2 of Article 26 of the PIL Act provides for the following connecting factors which shall be employed subsidiarily: the parties' common habitual residence, their common nationality and the place where the authority conducting the divorce formalities is located.[10] In addition, Article 27 of the PIL Act subjects divorce by litigation to the *lex fori*.[11]

Pursuant to Article 28 of the PIL Act,[12] the conditions and formalities of an adoption are governed by the law of the place of the adopting person's habitual residence and the law of the place of the adoptee's habitual residence (sentence 1). The effects of an adoption are governed by the law of the place of the adopting person's habitual residence at the time of

[7] Article 22 of the Chinese PIL Act provides: 'The formalities of a marriage are valid if they satisfy the *lex loci celebrationis*, the law of the place of either party's habitual residence, or the law of the country of either party's nationality.'

[8] Article 23 of the Chinese PIL Act provides: 'Personal relationships between spouses are governed by the law of the place of their common habitual residence; in the absence of a place of common habitual residence, the law of the country of their common nationality applies.'

[9] Article 24 of the Chinese PIL Act provides: 'With regard to property relationships between spouses, the parties may choose by agreement the law of the place of either party's habitual residence, the law of the country of either party's nationality, or the law of the place where the principal property is located, as applicable. In the absence of such a choice of law by the parties, the law of the place of their common habitual residence applies; in the absence of a place of common habitual residence, the law of the country of their common nationality applies.'

[10] Article 26 of the Chinese PIL Act provides: 'With regard to divorce by mutual consent, the parties may choose by agreement the law of the place of either party's habitual residence or the law of the country of either party's nationality as applicable. In the absence of such a choice of law by the parties, the law of the place of their common habitual residence applies; in the absence of a place of common habitual residence, the law of the country of their common nationality applies; in the absence of a common nationality, the law of the place where the authority conducting the divorce formalities is located applies.'

[11] Article 27 of the Chinese PIL Act provides: 'Divorce by litigation is governed by the *lex fori*.'

[12] Article 28 of the Chinese PIL Act provides: 'The conditions and formalities of an adoption are governed by the law of the place of the adopting person's habitual residence and the law of the place of the adoptee's habitual residence. The effects of an adoption are governed by the law of the place of the adopting person's habitual residence at the time of the adoption. The dissolution of an adoption relationship is governed by the law of the place of the adoptee's habitual residence at the time of the adoption or by the *lex fori*.'

the adoption (sentence 2). The dissolution of an adoption relationship is governed by the law of the place of the adoptee's habitual residence at the time of the adoption or by the *lex fori* (sentence 3).

Pursuant to Article 25 of the PIL Act,[13] personal relationships and property relationships between parent and child are governed by the law of the place of their common habitual residence. Absent a place of common habitual residence, the law of the place of either party's habitual residence or the law of the country of either party's nationality shall apply, provided that such a law favours the protection of the weaker party's rights and interests.[14] Pursuant to Article 29 of the PIL Act,[15] maintenance is governed by the law of the place of either party's habitual residence, the law of the country of either party's nationality or the law of the place where the principal property is located, provided that such a law favours the protection of the rights and interests of the person to be supported. Pursuant to Article 30 of the PIL Act,[16] guardianship is governed by the law of the place of either party's habitual residence or the law of the country of either party's nationality, provided that it is the law favouring the protection of the ward's rights and interests.[17]

III. Recognition and Enforcement of Foreign Court Decisions on Family Law Matters

The general system of the recognition and enforcement of foreign court decisions in China is established in Articles 288 and 289 of the PRC Civil Procedure Law and Articles 541, 542 and 544–48 of the Interpretation of the Supreme People's Court on the Application of the PRC Civil Procedure Law.[18] Such provisions only apply to those foreign court judgments or written orders not covered by one of the bilateral or multilateral treaties establishing recognition and enforcement rules that are in force in China, because Article 267 of the PRC Civil Procedure Law gives priority to international treaties to which China is a contracting party as regards civil proceedings involving a foreign element.[19]

[13] Article 25 of the Chinese PIL Act provides: 'Personal relationships and property relationships between parent and child are governed by the law of the place of their common habitual residence; in the absence of a place of common habitual residence, the law of the place of either party's habitual residence or the law of the country of either party's nationality applies, provided that such a law favours the protection of the weaker party's rights and interests.'

[14] Z Huo, 'An Imperfect Improvement: The New Conflict of Laws Act of the People's Republic of China' (2011) 60(4) *International and Comparative Law Quarterly* 1065, 1082.

[15] Article 29 of the Chinese PIL Act provides: 'Maintenance is governed by the law of the place of either party's habitual residence or the law of the country of either party's nationality, or by the law of the place where the principal property is located, provided that such a law favours the protection of the rights and interests of the person to be supported.'

[16] Article 30 of the Chinese PIL Act provides: 'Guardianship is governed by the law of the place of either party's habitual residence or the law of the country of either party's nationality, provided that such a law favours the protection of the ward's rights and interests.'

[17] M Blumer, *Chinese Private International Law* (Fajus Verlag, 2013) 29–31.

[18] The Interpretation of the Supreme People's Court on the Application of the PRC Civil Procedure Law was adopted on 18 December 2014. It was amended for the first time on 23 December 2020 and for the second time on 22 March 2022 (effective as of 10 April 2022).

[19] Article 267, which is contained in Part Four, 'Special Provisions for Civil Procedure of Cases Involving a Foreign Element', Chapter XXIII 'General Principles', of the PRC Civil Procedure Law, reads as follows: 'If an

In most cases, the recognition and enforcement of a foreign court judgment or written order in China will be resolved by recourse to international treaties and implemented by a Chinese court in accordance with the PRC Civil Procedure Law under the direction of the Interpretation of the Supreme People's Court on the Application of the PRC Civil Procedure Law. Absent an international treaty, a Chinese court will recognise or enforce foreign courts judgments and written orders on the basis of the principle of reciprocity, ie, only if a similar judgment or written order rendered by a Chinese court would be recognised or enforced in the relevant foreign country.

If a foreign court judgment or written order having *res judicata* effect requires recognition and enforcement by a Chinese court, the party concerned may directly apply for recognition and enforcement to the intermediate people's court having jurisdiction. The foreign court having rendered the judgment or written order may also, in accordance with an international treaty to which both the relevant foreign country and China are contracting parties or on the basis of the principle of reciprocity, request a Chinese court to recognise and enforce it (Article 288 of the PRC Civil Procedure Law).[20]

Only those foreign court judgments or written orders having *res judicata* effect may be recognised or enforced in China. The question whether a foreign judgment or written order has *res judicata* effect shall be determined by the international treaties to which China is a contracting party, the principle of reciprocity or Chinese law.

In the case of an application directly filed by the party concerned or a request made by the foreign court having rendered the judgment or written order for the recognition and enforcement thereof, the people's court having jurisdiction shall – after examining the foreign court judgment or written order in accordance with the international treaties to which China is a contracting party or on the basis of the principle of reciprocity and arriving at the conclusion that the recognition and enforcement of the foreign judgment or written order would neither contradict the primary principles of the law of the PRC nor violate the state's sovereignty, security and social and public interest – rule that the validity of the foreign judgment or written order should be recognised. If required, the Chinese court having jurisdiction shall also, in accordance with the relevant provisions of the PRC Civil Procedure Law, issue a writ of execution to enforce the foreign court judgment or written order (sentence 1 of Article 289 of the PRC Civil Procedure Law).[21]

international treaty concluded or acceded to by the PRC contains provisions that differ from the provisions of this Law, the provisions of the international treaty shall apply, except for those on which the PRC has made reservations.'

[20] Article 288 of the PRC Civil Procedure Law provides: 'If a judgment or written order having *res judicata* effect which was rendered by a foreign court requires recognition and enforcement by a people's court of the PRC, the party concerned may directly apply for recognition and enforcement to the PRC intermediate people's court having jurisdiction; the foreign court may also, in accordance with the provisions of an international treaty concluded or acceded to by the relevant foreign country and the PRC or on the basis of the principle of reciprocity, request recognition and enforcement by a people's court.'

[21] Article 289 of the PRC Civil Procedure Law provides: 'In the case of an application or request for the recognition and enforcement of a judgment or written order having *res judicata* effect which was rendered by a foreign court, the people's court shall, after examining it in accordance with the international treaties concluded or acceded to by the PRC or on the basis of the principle of reciprocity and arriving at the conclusion that it does not contradict the primary principles of the law of the PRC nor violates the State's sovereignty, security and social and public interest, order to recognise the validity of the foreign judgment or written order, and, if required, issue a writ of execution to enforce it in accordance with the relevant provisions of this Law. If the recognition and enforcement of the foreign judgment or written order would contradict the primary principles of the law of the PRC or violates the State's sovereignty, security and social and public interest, the people's court shall refuse to recognise and enforce it.'

Finally, if the recognition and enforcement of a foreign court judgment or written order having *res judicata* effect would contradict the primary principles of the law of the PRC or violate state's sovereignty, security and social and public interests, the Chinese court shall decline to recognise and enforce it (sentence 2 of Article 289 of the PRC Civil Procedure Law). This is in fact a public policy exception provided for by the Chinese rules on the recognition and enforcement of foreign court decisions.[22]

IV. Concluding Remarks

The Chinese PIL Act contains only choice-of-law rules, including those governing family law relationships involving a foreign element. Such choice-of-law rules are fairly modern and progressive for three reasons. First, habitual residence of a person is the main connecting factor in determining the laws applicable to family law relationships involving a foreign element. Second, the choice of the applicable law by the parties (party autonomy) is allowed when determining the laws applicable to the property relationships between spouses, and to divorce by mutual consent. Finally, Articles 25, 29 and 30 of the PIL Act introduce specific choice-of-law rules as regards personal and property relationships between parent and child, maintenance, and guardianship. These articles establish that the court should apply the law favouring the protection of the rights and interests of the weaker party, the person to be supported or the ward.[23] Compared with the majority of the PIL Act's choice-of-law rules which are the traditional 'jurisdiction-selecting rules', the specific choice-of-law rules contained in the above-mentioned three articles can be regarded in part as 'result-selecting rules'.[24]

As regards international civil procedural law, there are no special rules on the international jurisdiction of Chinese courts over family law matters. Though the general territorial jurisdiction rules contained in the above-mentioned Articles 22 and 23 of the PRC Civil Procedure Law are jurisdictional rules on domestic matters, they are to be applied by analogy by Chinese courts to international matters including international family law matters.

The Chinese rules on the recognition and enforcement of foreign court decisions are rudimentary. In practice, both the relevant international treaties to which the PRC is a contracting party and the principle of reciprocity play a role in the recognition and enforcement of foreign court decisions in family law matters. From a European/Swiss perspective, the use of the principle of reciprocity for the recognition and enforcement of foreign court decisions does seem a bit 'old-fashioned' and is disadvantageous to the cross-border circulation of judicial documents between China and the outside world. Moreover, China is expected to take part in more multilateral mechanisms taking the

[22] W Chen, 'National Report – China' in Basedow et al (n 1) 1970–80.

[23] K Boele-Woelki, 'International Private Law in China and Europe: A Comparison of Conflict-of-Law Rules Regarding Family and Succession Law' in J Basedow and KB Pißler (eds), *Private International Law in Mainland China, Taiwan and Europe* (Mohr Siebeck, 2014) 307–27.

[24] W Chen, 'La nouvelle codification du droit international privé chinois' in *Recueil des cours de l'Académie de droit international de La Haye*, vol 359 (Martinus Nijhoff Publishers, 2013) 217–22.

form of an international convention regarding the recognition and enforcement of foreign courts decisions.

In conclusion, there is a strong need for China to modernise its international civil procedural law rules on international jurisdiction and the recognition and enforcement of foreign court decisions in family law matters. It is to be hoped that the ongoing second decade of the twenty-first century will see far-reaching and effective reform in this field.

13

Some Recent Issues in Family Law and International Family Law in Japan

MARI NAGATA

I. Introduction

During the transition from the twentieth to the twenty-first century, numerous countries worldwide underwent significant alterations in their family perspectives and arrangements. However, despite this global trend, Japan has not fully embraced these transformations within its legal system. After the Second World War, the family law of Japan was amended to include contemporary constitutional values, including gender parity, yet it still embraces certain Confucian undertones. An example of this is the family registration system, which perceives the family as a collective entity rather than an assemblage of individuals. This so-called 'house (家 [*ie*])' system has given rise to a pre-eminence of legal marriage founded upon the patriarchal system and has constituted a substantial hindrance to the reform of family law in Japan.[1] Nevertheless, in an era where international travel is common, Japan cannot exist in complete isolation from the progressive changes of the world. Consequently, a conflict has emerged between Japan's reluctance to adapt and the dynamic movements of the rest of the world.

The aim of this chapter is to explain the current situation and challenges in Japan regarding two pertinent issues: (1) surrogacy (代理母出産 [*dairi-haha-shussan*]); and (2) same-sex marriage (同性婚 [*dosei-kon*]), in relation to both substantive law and private international law.

[1] For example, the introduction of separate surnames for married couples and the abolition of the distinction between children born in and out of wedlock have been discussed for many years, but there is no prospect that they will be enacted into law. The Japanese Civil Code was introduced in 1890, but due to the strong influence of French law, which reflected individualistic and liberal values, it faced significant opposition for disrupting the traditional Japanese 'house' system. Consequently, its enforcement was delayed indefinitely in 1892 and ultimately was never implemented. It was commonly believed at the time that the 'Civil Code came into force and loyalty and filial piety perished'. For example, see S Ninomiya, 'Josetsu [Introduction]' S Ninomiya (ed), *Shin Chushaku Minpou* [*New Commentary on the Civil Code of Japan*] vol 17 (Yuhikaku, 2017) 6–7.

II. Surrogacy within the Framework of Japanese Law

A. Establishment of a Legal Mother–Child Relationship in Japan

Before delving into the intricacies of surrogacy, it is imperative to provide an overview of the substantive law concerning the establishment of the mother–child relationship in Japan. It is worth noting that under Japanese law, the distinction between legitimate and illegitimate children still exists within the legal framework. A legitimate child is a child born within the confines of a marital union between a man and a woman. In contrast, an illegitimate child is a child born outside the bonds of marriage. While the legal relationship between a parent and a legitimate child is established at the moment of birth, the same does not hold true for an illegitimate child, unless the father acknowledges the child. The original Civil Code drew a clear distinction between the legal treatment of legitimate and illegitimate children, including differences in their inheritance rights. However, subsequent amendments were made to the Civil Code in response to the Japanese Supreme Court's ruling that such differences were unconstitutional. Nevertheless, some distinctions persist to this day, particularly in the way in which they are registered in official family records.

Furthermore, there is no statutory law that specifically regulates the relationship between a mother and her child. Hence, the Civil Code remains silent on whether the determination of the legal relationship between a mother and child should prioritise the circumstances of childbirth or the genetic connection. With the growing use of assisted reproductive technologies, this matter has become a critical concern. As a result, in 2020, the Japanese government implemented specialised legislation (see below) to establish a legal parent–child relationship for children conceived via assisted reproductive technologies involving the use of third-party sperm or eggs.

With respect to the establishment of legitimate parent–child relationships, the Japanese Civil Code defines them as follows:

> Article 772[2]
>
> (1) A child conceived by a wife during marriage shall be presumed to be a child of her husband.
> (2) A child born after 200 days from the formation of marriage or within 300 days of the day of the dissolution or rescission of marriage shall be presumed to have been conceived during marriage.

The illegitimate parent–child relationship is established only by acknowledgement of the child under Japanese law, which is based on the following Article 779 of the Civil Code:

> Article 779
>
> A father or a mother may affiliate his/her child out of wedlock.

In essence, Article 779 dictates that the father or mother must acknowledge ('affiliate' 認知 [*ninchi*]) the child, as the legal paternity of the illegitimate child can only be established

[2] The English translations of the articles of the Japanese Civil Code and the Act on General Rules for Application of Laws presented in this chapter are all translations from the Japanese Law Translation Database System operated by the Japanese Ministry of Justice (www.japaneselawtranslation.go.jp). At the time of writing, this article is in the final stages of revision. After April 2024, a flexible presumption of legitimacy will be applied to children conceived prior to the parents' marriage or born after remarriage.

through acknowledgement. However, in terms of the legal mother–child relationship of an illegitimate child, the Supreme Court has held that 'in principle, it is reasonable to conclude that the parent-child relationship between a mother and her illegitimate child naturally arises from the fact of the delivery of the child, without requiring acknowledgment by the mother'.[3] Thus, the prevalent view in both legal practice and academic discourse is that acknowledgement by the mother is not a prerequisite for establishing the legal maternity of the illegitimate child.[4]

These provisions were inherited from the Civil Code of 1889 with naturally conceived children in mind. However, recent advancements in medical technology have resulted in an increase in children born through assisted reproductive technology, requiring the implementation of new legal measures. In response to this trend, the Law on Special Provisions of the Civil Code Concerning the Provision, etc of Assisted Reproductive Technologies and the Parent-Child Relationship of a Child Born Thereby (hereinafter referred to as 'the ART-Law') was passed in 2020 and came into force in 2021. Under this special law, in cases of assisted reproductive medical treatment utilising another person's eggs, '[i]f a woman conceives and gives birth to a child through assisted reproductive medical treatment using the eggs (including embryos derived from such eggs) of a woman other than herself, the woman who has given birth shall be the mother of such child' (Article 9).

B. Surrogate Motherhood in Japanese Substantive Law

According to the aforementioned provisions, it becomes apparent that the fact of giving birth to a child is the decisive element in establishing the mother–child relationship under Japanese law. Therefore, what is the legal relationship between a mother and a child in the case of surrogate motherhood? Japanese law lacks provisions regarding the establishment of a parent–child relationship in cases where a surrogate mother gives birth to a child. The ART-Law covers assisted reproductive medical treatment, which involves medical treatment through artificial insemination, in vitro fertilisation or in vitro fertilisation embryo transfer, but surrogate motherhood is not included. Japanese law does not expressly permit or prohibit surrogate conception, remaining silent on the issue. Nevertheless, the Japan Society of Obstetrics and Gynecology does not allow for surrogate conception, and in 2003 it released a bulletin indicating that it does not condone surrogate conception. It noted as reasons for this the primacy of the interests of the unborn child, the possible threat to the physical and emotional health of the surrogate mother, the danger of adding complexity to familial relationships, and society's general stance towards surrogacy as unethical.[5] Despite this, there are still physicians in Japan who practise assisted reproductive technology for surrogate conception, even if it is not a widely accepted medical practice. In August 2022, certain newspapers reported that a project team of the ruling Liberal Democratic Party

[3] Judgment of the Japanese Supreme Court, 27 April 1962, *Minshu* Vol 16 No 7,1247.

[4] Y Maeda, 'Ninchi [Acknowledgement]' in S Ninomiya (ed), *Shin Chushaku Minpou* [*New Commentary on the Civil Code of Japan*] vol 17 (Yuhikaku, 2017) 603.

[5] The Society also asserts that, particularly with respect to the justification based on the welfare of the child, the act of delivering the child to the client after birth by the surrogate mother who has conceived and given birth based on the request may run afoul of art 35 of the 1989 Convention on the Rights of the Child.

(自由民主党 [*Jiyu Minshu To*]) had suggested that surrogacy should be permitted under specific conditions.[6] However, no specific legislation has been reported since then.

C. Surrogate Motherhood in Japanese Private International Law

Despite the absence of official recognition of surrogate motherhood in Japan, there exist individuals who yearn to bring a child into the world through surrogacy, often resorting to overseas surrogate mothers. However, in Japan, the registration of births is commonly accepted without strict scrutiny, except in cases where the listed mother is over 50 years old.[7] This lack of oversight renders it impossible to determine whether Japanese nationals have resorted to surrogacy abroad or if the listed mother is indeed the biological mother. Consequently, the prevalence of cross-border surrogacy in Japan remains unknown. Nonetheless, given the numerous accounts of international surrogate mothers of Japanese nationality since the late 2000s[8] and the proliferation of cross-border surrogacy agencies accessible via online search engines by typing in 'surrogacy' in Japanese, it is probable that a significant number of Japanese families have resorted to surrogacy abroad.

In reference to the legal system, in line with the lack of provisions regarding surrogate motherhood under Japanese substantive law, Japanese private international law also lacks provisions governing the parent–child relationship of a child delivered by a surrogate mother. The Act on General Rules for Application of Laws (hereinafter 'the Act'), which is a choice-of-law norm in Japan, only stipulates the rules for determining the governing law in each case of the formation of a legitimate parent–child relationship, the formation of an illegitimate parent–child relationship, and legitimation. Consequently, there is no explicit provision to which direct reference should be made regarding how the parent–child relationship in Japan should be considered, particularly when a child is born through surrogacy in a foreign country. In this regard, two major approaches have been presented in the academic literature, namely the governing law approach and the foreign judgment recognition approach. The governing law approach applies the governing law applicable to the establishment of the parent–child relationship, as in the case of an ordinary parent–child relationship, regardless of whether or not the court in the country of birth has made a judgment.[9] In accordance with this approach, when the establishment of the parent–child relationship of a child born through surrogacy is in question, the first step is to apply Article 28 of the Act,[10] which pertains to the establishment of a legitimate parent–child relationship.

[6] *The Asahi*, 31 August 2022. The envisioned parameters encompass constraints such as confining surrogate conception to women who are congenitally without a uterus, and surrogate conception is deemed to be an interim solution until the practical application of uterine transplants is established.

[7] Circular Notice ('Tsutatsu') No 2008 issued by the Director-General of the Civil Affairs Bureau, Ministry of Justice on 5 September 1961.

[8] The *Manji Yamada* case is one of the most famous cases that happened in India. See *Baby Manji Yamada v Union of India and Another* [2008] 13 SCC 518. This case is said to have been one of the triggers for the tightening of regulations on cross-border surrogacy in India. See J Reddy, 'Indian Surrogacy: Ending Cheap Labor' (2020)18 *Santa Clara Journal of International Law* 92.

[9] Y Sato, 'Case Note' in Y Sakurada and M Dogauchi (eds)., *Kokusai Shiho Hanrei Hyakusen, Shimpo Taio Hoseiban* [*Collection of Cases on Private International Law of Japan, Revised Version to Comply with the New Law*] (Tokyo, Yuhikaku, 2007) 123.

[10] Article 28 of the Act provides as follows: '(1) If a child is treated as a child born in wedlock under the national law of either the husband or wife at the time of the child's birth, the child is deemed to be a child born in wedlock.'

In cases where the establishment of such parent–child relationship is not recognised, the second step involves the application of provisions regarding the establishment of illegitimate parent–child relationships as stipulated in Article 29 of the Act[11] to determine whether or not a parent–child relationship has been established. This approach, which pertains to adoptions formed in foreign countries, has traditionally been adopted in Japanese jurisprudence.[12] The second approach determines whether or not the parent–child relationship has been established based on whether or not the foreign judgment is recognised in Japan in cases where a child is born through surrogacy using a foreign surrogate mother in a foreign country and the court of that country has issued a judgment recognising the parent–child relationship between the client parent and the child born.[13] The question is whether the effect of the foreign court's judgment can be recognised in Japan by applying Article 118 of the Code of Civil Procedure, which regulates the recognition of foreign judgments, or by analogy. The second approach is the more prevailing view.

Two cases related to surrogacy in foreign countries have been published by Japanese courts to date. One of these cases was adjudicated in accordance with the governing law approach, albeit without any decision by the Supreme Court being indicated, while the other was adjudicated by the Supreme Court under the foreign judgment recognition approach.

On 20 May 2005, the Osaka High Court rendered a decision in the first published Japanese case involving the use of a surrogate mother in California.[14] In this case, a Japanese couple sought to conceive a child through surrogacy in California, using an egg donated by an American woman and the sperm of the Japanese husband to create a fertilised egg in an in vitro fertilisation process, which was then implanted in another American woman. This process resulted in the birth of twins. Prior to the birth of the children, the Japanese couple obtained a judgment in the Superior Court of California, County of Los Angeles, which recognised them as the legal parents of the children and ordered that their names be listed as parents on the children's birth certificates. Immediately after the children's birth on 17 October 2002, the couple began fostering the children, named them and returned to Japan with them four months later in February 2003. In January 2004, the couple submitted a birth registration for the children, but due to the wife being over 50 years old, a detailed

[11] Article 29 of the Act provides as follows: '(1) In the case of a child born out of wedlock, the formation of a parent-child relationship with regard to the father and the child is governed by the father's national law at the time of the child's birth, and with regard to the mother and the child by the mother's national law at the time. In this case, when establishing a parent-child relationship by acknowledgment of parentage of a child, if obtaining the acceptance or consent from the child or a third party is required for acknowledgement under the child's national law at the time of the acknowledgement, the requirement is also be satisfied.

(2) Acknowledgement of parentage of a child is governed by the law designated in the first sentence of the preceding paragraph, or by the national law of the acknowledging person or of the child at the time of the acknowledgement. In this case, if the acknowledging person's national law is to govern, the second sentence of the preceding paragraph applies mutatis mutandis.'

[12] Sato (n 9) 123, Traditionally, the majority view, both in theory and in practice, has been that even if the adoption was concluded in a foreign court, the validity of the adoption is determined by the governing law as determined by the Act. See K Nishioka and Y Nishitani, *Japanese Private International Law* (Hart Publishing, 2021) 225.

[13] D Yokomizo, 'Recognition of a Foreign Judgment on Children Born through Surrogate Pregnancy' (2017) 60 *Japanese Yearbook of International Law* 399, 402; H Sano, 'Chakushutsu de aru Ko no Oyako Kankei no Seiritsu [Establishment of Legitimate Parent-Child Relationship]' in Y Sakurada and M Dogauchi (eds), *Chushaku Kokusai Shiho* [*Private International Law Annotated*], vol 2 (Yuhikaku, 2011) 83.

[14] Judgment of Osaka High Court, 20 May 2005, *Hanrei-Jiho* vol 1919,107.

investigation was conducted. As a result, the registration was not accepted on the grounds that she had not given birth to the children. The couple subsequently filed a petition requesting that the birth registration be accepted.

Although the content of the unpublished first instance court's decision remains uncertain, the Osaka High Court employed a governing law approach in handling the case. The Court stipulated that, when determining the existence of a parent–child relationship between the children in question and the Japanese couple, the legitimacy of said relationship should first be assessed under the governing law outlined in Article 17 of the previous Act (Article 28 of the amended Act). If this is not recognised, the existence of an illegitimate parent–child relationship should then be examined under the governing law stipulated in Article 18 of the Act (Article 29 of the amended Act). The Court concluded that the California court's ruling was only relevant insofar as it pertained to the contents of Californian law serving as the governing law. Consequently, the Court determined that the children in question could not be legally regarded as the legitimate offspring of any party. To arrive at its decision, the Court initially assessed whether a legitimate parent–child relationship existed between the Japanese couple and their children under the governing law stipulated in Article 17 of the previous Act (Article 28 of the amended Act) and ultimately rejected its validity. Subsequently, the Court evaluated the legitimacy of the parent–child relationship between the American woman who delivered the children and her spouse, as well as the children themselves, in accordance with the governing law outlined in Article 17 of the previous Act (Article 28 of the amended Act) under Californian law and denied it based on the decision of the California court.

Regarding the examination of the illegitimate parent–child relationship, even if Californian law governs the case pursuant to Article 18 of the previous Act (Article 29 of the amended Act), recognising the parent–child relationship between the Japanese wife and the children in Japan would contravene Japanese public policy. Therefore, such recognition could not be applied and, instead, Japanese law should be implemented, with the American woman who delivered the children being regarded as their mother. The Court initially determined that, with respect to the non-legitimate parent–child relationship between the Japanese wife and her children, the birth mother is recognised as the mother under Japanese law, which is the applicable law under Article 18 of the previous Act (Article 29 of the amended Act), meaning that the Japanese wife who did not give birth is not considered the mother. Subsequently, with respect to the non-legitimate parent–child relationship between the American woman who gave birth to the children and the children, the Court determined that under the law of California, which is the applicable law under Article 18 of the previous Act (Article 29 of the amended Act), the Japanese wife is considered the mother. However, it found that this conclusion was against Japanese public policy. As a result, the birth registration that identifies the children in question as the offspring of the Japanese couple was deemed unacceptable.

The second case pertains to a famous couple who opted for surrogacy in Nevada in the US. The Supreme Court passed a verdict on 23 March 2007.[15] In this instance, a Japanese

[15] Decision by the Supreme Court, 23 March 2007, *Minshu* Vol 61, No 2, 619. An English translation of this decision can be found at www.courts.go.jp/app/hanrei_en/detail?id=883 and in (2008) 51 *Japanese Yearbook of International Law* 552. See also Yokomizo (n 13) 399–409.

couple travelled to the US to pursue surrogacy using their own sperm and eggs. There, they signed a surrogacy agreement with an American couple residing in Nevada, according to which the legal parents of the child would be the Japanese couple. The surrogate mother was impregnated using the sperm and egg of the Japanese couple and delivered the children in November 2003. In December of the same year, the Domestic Relations Division of the Second Judicial District Court of Nevada, District of Washoe County, Nevada, responded to a petition by the Japanese couple, confirming that they were the legal parents of their children. In January 2004, the Japanese couple submitted a birth registration of children born in Nevada to the Japanese authorities, declaring them as their legitimate children, but it was not accepted due to the known fact that they had used a surrogate mother. Consequently, the Japanese couple filed a petition seeking an order to accept the registration. The court of first instance followed the governing law approach, as in the 2005 Osaka High Court decision, and declined to establish a parent–child relationship between the Japanese couple and the children in question.[16]

Conversely, the Tokyo High Court, as the court of the second instance, adopted the approach of recognising foreign judgments. It ordered the acceptance of the birth registration of the children, presuming that the Nevada court judgment is effective under Article 118 of the Code of Civil Procedure or by analogical application and that the children are the legitimate children of the Japanese couple.[17]

Ultimately, however, the Supreme Court reversed the decision of the Tokyo High Court. The Supreme Court's decision can be summarised as follows.

A judicial decision rendered by a foreign court acknowledging the establishment of a natural parent-child relationship between persons who are not eligible for such relationship under the Japanese Civil Code is contrary to public policy as prescribed in Article 118, item 3 of the Code of Civil Procedure and cannot be recognised in Japan. Therefore, it is not effective in Japan.

When children are conceived and delivered through assisted reproductive medical treatment using another woman's eggs, even if a genetic relationship exists between the children born and the woman who donated the eggs, the mother of the children is the woman who conceived and delivered them, and no maternal-child relationship is established with the woman who did not conceive and deliver them.

The following statement is apparent from the decision of the Supreme Court – namely, unlike the Osaka High Court decision discussed previously, the Supreme Court has embraced the foreign judgment recognition approach. Consequently, in practical terms, the foreign judgment recognition approach is employed in cases where the court in the country where the surrogate mother has given birth to the client's child has recognised the parent–child relationship between the client and the child born through surrogacy. Nevertheless, the Supreme Court's position on the criteria for determining public policy as a requirement for foreign judgment recognition remains somewhat unclear. When the public policy requirement regarding foreign judgment recognition is substantially at issue, the common academic perspective is that a two-pronged test should be utilised, meaning that the incompatibility of the effect of foreign judgment recognition with the Japanese legal

[16] Decision by Tokyo Family Court, 30 November 2005, *Minshu* Vol 61, No 2, 658.
[17] Decision by Tokyo High Court, 29 September 2006, *Minshu* Vol 61, No 2, 671.

system and the strength of the connection between the case in question and Japan should be examined.[18] If either of these factors is deemed to be significant or both of them are to a considerable extent, then the foreign judgment in question should not be viewed as a violation of public policy. Under this two-pronged test, the mere fact that the content of a foreign judgment is different from Japanese law does not make its recognition a violation of public policy. The 2007 Supreme Court decision can be interpreted as stating that foreign judgments that acknowledge a parent–child relationship differing from Japanese law violate public policy and has drawn much criticism in this regard.[19] Nevertheless, even if one were to accept the two-pronged test, it is unlikely that the 2007 Supreme Court decision would alter the conclusion that the recognition of a foreign judgment is not permissible due to a violation of public policy since the case is also closely linked to Japan, and numerous comments corroborate this notion.[20]

D. Impacts on East Asian Countries

The foregoing presents an outline of theories and practices on the subject of surrogate mothers under Japanese law, particularly under Japanese private international law. This condition is not exclusive to Japan, but is almost identical in other East Asian jurisdictions. As a matter of fact, surrogate motherhood is not positively illegal or legal in East Asian countries, and most countries have de facto prohibited the use of surrogate mothers either in practice or through judicial precedents. Moreover, there are no clear codified laws governing the legal treatment of parent–child relationships in cases where surrogate mothers are utilised outside the country, even though such cases have been increasingly reported.[21] In view of this situation, the precedents of Japanese courts and academic discussions may carry some significance in other East Asian jurisdictions.

III. Same-Sex Marriage in Japanese Law

A. Legal Marriage in Japan

Under the Japanese Civil Code, only civil marriages, established by submitting a marriage registration form to the municipal government, are legally recognised and have legal effect. Religious marriages or ceremonial marriages, on the other hand, have no legal effect and are not protected under the law. In spite of the introduction of registered partnership systems or civil unions in some countries, it has not been explicitly established in Japan and hence not officially implemented. Conversely, extra-marital cohabitation, though unacknowledged under codified law, is acknowledged in the judicial precedents and prevailing opinions in

[18] See Nishioka and Nishitani (n 12) 212.

[19] For example, see Yokomizo (n 13) 405.

[20] ibid 409; M Iwamoto, 'Case Note' in M Dogauchi and Y Nakanishi (eds), *Kokusai Shiho Hanrei Hyakusen, 3rd* [*Collection of Cases on Private International Law of Japan, 3rd edn*] (Yuhikaku, 2021) 117.

[21] One of Japan's most prominent daily newspapers, the *Mainichi*, reported that there are growing number of Chinese who come to Japan and hire surrogate mothers there (mainichi.jp/english/articles/20160319/p2a/00m/0na/011000c).

scholarly literature as a relationship that can obtain legal protection, such as the obligation of fidelity and the duty of cohabitation, mutual cooperation and assistance, provided that specific conditions are met. As per the prevailing opinions and judicial precedents, the prerequisites for obtaining legal protection for an extra-marital cohabitation consist of a shared intention to form an extra-marital cohabitation and the presence of joint habitation (not necessarily in the same abode).[22]

B. Same-Sex Marriage in Japanese Substantive Law

The Japanese legal system comprises a multitude of statutes that govern the concept of marriage. One such provision is outlined in Article 24 of the Constitution of Japan, which stipulates the following:

> (1) Marriage shall be based only on the mutual consent of both sexes and it shall be maintained through mutual cooperation with the equal rights of husband and wife as a basis.
> (2) With regard to choice of spouse, property rights, inheritance, choice of domicile, divorce and other matters pertaining to marriage and the family, laws shall be enacted from the standpoint of individual dignity and the essential equality of the sexes.

Furthermore, prior to the 2022 amendment, Article 731 of the Civil Code established that legal marriage was only permissible for a man who had reached the age of 18 and a woman who had reached the age of 16.[23] While there is no codified law that explicitly prohibits same-sex marriages, these provisions suggest that legal marriage under Japanese law is exclusively reserved for opposite-sex couples – that is, individuals of opposite biological sexes.[24]

The question of whether the lack of legal recognition for same-sex marriage violates Article 14, paragraph 1 of the Japanese Constitution, which guarantees equality before the law, has been repeatedly brought before the courts. Notably, three lower court cases in recent years have addressed this issue. In the first case, the Sapporo District Court held on 17 March 2021[25] that although the institution of marriage provides heterosexuals with legal benefits, it denies homosexuals the legal means to enjoy even a portion of these benefits. The Court found that even assuming that the legislature has broad legislative discretion, discriminatory treatment in this case exceeds that discretionary power and must be interpreted as discriminatory treatment without a rational basis. The Court thus concluded that to the extent described above, the provision violates Article 14, paragraph 1 of the Constitution.

The second case, the Osaka District Court's judgment of 20 June 2022,[26] rejected the plaintiffs' claim that current laws and regulations violate the Constitution because the provisions of the current law that make same-sex marriage impossible are within the

[22] T Matsukawa, *Mimpo, Shinzoku-Sozoku* [*Civil Code, Family Relationship and Succession*], 7th edn (Yuhikaku, 2022) 61; T Takahashi et al, *Mimpo 7, Shinzoku-Sozoku* [*Civil Code 7, Family Relationship and Succession*], 6th edn (Yuhikaku, 2020) 119.

[23] Article 731 of the Civil Code, as amended in 2022, states that a person must be 18 years old to be able to marry. It can be said that the current law has become difficult to be used as a basis for interpreting the recognition of marriage only between persons of the opposite sex.

[24] Matsukawa (n 22) 70.

[25] *Hanrei-Jiho*, No 2487, 3.

[26] Heisei 31(wa)1258, website on the *Saibansho* [Courts in Japan], www.courts.go.jp/app/hanrei_jp/detail4?id=91334.

reasonable legislative discretion of the Japanese Diet allowed by Article 14, paragraph 1 of the Constitution.

Lastly, the Tokyo District Court's judgment on 30 November 2022[27] ruled that the lack of a legal system for homosexuals to become partners and family members under current law is a severe threat and obstacle to their personal survival, which is a violation of Article 24, paragraph 2 of the Constitution. The Court concluded that there were reasonable grounds in light of personal dignity to recognise the absence of a legal system for homosexuals to become partners and family members as unconstitutional. However, it did not conclude that the current provisions violated the Constitution because there are various policies that do legally protect same-sex couples (such as the establishment of registered partnerships or the creation of a marriage-like institution for same-sex couples), but the choice of which protections should exist is left to the discretion of the legislature.[28]

All three judgments recognise the impossibility of same-sex marriage under the current laws and regulations. However, while the Osaka District Court ruled that it was not unconstitutional because there are other ways for same-sex couples to be protected besides legal marriage, the Sapporo District Court ruled that it was unconstitutional because it was not reasonably discriminatory. The Tokyo District Court, on the other hand, ruled that it was unconstitutional because there were no reasonable grounds in light of individual dignity. As such, Japanese precedents are divided on whether the treatment of same-sex marriage in the various provisions of the current law is unconstitutional or not.

In light of the circumstances, a notable case was adjudicated by Japanese courts, which addressed the issue of whether same-sex marriage constitutes a legally protected relationship under Japanese law. The case facts are as follows: in 2010, X and Y1 (both Japanese women) began living together in Japan and obtained a marriage registration certificate in New York in 2014, where same-sex marriage is legally recognised. Y1 became pregnant through micro-insemination after receiving sperm donation from Y2 (a Japanese male at the time), whom she met through social media, based on an agreement with X. X also purchased a residence with the intention of raising their children there. Unfortunately, Y1's initial pregnancy ended in a miscarriage. Nevertheless, Y1 continued to hold the desire to raise a child with X. Y1 considered sperm donation from Y2 using the syringe method and stayed at Y2's residence for a few days at the end of 2016. Upon returning home, Y1 informed X of her desire to have a relationship with both X and Y2, revealing that Y1 and Y2 had engaged in sexual intercourse. After promising X to cut off contact with Y2, Y1 continued to live with X. However, Y1 later confessed to X that she still had feelings for Y2 and left home, resulting in her separation from X in November 2017. In 2017, X filed a petition for mediation with the Family Court to dissolve their extra marital relationship, which was resolved in a trial in lieu of mediation. X and Y1 agreed to dissolve their marriage in the US, cooperate as needed and take necessary steps to end their marriage.[29] X subsequently filed a lawsuit against Y1 and Y2, claiming that the extra-marital cohabitation between

[27] Heisei31(wa)3465, *Hanrei-Jiho*, No 2547, 45.

[28] These decisions constitute a segment of a sequence of litigations instituted nationwide under the heading 'Marriage for All JAPAN' (www.marriageforall.jp/en). As of March 2023, there are several pending lawsuits yet to be determined, and since appeals have been lodged in relation to all three District Court verdicts discussed above, it is foreseen that the publication of legal precedents will persist for a considerable time.

[29] After this, Y1 and Y2 married in August 2018, but divorced the following month, and Y1 underwent gender re-assignment surgery and subsequently became a woman on the family register as well.

X and Y1 had broken down due to sexual relations between Y1 and Y2, and seeking payment of expenses and monetary compensation for the dissolution of the marriage based on joint tortious acts.

In its ruling of 18 September 2019, the Utsunomiya District Court, Maoka Branch,[30] held as follows:

- The Japanese Constitutional Law does not prohibit same-sex marriage.
- If the same-sex marriage in question can be considered a legally protected relationship similar to extra-marital cohabitation, it has interests that are worthy of legal protection.
- However, since marriage is currently restricted to a man and a woman, it is reasonable to interpret that extra-marital cohabitation (de facto marriage), which is similar to marriage, is also limited to a relationship between a man and a woman, at least for the time being. Therefore, same-sex marriages themselves cannot be considered extra-marital cohabitations.
- X and Y1 began cohabitation in 2010 and lived together for a significant period of time. They obtained a marriage registration certificate in New York State, where same-sex marriage is legal, and held a wedding ceremony in Japan, informing those close to them of their relationship. They also received a sperm donation from a third party in order to conceive a child to be raised by them. In light of these facts, they intended to make each other their future partner.
- Therefore, although they were not in an extra-marital cohabitation relationship, they had a living relationship that could be regarded as equivalent to an extra-marital cohabitation relationship.
- Considering that the relationship in question is a same-sex marriage that is currently not legally recognised, the level of legal protection granted to the plaintiff based on this relationship should be lower than that granted to heterosexual marriages or heterosexual extra-marital cohabitation relationships.

Both the plaintiff and the defendants appealed the District Court's decision. In its ruling as the second instance, the Tokyo High Court[31] concluded that:

- X and Y1 were trying to establish a relationship that was as similar to a married couple as possible, even though they could not register a legal marriage because they were of the same sex.
- As of 2016, it could be said that X and Y1 had a relationship that was similar to a union between a man and a woman who cooperate and live together as a couple.
- It is permissible for same-sex couples to have the same duty of chastity as married couples through agreement.

As previously stated, in Japan, although not sanctioned by written law, an extra-marital cohabitation is deemed to be a legally protected relationship if the couple intends to become husband and wife in the socially accepted sense and cohabit as such. Nevertheless, the debate over whether extra-marital relationships that may be subject to legal protection

[30] *Hanrei Jiho*, No 2473, 51.
[31] Judgment of Tokyo High Court, 4 March 2020, *Hanrei Jiho*, No 2473, 47.

should be limited to those without impediments to marriage has been ongoing.[32] In view of this discourse, there may be scope for debating whether same-sex extra-marital cohabitations can be legally protected.[33] However, unlike legal impediments to marriage, such as consanguineous marriage, which are clearly prohibited by codified law, the fact that both parties to a marriage are of the same sex is not regarded as an explicit impediment – the latter is merely a form of marriage that was not contemplated when the system was devised. Therefore, recognising the establishment of extra-marital cohabitation for same-sex couples, which has been acknowledged at least under judicial doctrine, as in the Tokyo High Court's decision, does not appear to present any issues.

C. Same-Sex Marriage and Civil Union in Japanese Private International Law

Just as substantive law lacks codified statutes that provide legal protection to same-sex couples in their union, Japan's conflict of laws also lacks codified laws that pertain to same-sex couples. However, while statistics are not entirely clear on this point, it is quite possible to imagine that the number of cases in which Japanese nationals or foreign residents in Japan are contracting same-sex marriages or civil unions in countries where they are legal is increasing. In fact, the Tokyo High Court case discussed above involved two Japanese women living in Japan who were legally married in New York. Unfortunately, in these decisions, the existence of a lawful marriage in New York was not evaluated in terms of private international law, but was merely considered as a fact, one of the factors used to determine the existence of the intention to marry, which is a requirement for an extra-marital cohabitation under Japanese law. On the other hand, there have been discussions in academic circles on how to treat same-sex marriages or civil unions under the conflict of laws.

Under Japanese private international law, the formation and validity of marriage are stipulated in Article 24 and 25 of the Act as follows:

> Article 24 Formation and Formalities of Marriage
>
> (1) The formation of a marriage is governed by the national law of each party.
> (2) The formalities for a marriage are governed by the law of the place where the marriage is celebrated (*lex loci celebrationis*).
> (3) Notwithstanding the preceding paragraph, the formalities that comply with the national law of either party to a marriage are valid; provided, however, that this does not apply where a marriage is celebrated in Japan and either party to the marriage is a Japanese national.
>
> Article 25 Effect of Marriage
>
> The effect of a marriage is governed by the national law of the husband and wife if their national law is the same, or where that is not the case, by the law of the habitual residence of the husband and wife if their law of the habitual residence is the same, or where neither of these is the case, by the law of the place most closely connected with the husband and wife.

[32] In particular, there are disputes over the establishment of extra-marital cohabitations in violation of the prohibition of consanguineous marriages and the prohibition of bigamy. See Takahashi et al (n 22) 119.

[33] See, eg, H Moriyama, 'Case Note' (2021) 1567 *Jurisuto* [*Jurist*] 63; S Ninomiya, 'Dosei-Kappuru no Kyodo Seikatsu [Co-living of Same-Sex Couples]' (2020) 804 *Koseki Jiho* [*Family Registration Bulletin*] 7–10.

There is debate surrounding whether these provisions apply to same-sex marriages or civil unions. With respect to same-sex marriage, the prevailing view is that the concept of 'marriage' in private international law is broader than that in Japanese substantive law and should be regarded as unique to private international law. Therefore, it is argued that same-sex marriage is included in the scope of these articles or, at the very least, these articles could be applied analogously.[34] Conversely, some argue that 'marriage' as provided for in the Act does not cover same-sex marriages.[35] This view holds that the rule regarding the governing law of 'marriage' in the Act cannot be extended to same-sex marriages and, instead, the subsidiary rule for determining the governing law of family relations in Article 33 of the Act[36] must be applied.

Regarding this matter, there exists an unpublished judgment that was issued by the Yokohama Family Court on 10 February 2022 that is worth mentioning.[37] The case concerns two women, one German and the other Japanese, who had been residing together in Japan for a number of years. During that period, they established and registered a cohabitation partnership in Germany in accordance with German law, which they subsequently legally transformed into a marriage in Germany, after the establishment of a legal framework in this country that allowed for the transformation of a cohabitation partnership into a marriage. Some years later, the two women ceased living together, and the German woman filed a petition with the Japanese woman in the Yokohama Family Court for the division of property during the time of their extra-marital cohabitation, after which she returned to Germany.

In making its decision, the Yokohama Family Court initially determined that the establishment of an extra-marital cohabitation should be governed by Article 24 of the Act, which is the same as the formation of a marriage. The Court then evaluated whether the aforementioned extra-marital cohabitation relationship was legitimately established by applying the national law of each party in accordance with this provision. The Court discovered that while the prerequisite for the establishment of an extra-marital cohabitation is that there must be no marriage, according to German law (the national law of the petitioner), same-sex marriage has been established and, as a result, the prerequisite for the establishment of an extra-marital cohabitation is not met. Additionally, under Japanese law, which is the national law of the respondent, it is a fundamental requirement for marriage that the parties be of opposite genders, and an extra-marital cohabitation lacking such a fundamental requirement cannot be considered legitimately established under Japanese law.

Although the soundness of the conclusion reached by the Yokohama Family Court and its interpretation of the prerequisites for the establishment of extra-marital cohabitation under Japanese law is open to discussion, it is noteworthy in terms of private international law that the Court did not evaluate the validity of a marriage that was legally established in

[34] T Hayashi, 'Doseikon/Toroku Patonashippu o Meguru Kokusai Shiho Mondai [Issues of Private International Law on Same-Sex Marriage/Registered Partnership]' in S Ninomiya and S Watanabe (eds), *Gendai Kazoku-ho Koza vol.5, Kokusaika to Kazoku* [*Contemporary Family Law Lecture Series, Volume 5: Internationalisation and the Family*] (Nihon-Hyoron Sha, 2021) 115, 135; D Yokomizo, 'Konin no Seiritsu oyobi Hoshiki [Formation and Forms of Marriage]' in Sakurada and Dogauchi (n 13) 10.

[35] J Yokoyama, *Private International Law in Japan*, 2nd edn (Kluwer, 2019) 277–81.

[36] Article 33 of the Act provides as follows: 'Family relationships or rights and obligations arising therefrom other than those provided for in Article 24 through Article 32 are governed by the national law of the party concerned.'

[37] Adjudication by Yokohama Family Court, 10 February 2022 (Reiwa 2(wa) No 2098).

Germany, but instead dealt with the matter of extra-marital cohabitation as the parties had requested. Additionally, it seems important to observe that the Court, in examining the law applicable to an extra-marital cohabitation, arrived at its decision in accordance with Article 24 of the Act on the formation of marriage, without any consideration of whether the extra-marital cohabitation was between individuals of the opposite sex or the same sex. The determination of the applicable law for extra-marital cohabitation relationships of this kind appears to be closely aligned with the academic theory that includes same-sex marriage within the scope of Article 24, or that this provision should be applied by analogy to same-sex marriage.[38]

Regarding same-sex civil unions, some argue that they should be treated in the same manner as same-sex marriages. Those who make this argument assert that the provisions of Article 24 and subsequent provisions of the Act should be applied or analogously applied to same-sex marriages, and that this interpretation is also appropriate for civil unions.[39] Those who argue that Article 33 of the Act should be applied to same-sex marriages also contend that the same treatment should be applied to civil unions.[40]

Conversely, others argue that the determination of the governing law for civil unions cannot be made in the same manner as for marriage or same-sex marriage. They advocate for a separate rule to determine the governing law for civil unions, using the place of registration as the connecting factor.[41] The following points have been raised from this perspective: if the provisions of Articles 24 et seq of the Act, which regulate marriage, or Article 33, which regulates family relationships, were to govern the determination of the governing law for civil unions, there would be many cases where the national law of the parties or the law of the common habitual residence of the parties would apply. If civil unions are not legalised in those countries, there is a possibility that the outcome may lack foreseeability as to how to treat civil unions in the eyes of the parties.

Of these arguments, the prevailing view in recent years has been that the place of registration should be the connecting factor. This appears to be reasonable.

D. Impacts on East Asian Countries

Considering the aforementioned discourse pertaining to same-sex marriage in substantive law and private international law in Japan, is there anything that can be delineated which could have a reverberating effect on other East Asian nations? In point of fact, Taiwan has been at the vanguard of this issue within East Asia. In 2019, Taiwan legitimised same-sex marriage[42] and promptly afterwards, same-sex marriages between a Taiwanese citizen and a foreigner have been deemed valid in Taiwan provided that the national law of the foreigner

[38] It seems that there is almost no disagreement regarding the application of art 24 to the extra-marital cohabitation, especially those between opposite-sex partners, at present. See Yokomizo (n 34) 9.

[39] ibid 10.

[40] Yokoyama (n 35) 304.

[41] Nishioka and Nishitani (n 12) 163 also insist that as for civil union, the law of the place of registration will be applied unilaterally, not bilaterally. See Hayashi (n 34) 140–41.

[42] S Friedman and C Chen, 'Same-Sex Marriage Legalization and the Stigmas of LGBT Co-parenting in Taiwan' (2022) *Law & Social Inquiry* 1, doi:10.1017/lsi.2022.32.

permits same-sex marriage. Nevertheless, following a series of court verdicts recognising the validity of same-sex marriages in Taiwan for numerous cross-border same-sex couples, such as a Japanese-Taiwanese couple, the Taiwanese authorities modified their previous interpretation in January 2023 to recognise all same-sex marriages, irrespective of the content of national law.[43] Such a treatment of same-sex marriage in Taiwan could serve as a milestone in East Asia.

In the aforementioned Sapporo District Court, Osaka District Court and Tokyo District Court rulings, the courts provided a comprehensive list of jurisdictions where same-sex marriage is recognised, and it was quite extensive. However, Japan remains the only G7 nation where same-sex marriage is not legally recognised. In contrast, in other East Asian countries, including China, there have been recent reports of significant enforcement of anti-homosexual policies, despite the fact that same-sex marriage is not prohibited.[44] Like China, there is still substantial resistance to legalising same-sex marriage in many East Asian regions, and Japan finds itself caught between the values of these jurisdictions and the more progressive values of other areas, particularly those considered to be developed countries. Against this backdrop, Japanese Prime Minister Fumio Kishida stated in the Diet on 1 February 2023 that the legalisation of same-sex marriage is an issue that requires extremely careful consideration and that he would not pursue any recent legislation, arguing that it would challenge fundamental views of family, values and society.[45] Based on Prime Minister Kishida's statement and the actions of the Ministry of Justice's Legislative Council, it seems unlikely that same-sex marriage or civil unions will be legalised in Japan any time soon. Nevertheless, despite the central government's stance, an increasing number of local governments are issuing partnership certificates to same-sex couples upon request. Although these certificates have no legal effect, they are believed to have certain practical benefits, such as enabling same-sex partners to receive life insurance benefits and serving as proof of spousal status in public hospitals. According to the Gender Equality Bureau Cabinet Office's data released in February 2022, 147 local governments, including prefectures and cities, have introduced partnership certificates, and as of 31 December 2021, certificates had been issued to 2,537 couples.[46] These data suggest that a certain proportion of same-sex couples in Japan are in long-term relationships that require official recognition and that society has recognised the existence of such relationships. Considering these social changes and needs, even if a substantive legal response is not feasible at present, it would be preferable to apply value-neutral choice-of-law rules to same-sex marriages that have been performed in foreign countries and to recognise them as valid in Japan if they are valid under the applicable law rather than treating them a priori as a breach of public policy.

[43] However, for couples involving a Mainland Chinese and a Taiwanese, same-sex marriages will continue to be invalid (taiwaninsight.org/2023/01/18/the-procrastinating-progress-of-transnational-same-sex-marriage-rights-in-taiwan).

[44] www.nytimes.com/2020/10/28/business/international/china-gay-homosexuality-textbooks-lawsuit.html.

[45] www.bloomberg.com/news/articles/2023-02-02/japan-s-kishida-rebuffs-calls-for-marriage-equality-ahead-of-g-7?leadSource=uverify%20wall.

[46] Gender Equality Bureau Cabinet Office, *Jinsei 100nen Jidai no Kekkon to Kazoku ni Kansuru Kenkyukai* [*Study Group on Marriage and Family in the Age of 100 Years of Life*], Eighth Meeting Materials, available at www.gender.go.jp/kaigi/kento/Marriage-Family/8th/pdf/2.pdf.

IV. Conclusion

The foregoing provides an exposition of judicial precedents and theories pertaining to issues that pose ongoing difficulties within Japan's family law system. While a number of subcommittees under the Legislative Council are currently engaged in discussions concerning family law, the Subcommittee on Assisted Reproductive Technology has not yet progressed in its deliberations regarding the legalisation of surrogacy, and same-sex marriage has not even been the subject of a subcommittee meeting. Nevertheless, given the current era of increased international mobility and the growing prevalence of international families, it appears imperative to establish certain legal frameworks, particularly as they relate to the international dimensions of family law. In this context, the precedents set forth by Japan appear to highlight a complex and perplexing situation; nonetheless, I remain optimistic that these cases may offer instructive lessons.

14

The Applicable Law in Succession Matters in China, Japan and South Korea

The Professio Iuris *as a Bridge?*

OLIVIER GAILLARD

I. Introduction

In inheritance matters, civil law systems have historically struggled to select the connecting factor that reflects the closest connection between a person's succession and a state or, to express it in classical Savignyan terms, to find the 'seat' ('Sitz') of an estate according to its 'inherent nature' ('eigenthümliche Natur'). Nationality, on the one hand, and a territorial factor (domicile or habitual residence), on the other hand, have alternately – like the oscillations of a pendulum – been favoured to designate the law that best embodies the principle of proximity or the cultural identity of the deceased.

Discrepancies between jurisdictions may also arise from the adoption of a unitary or scissionist approach to succession, or from the admission of party autonomy, which is controversial in this legal area.

The absence of international harmony as regards the designation of the law applicable to the succession (*lex successionis* or *lex hereditatis*) gives rise to great uncertainty, which is detrimental to the *de cuius* as well as to the presumptive heirs.

After the failure of the Hague Convention of 1 August 1989 on the Law Applicable to Succession to the Estates of Deceased Persons (hereinafter the '1989 Hague Convention'), which never came into force for lack of sufficient ratifications, European Regulation No 650/2012 on Succession (hereinafter the 'European Succession Regulation') has managed to bring together under the same aegis conflict-of-law systems that were deemed irreconcilable. In East Asia, however, there is no such convention and the Asian Principles of Private International Law have not yet found concrete legislative expression.

The jurisdictions of this region thus provide a fascinating illustration of the difficulties of identifying the proper connecting factor in succession matters. We will analyse the conflict-of-law rules of three jurisdictions, namely China, Japan and South Korea, in order to highlight the underlying objectives of these provisions. We will see that China and Japan adopt diametrically opposed solutions, whereas South Korea has succeeded in distancing itself from foreign influences to develop an innovative mechanism, in the form of a choice of law of *de cuius* (*professio iuris*), which could serve as a bridge between the different approaches and as a source of inspiration for future legal developments in the neighbouring jurisdictions.

II. Conflict-of-Law Rules in Succession Matters

A. China

i. Habitual Residence as the Main Connecting Factor

The determination of the applicable succession law in international cases has undergone numerous changes over the course of China's private international law reforms, with rules scattered across several laws whose coordination has not always been free from controversy. This legal situation was further complicated by the fact that these laws had to be supplemented by opinions (意见 *yijian*) and judicial interpretations (司法解释 *sifa jieshi*) of the Supreme People's Court of the People's Republic of China (SPC),[1] which are regarded as sources of law and play a crucial role in practice.[2]

Without delving into the details of the Chinese legal system,[3] we will briefly present the various key stages in the development of the conflict-of-law rules for succession. The following highlights the underlying objectives that prompted the changes made to the current legal system.

One of the milestones for the determination of the *lex hereditatis* was the Succession Act of 10 April 1985 (hereinafter the '1985 Succession Act').[4] This Act mainly covered Chinese substantive inheritance law, which is now governed by Articles 1119 ff of the Chinese Civil Code of 28 May 2020 (民法典 *minfadian*).[5] The question of the applicable law to an estate with foreign elements was relegated to the penultimate article of this Act, in the 'supplementary provisions' (附则 *fuze*; Article 36). The exact scope of this provision was highly controversial. Specifically, it was not clear whether it applied solely to legal succession (法定继承 *fading jicheng*) or whether it also applied – directly or by analogy – to testamentary succession (遗嘱继承 *yizhu jicheng*).[6] Although rather rudimentary and worded in an unnecessarily convoluted manner, this provision already contained some of the guiding principles that would be retained by Chinese private international law, such as the use of a territorial criterion as the main connecting factor (at that point the domicile [住所 *zhusuo*] of the deceased)[7] and the application of different laws depending on the nature (movable or

[1] 中华人民共和国最高人民法院 *zhonghua renmin gongheguo zuigao renmin fayuan.*

[2] These rules must be distinguished from the court's interpretation in a specific case; see B Ahl, 'Die Justizauslegung durch das Oberste Volksgericht der VR China' (2007) *Zeitschrift für Chinesisches Recht*, 251.

[3] For more details, see H von Senger, ch 2 in this volume.

[4] 继承法 *jichengfa.*

[5] This new version of the Chinese Civil Code came into force on 1 January 2021.

[6] Z Huo, *Private International Law in China* (Law Press, 2010) 238; Z Liu, *Das chinesische Internationale Erbrecht gestern-heute-morgen* (Peter Lang, 2005) 225.

[7] In an Opinion of the SPC of 11 September 1985 on the implementation of the Succession Act, it was specified that art 36 referred to the law of the last domicile of the *de cuius* (*lex ultimi domicilii*).

immovable) of the assets concerned, real property being governed by the law of the situation (*lex rei sitae*), in accordance with the principle of the scission of the succession.[8]

Promulgated a year later on 12 April 1986, the General Principles of Civil Law (民法通则 *minfa tongze*), supplemented by an Opinion of the SPC,[9] contain several conflict-of-law rules, including in matters of succession. The rule determining the applicable *lex hereditatis* was in every respect similar to that provided for in the 1985 Succession Act, with the exception of its scope, which was expressly limited to intestate succession (Article 149).[10] The coordination between these two acts was controversial, some authors giving priority to the General Principles of Civil Law based on the Latin adage *lex posterior derogat priori*.[11]

In view of the complexity of this system, a single specific law covering legal situations with foreign elements was urgently needed. Thus, after a codification process lasting several decades,[12] the Law of the People's Republic of China on the Application of Laws to Civil Relationships Involving a Foreign Element (hereinafter the 'PIL Act')[13] was promulgated on 28 October 2010 and came into force on 1 April 2011.

In addition to bringing the conflict-of-law rules together in one piece of legislation – avoiding any unnecessary and confusing overlap – the PIL Act clarified certain ambiguities of the previous provisions and filled in several lacunae.[14] As we shall see, these improvements are particularly noticeable when it comes to the determination of the law applicable to a cross-border succession. However, despite these undeniable improvements, the five provisions dealing with successions (Articles 31–35 of the PIL Act) remain relatively rudimentary and are not free from ambiguity. To clarify certain points, on 28 December 2012 the SPC published a first set of Interpretations of the PIL Act (hereinafter the 'PIL Act Interpretations'), mainly focusing on the general rules of the Act and not on its special provisions.[15]

While the new rule for the determination of the *lex hereditatis* retains the fundamental principles of the previous acts, it modifies the main criterion. The factor of the domicile now gives way to that of the habitual residence (经常居所 *jingchang jusuo*) of the *de cuius* at the time of death to designate the law applicable to movable property. On the other hand, the law applicable to the succession of immovable property (不动产 *budongchan*) continues to be governed by the law of the place where this property is located (Article 31 of the PIL Act).[16] This change is due to the fact that the notion of 'domicile' is closely linked, under

[8] SK Stork genannt Wersborg, *Welches Recht gilt? Die Bestimmung des anzuwendenden Rechts im chinesischen, im deutschen und im europäischen internationalen Erbrecht* (Zerb Verlag, 2018) 14 ff.

[9] This Opinion of 26 January 1988 specified, for example, the fate of an estate with no known heir (*bona vacantia*; art 191).

[10] Liu (n 6) 210.

[11] Stork genannt Wersborg (n 8) 16. *Contra* W Chen, *Chinese Civil Procedure and Conflict of Laws* (Homa & Sekey Books, 2013) 127.

[12] The initial impetus to create such a law dates back to the 1990s. For more details, see J Huang, 'Creation and Perfection of China's Law Applicable to Foreign-Related Civil Relations' (2012–13) *Yearbook of Private International Law*, 269, 281 ff.

[13] 中华人民共和国涉外民事关系法律适用法 *zhonghua renmin gongheguo shewai minshi guanxi falü shiyonfa*.

[14] R Süß, 'VR China: Gesetz zum Internationalen Privatrecht' (2012) *Zeitschrift für Erbrecht und Vermögensnachfolge* 199. The PIL Act specifies expressly that it takes precedence over art 36 of the 1985 Succession Act in the event of discrepancies (art 51 of the PIL Act).

[15] These first Interpretations came into force on 7 January 2013; T Xue, 'Neue Regeln des Obersten Volksgerichts: Die erste justizielle Interpretation des chinesischen IPR-Gesetzes' (2014) *Praxis des Internationalen Privat- und Verfahrensrechts* 206; P Leibküchler, 'Erste Interpretationen des Obersten Volksgericht zum neuen Gesetz über das Internationale Privatrecht der VR China' (2013) *Zeitschrift für Chinesisches Recht* 89, 107 ff.

[16] For our analysis of the principle of the scission, see section II.A.ii below.

Chinese substantive law, to a system of household registration (户口 *hukou* or 户籍 *huji*),[17] which was deemed unsuitable in an international context, given that foreigners are precisely not subject to this registration system. As a result, the habitual residence naturally emerged as the main connecting factor in the PIL Act.[18] On the other hand, the nationality plays only a subsidiary role. One of the underlying reasons is to prevent Chinese nationals resident abroad from having Chinese law applied to them, with which they are, by assumption, unfamiliar.[19]

The adoption of the connecting factor of the habitual residence has been seen as a major step forward in Chinese law and is in line with the trend set by the Hague Conventions and European law, including the Succession Regulation (Article 21).

Despite its importance, the concept of 'habitual residence' is not defined in the Act itself. Instead, the PIL Act Interpretation indicates that it is the place where a person has lived continuously for more than a year and that serves as their centre of life (生活中心 *shenghuo zhongxin*; *Lebensmittelpunkt*) (Article 15 of the PIL Act Interpretation).[20]

Determining the actual centre of life of the *de cuius* includes examining his or her family, social and professional relationships.[21] In addition, the majority of his or her assets are frequently located in the state where he or she resides.[22] These elements are crucial in terms of the concretisation of the principle of proximity.[23] Furthermore, the application of the law of the state where the *de cuius* has his or her habitual residence allows the competent authorities to apply, in most cases, their own law (*Gleichlauf*) to the settlement of the successions of all the inhabitants of the same country, thus promoting integration and equality.[24]

It should also be pointed out that Chinese private international law does not recognise the institution of *renvoi*. This means that the applicable law that it designates refers exclusively to the substantive provisions of the *lex causae* (*Sachnormverweisung*; Article 9 of the PIL Act). The conflict-of-law rules are excluded, so they cannot interfere with the principles set out above.[25]

Notwithstanding its undeniable benefits, the connecting factor of the habitual residence has several shortcomings, mainly due to its lack of stability during the lifetime of the deceased.[26] First, it does not systematically embody the principle of proximity, in particular

[17] See art 15 of the General Principles of Civil Law and art 9(1) of the supplementing Opinion.

[18] Q He, 'Changes to Habitual Residence in China's *Lex Personalis*' (2012–13) *Yearbook of Private International Law* 323, 326 ff; W Long, 'The First Choice-of-Law of China's Mainland: An Overview' (2012) *Praxis des Internationales Privat- und Verfahren* 273, 277.

[19] Stork genannt Wersborg (n 8) 41 ff.

[20] There are exceptions, the scope of which is controversial, in particular for hospital stays and dispatched labour; E Wan [万鄂湘] (ed), *Zhonghua Renmin Gongheguo Shewai Minshi Guanxi Falü Shiyong Fa Tiaowen Lijie yu Shiyong* (China Legal Publishing House, 2011) 243.

[21] GA Capaul, 'Zum Anknüpfungszeitpunkt im internationalen Erbrecht' in P Grolimund et al (eds), *Festschrift für Anton K Schnyder zum 65 Geburtstag* (Schulthess, 2018) 49, 61.

[22] M Pfeiffer, 'Legal Certainty and Predictability in International Succession law' (2016) 12 *Journal of Private International Law* 566, 571 ff.

[23] O Gaillard, 'The *Professio Iuris* in Swiss Private International Law' (2021–22) *Yearbook of Private International Law*, 393, 413; He (n 18) 323.

[24] J Huang [黄进] and R Jiang [姜茹娇] (eds), *Zhonghua Renmin Gongheguo Shewai Minshi Guanxi Falü Shiyong Fa Shiyi yu Fenxi* (Wangjing, 2012) 2.

[25] ES Kim, 'Cross-border Succession in Japan, Korea and China and Related Legal Issues' (2015) *Chonnam Law Review* 27, 30; Stork genannt Wersborg (n 8) 52; Chen (n 11) 153. For the limited admission of *renvoi* in Japanese and Korean law, see sections II.B.ii and II.C.i below.

[26] Capaul (n 21) 51 ff.

when the *de cuius* changes his or her habitual residence shortly before his or her death or if he or she does so for professional reasons with the intention of returning to his or her country of origin.[27] It is also more susceptible to fraudulent manipulations by the *de cuius* to influence indirectly the applicable law to his or her own succession.[28] Furthermore, the systematic application by the authorities of their own law, which can be induced by this connecting factor, in addition to being detrimental in terms of international uniformity of the applicable law, may be seen as akin to an inward-looking attitude, sometimes ironically referred to as 'lex forism'.[29]

Finally, the connecting factor of the habitual residence is a protean notion, the definition of which is likely to vary from state to state.[30] The definition of the concept in Chinese law is unique in that it includes, as we have shown above, a minimum duration, determined *in abstracto*, of one year. This means that during this first year, the concrete determination of the *lex successionis* is in a state of limbo and may change after the minimum period has elapsed, without the *de cuius* realising it or even against his or her will. The legal uncertainty is accentuated by the fact that Article 15 of the PIL Act Interpretation is a discretionary provision (*Kann-Vorschrift*), so the judge may waive the one-year requirement in a specific case in the light of all the circumstances.[31]

Because of the legal uncertainty that the determination *in concreto* of habitual residence can cause, particularly when there is a discrepancy between the *de cuius*' centre of life and place of residence, or when he or she divides his or her life equally between several states,[32] some legal systems have rejected this connecting factor. This was the case in 2020 during the reform of Swiss private international law, which is still in progress at the time of writing.[33]

However, the pre-eminence of the connecting factor of the habitual residence is tempered in two provisions dealing with testamentary succession, which, as we have seen, was not covered by the previous acts.[34] Here, the conflict-of-law objective of proximity gives way to considerations of a substantive nature.

The first of these provisions concerns the form of wills (遗嘱方式 *yizhu fangshi*). According to Article 32 of the PIL Act, a will is formally valid if it complies with the law of the habitual residence of the testator when he or she made the disposition (*tempore designationis*) or at the time of his or her death (*tempore mortis*), with the law of his or her nationality,[35] or with the law of the place where the act of creating the will occurs.

[27] A Bonomi, 'Successions internationales: conflits de lois et de juridictions', (2010) *Collected Courses of The Hague Academy of International Law*, 71, 182 ff.

[28] ibid 194. However, art 11 of the PIL Act Interpretations sets aside any fraudulent creation of a connecting factor, but only if this was intended to circumvent Chinese mandatory rules; Stork genannt Wersborg (n 8) 55 ff.

[29] O Gaillard, *La professio juris en droit international privé suisse – Contexte, fondements et limites de l'élection de la loi successorale* (Schulthess, 2022) § 450 ('parochialism' or 'Heimwärtsstreben').

[30] ibid §§ 444 ff; Capaul (n 21) 51 ff; Bonomi (n 27) 182 ff.

[31] Stork genannt Wersborg (n 8) 43 ff and 71; Leibküchler (n 15) 97.

[32] KB Pißler, 'Das neue internationale Privatrecht der Volksrepublik China' (2012) *Rabels Zeitschrift für ausländisches und internationales Privatrecht* 1, 15; Stork genannt Wersborg (n 8) 70 ff; Huang and Jiang (n 24) 109. These authors suggest referring to the current residence (现在居所 *xianzai jusuo*; art 20 of the PIL Act) in cases where the habitual residence cannot be determined.

[33] See O Gaillard, 'La flexibilisation de la *professio juris* dans le projet de réforme du chapitre 6 de la LDIP' (2023) *iusNet – Droit civil*; Gaillard (n 29) §§ 156 ff and 175 ff.

[34] This is one of the lacunae that the PIL Act has filled; X Qi [齐湘泉], *'Shewai Minshi Guanxi Falü Shiyong Fa' Yuanli yu Jingyao* (Wangjing, 2012) 260.

[35] Although this is not expressly stated in the legal text, the majority view considers that nationality may be considered both at the time of the making of the will and at the time of death; W Zhu, 'The New Conflicts Rules for

Although China has been a Member State of the Hague Conference since 1987, it has not ratified the Convention of 5 October 1961 on the Conflicts of Laws Relating to the Form of Testamentary Dispositions (hereinafter the '1961 Hague Convention').[36] However, it should be noted that Article 32 of the PIL Act is very similar to its conventional counterpart, but with a reduced number of connecting factors.

The multiplication of alternative connecting factors is undoubtedly intended to favour as far as possible the formal validity of wills (*favor* [*validitatis*] *testamenti*). It is therefore sufficient that a will complies with the formal requirements of one of the legal orders designated alternatively to be considered formally valid.[37]

As for the effects of the will (遗嘱效力 *yizhu xiaoli*), also known as the material validity, Article 33 of the PIL Act states that it is governed by the law of the habitual residence or the law of the *de cuius*' state of origin at the time the will was made or at the time of death.[38] Following the same approach as the rule on formal validity, the multiplication of connecting factors is intended to favour the material validity of the will in order to avoid as far as possible that it is invalidated, for example, on account of a lack of testamentary capacity in one of the states concerned.[39]

While the PIL Act does not define the scope of material validity, the majority view considers that it covers testamentary capacity, defects in consent, interpretation and revocation of the will.[40] On the other hand, the existence, nature and extent of a statutory share should remain governed by the *lex hereditatis*.[41] It may be surprising that the PIL Act does not expressly specify which provision determines the law applicable to the statutory share, as it is such a crucial mechanism in cross-border estates.[42] This absence can be explained by the fact that Chinese substantive inheritance law does not recognise statutory shares *stricto sensu*, such as it exists in other civil law countries.[43] The Chinese Civil Code mainly provides for a system of flexible protection for legal heirs who have special financial needs,[44] a mechanism somewhat similar, mutatis mutandis, to the so-called 'family provisions' of some common law systems, such as English law.[45]

Family and Inheritance Matters in China' (2012–13) *Yearbook of Private International Law* 369, 383; Stork genannt Wersborg (n 8) 98 ff; Pißler (n 32) 28.

[36] As a Special Administrative Region of China, Hong Kong is a member of this Convention.

[37] Y Huang [黄亚英], *Zhongguo Guoji Sifaxue* (Xiamen University Press, 2017) 227; Wan (n 20) 241 ff.

[38] Here again, the majority view considers that both connecting factors can be assessed at the two points in time: Zhu (n 35) 383; Pißler (n 32) 28.

[39] L Jia, Q Wu and Z Zhang, 'Law of Property' in X Liu and Z Zhang (eds), *Chinese Private International Law* (Hart Publishing, 2021) 91, 106; Huang and Jiang (n 24) 195. However, the question of the coordination of the different connecting factors is controversial: Stork genannt Wersborg (n 8) 103 ff; Qi (n 34) 262.

[40] However, the exact scope of the material validity is controversial; S Li [李双元] and F Ou [欧福永] (eds), *Guoji Sifa*, 5th edn (Beijing University Press, 2018) 340.

[41] Stork genannt Wersborg (n 8) 129 ff.

[42] See eg art 23(2)(h) of the European Succession Regulation and art 95b(2) of the Swiss Draft of Private International Law of 13 March 2020 (still under review by the Swiss Parliament); Gaillard (n 23) 405 ff.

[43] Stork genannt Wersborg (n 8) 129 ff and 169 ff.

[44] Article 1141 of the Chinese Civil Code states that a will should provide for a share of the estate for legal heirs who are incapable of working or otherwise unable to earn an income.

[45] See, eg, the 'maintenance standard' of the Inheritance (Provision for Family and Dependants) Act 1975; Gaillard (n 29) §§ 1508 ff.

ii. Scission of the Succession

One of the most salient features of the Chinese inheritance conflict-of-law rules is the principle of the scission or splitting of the succession (*Nachlassspaltung*). This principle already existed in Chinese law under the 1985 Succession Act and the General Principles of Civil Law. Although the influence of the private international law of the Soviet Union is often mentioned,[46] the similarity with the conflict-of-law rules of common law jurisdictions – which traditionally adopt this principle, even in mixed jurisdictions such as Louisiana[47] – is undeniable.[48]

Real estate is thus subject to the law of its location (*lex rei sitae*; 不动产所在地法律 *budongchan suozaidi falü*; Article 31 of the PIL Act *in fine*). As a result, the settlement of the succession may be governed simultaneously by several laws, depending on the location of the *de cuius*' real property. The law of the situation also applies to movable property, subject to the fiction of it being located in the state of the deceased's habitual residence, according to the adage *mobilia sequuntur personam*.

The main advantage of applying the *lex rei sitae* to immovable property is to promote the circulation of decisions on such property by facilitating their recognition in the state where it is located (*Verkehrsinteressen*). By encouraging the coincidence of the law applicable to both inheritance and property, the whole process of transferring ownership of land is facilitated.[49] The application of Chinese substantive law to property located in China also makes it possible to take account of the system of collective ownership of land (集体所有制 *jiti suoyouzhi*), which is a distinctive feature of this legal system.[50]

On the other hand, the simultaneous application of several inheritance laws depending on the movable or immovable nature of each asset considerably complicates the settlement of a succession, especially as regards the coordination of several approaches to the concept of statutory share.[51] From a Chinese law perspective, this is less problematic, given its conception of a flexible and limited protection of heirs with specific financial needs.

The principle of scission finds its limits when assessing the formal and material validity of a will (Articles 32 and 33 of the PIL Act), since it would not be conceptually convincing for a will to be deemed valid in relation to certain assets, but not in relation to others.[52]

Finally, reference is also made to the location of the property in two legal provisions relating to the administration of the estate (遗产管理 *yichan guanli*; Article 34 of the PIL Act) and to estates without known heirs (Article 35 of the PIL Act). However, doctrinal opinions are divided as to the scope of the *lex rei sitae* and the application of scission in this context.[53]

[46] Stork genannt Wersborg (n 8) 72.

[47] Articles 3532 ff of the Louisiana Civil Code.

[48] However, these legal systems refer to the domicile for the applicable law to movable property. See *ex multis* §3-5.1(b) of the New York Estates, Powers and Trusts Law.

[49] Gaillard (n 29) §§ 565 ff.

[50] See art 10 of the Chinese Constitution; Stork genannt Wersborg (n 8) 72.

[51] Gaillard (n 29) § 559.

[52] Huang and Jiang (n 24) 186 ff; Wan (n 20) 248 ff.

[53] See Stork genannt Wersborg (n 8) 139 f and 149 ff.

B. Japan

i. The Importance of Nationality and Unity of Succession

The history of Japanese private international law dates back to the mid-nineteenth century, after the Meiji Restoration, when Japan was forced as from 1858 to conclude so-called unequal treaties (不平等条約 *fubyōdō jōyaku*) by various Western powers. One of the main features of these treaties was that they established consular jurisdictions for foreigners, on the grounds that the Japanese legal system of the time, which consisted of non-unified feudal customary law, was considered underdeveloped.[54] With a view to abolishing these treaties, the last of which remained in force until 1911, Japan set about modernising its legal system as a whole, consciously and selectively drawing on Western examples.[55] The codification of the first conflict-of-law rules was part of this endeavour, in order to demonstrate Japan's ability to manage cross-border relations.[56]

The first piece of legislation on private international law (法例 *Hōrei*) was promulgated on 21 June 1898, thereby enabling Japan to catch up with several Western states. This law was largely modelled on early drafts of the German Private International Law Act (Einführungsgesetz zum Bürgerlichen Gesetzbuche; hereinafter 'EGBGB'), enacted in 1896.[57] Virtually unchanged for almost a hundred years, the *Hōrei* has been significantly amended twice. The first time was in 1989; the second amendment, in 2006, led to the conflict-of-law rules that are now in force, under the new name of Act on General Rules for Application of Laws (法の適用に関する通則法 *hō no tekiyō ni kansuru tsūsoku hō*; hereinafter 'AGRAL').[58]

It should be noted that the Japanese conflict-of-law rules in matters of succession are reduced to their essentials. AGRAL only provides two provisions: one dealing with intestate succession and the other with the material validity and revocation of wills.

The *lex hereditatis* is determined by a bilateral rule in the purest Savignian classicism, referring to the national law of the deceased (本国法 *honkokuhō*; *lex patriae*; Article 36 AGRAL); this principle has been carried out since the *Hōrei* of 1898.[59] Similarly, the formation and effects of the will (遺言の成立及び効力 *yuigon no seiritsu oyobi kōryoku*), as well as its rescission (取消し *torikeshi*), are governed by the *de cuius*' national law, but at the time of the relevant action also called 'hypothetical succession law' (Article 37 AGRAL).[60]

[54] For an in-depth analysis of these treaties, see M Bälz and F Dröll, 'Japans "Ungleiche Verträge": Von der Diskriminierung durch das Völkerrecht zur Modernisierung des Rechts' (2022) *Journal of Japanese Law* 43; B Jaluzot, 'Les traités inégaux japonais, de leur signature à leur renégociation' (2021) *Journal of Japanese Law* 1.

[55] See B Jaluzot, ch 3 in this volume. See also O Gaillard, 'Le droit des successions japonais' (2014) *Successio* 328; Y Nishitani, 'Mancini and the Principle of Nationality in Japanese Private International Law' in H-P Mansel et al (eds), *Festschrift für Erik Jayme* (Sellier, 2004) 627, 630.

[56] K Nishioka and Y Nishitani, *Japanese Private International Law* (Hart Publishing, 2021) 3 ff.

[57] ibid 4; Nishitani (n 55) 630 ff. This Act was first drafted in 1890 based on Italian, French and Belgian law, but this version never came into force.

[58] For more details, see Y Nishitani, 'Die Reform des internationalen Privatrechts in Japan' (2007) *Praxis des Internationalen Privat- und Verfahrensrechts* 552.

[59] H Matsuoka [松岡 博], *Kokusai Kankei Shihō Nyūmon*, 4th edn (Yuhikaku, 2019) 242 ff and 247 ff; Kim (n 25) 29. As far as inheritance rules are concerned, the only change has been a modernisation of the language (現代語化 *gendaigoka*); T Hayashi, 'International Succession in Japan' (2009) *Japanese Yearbook of International Law* 433, 434.

[60] Nishioka and Nishitani (n 56) 197 ff.

The influence of Mancini's theories is here patent. Since the second half of the nineteenth century, the nationality factor has indeed played a key role in the theory of private international law in the area of personal status *largo sensu*, including inheritance law. In his lectures, Mancini believed that a person should remain subject to his or her *lex patriae* in these areas of law, even outside that person's country of origin.[61] His ideas flourished in continental Europe at the time,[62] with the notable exception of Switzerland. Nationality was then considered the 'natural' connecting factor for inheritance cases, insofar as it was thought to best embody the principle of proximity.[63] The close link between nationality and cultural identity that can be highlighted is particularly appropriate for a legal area as deeply rooted in a country's culture and traditions as inheritance law. Japanese authors confirm this objective of applying Japanese inheritance law to Japanese citizens residing abroad (在外邦人 *zaigai hōjin*).[64] Conversely, it has been argued that applying the same inheritance law to all inhabitants of the same country regardless of their nationality could be perceived as an improper attempt to 'assimilate' resident aliens.[65]

Nationality is also characterised by its stability throughout the life of the *de cuius* and the relative ease with which it can be ascertained, even years after the death. Finally, this connecting factor is less likely to be manipulated in order to indirectly influence the applicable law.[66]

However, a paradigm shift has gradually taken place in favour of the habitual residence in several Hague Conventions and, more recently, in the European Succession Regulation. In the light of this trend to the detriment of the nationality – sometimes described as a 'fossil'[67] – the continuous use of this connecting factor in Japanese law for almost 130 years may seem outdated, at least from a European point of view.[68]

Among the shortcomings of this connecting factor, it should be noted that the systematic and *in abstracto* presumption of a strong connection between nationality and cultural identity has been criticised as being a manifestation of legal reductionism, as state borders do not necessarily correspond to the boundaries of cultural groups present in the country. Moreover, this factor loses part of its effectiveness when the deceased possessed more than one nationality or, a fortiori, when he or she was a refugee or stateless.[69]

In this respect, Article 38 (1) AGRAL aims to regulate situations with multiple nationalities with cascading solutions. If the person in question is of Japanese nationality, Japanese law will automatically apply. This irrebuttable presumption is very practical, as it avoids

[61] For more details, see Nishitani (n 55) 628 ff.

[62] For example, Greek law attached great importance to designating the *lex successionis* by reference to the nationality of the *de cuius*, which was regarded as the 'umbilical cord' between emigrants and their homeland (*ομφάλιος λώρος των ξενητεμένων*); O Gaillard, 'Les relations entre la Grèce et la Suisse en matière successorale: la Convention d'établissement et de protection juridique du 1er décembre 1927' (2016) *Swiss Review of International and European Law* 53, 59.

[63] Gaillard (n 29) §§ 415, 454 and 683.

[64] K Koide [小出邦夫], *Chikujō Kaisetsu Hō no Tekiyō ni Kansuru Tsūsokuhō* (Shouji-houmu, 2015) 150; Hayashi (n 59) 447.

[65] Nishitani (n 55) 636 ff.

[66] Gaillard (n 23) 412; Nishioka and Nishitani (n 56) 14.

[67] For more details, see Gaillard (n 29) § 457.

[68] However, it is noteworthy that Japanese authors have criticised the exclusive reference to the nationality; for more details, see Nishitani (n 55) 635; Hayashi (n 59) 448.

[69] Gaillard (n 23) 412.

reference to the effective nationality, the determination of which generates legal uncertainty (particularly in matters of succession where the *de cuius* is, by definition, no longer available). However, this approach does not take into account conflict-of-law considerations, given that it is not based on the concretisation of the principle of proximity.[70] In other cases, the national law is that of the country of origin where the person has his or her habitual residence. If this condition is not met, the provision uses the closest connection test. In addition, Article 38(2) AGRAL reserves a subsidiary role for the law of the habitual residence in cases of statelessness of the person in question.

An additional problem arises in Japan with respect to the status of 'Special Permanent Resident' (特別永住者 *tokubetsu eijū-sha*) granted to nationals of former Japanese colonies – Korea and Taiwan – who lost their Japanese nationality following the entry into force on 28 April 1952 of the Treaty of San Francisco. For these specific cases, the factor of nationality alone does not give satisfactory results. For example, what should be considered the *lex patriae* of a person whose identity documents only state 'Chōsen' (朝鮮) – ie, the name of Korea before the division? The Japanese courts have resolved this issue by adopting various approaches, including using the closest connection test,[71] which leads to a lack of legal certainty.

The Japanese conflict-of-law rules abandon the exclusivity of nationality only when considerations of a substantive nature come into play, such as favouring the formal validity of a will. Unlike China and South Korea, Japan ratified the 1961 Hague Convention as early as 1964 and incorporated it into its legal system through a domestic law.[72] This law provides for no less than eight alternative connecting factors in order to increase the likelihood that the will can be found formally valid (*favor testamenti*). Contrary to Chinese law, the law of the domicile at the time when the disposition is made or at the time of the testator's death and the law of the situation of immovables, so far as such property is concerned, are also taken into consideration (Article 2).[73]

The scope of the *lex successionis* designated by the factor of nationality is very broad and encompasses the question of the statutory shares.[74] In line with the principle of the unity of succession, which is also deeply rooted in European law, the *lex patriae* applies to all assets, irrespective of their location or nature (movable or immovable).[75]

In this respect, the Japanese conflict-of-law rules are diametrically opposed to those of the Chinese legal system, which is likely to lead to international disharmony, with the application of different laws depending on the jurisdiction under consideration. A simple example of a Japanese citizen habitually resident in China and owning real property in Switzerland illustrates this. From the Japanese perspective, the Japanese citizen's entire estate is governed solely by his or her Japanese national law. On the other hand, the Chinese conflict-of-law rules consider that Chinese law applies to movable property, whereas Swiss law applies to the inheritance of the real estate located in that state.

[70] The priority of the national law corresponding to the law of the forum has been abandoned in several systems, such as Swiss law (art 23(2) of the PIL Act).

[71] For different approaches, see Tokyo District Court, 7 June 2011, *Hanrei Times* 1368, 233 (Korean citizen) and Tokyo District Court, 19 October 2016, 2016WLJPCA10198016 (Taiwanese citizen). For more details, see Kim (n 25) 39 ff.

[72] Act on the Law Governing Formalities of a Will of 10 June 1964 (遺言の方式の準拠法に関する法律).

[73] Nishioka and Nishitani (n 56) 199 ff.

[74] Hayashi (n 59) 444.

[75] Nishiola and Nishitani (n 56) 193 ff.

However, the predominance of the connecting factor of the nationality and the principle of the unity of succession in Japanese law is mitigated by the partial admission of the doctrine of *renvoi*, the consequences of which on the coordination with the Chinese conflict rules are complex.

ii. Partial Admission of Renvoi *and its Consequences*

As a general rule, Japanese conflict-of-law provisions refer directly to the substantive law of the *de cuius*' state of origin. One exception arises from the partial admission of the doctrine of *renvoi* (反致 *hanchi*).[76] If the conflict-of-law rules of the designated national law refer back to Japanese law, the substantive provisions of this legal order will apply as the *lex fori* (Article 41 AGRAL). In other cases, the conflict rules of the *lex causae* are inoperative. This is a case of remission (*Rückverweisung*; *renvoi au premier degré*) and not transmission (*Weiterverweisung*; *renvoi au second degré*).[77]

The objective of the partial admission of this mechanism is to foster international harmony with the state of origin of the person concerned. However, this harmony is only sought when Japanese law is designated. This remission to Japanese law also provides some relief for the Japanese courts, which will apply their own law. Finally, this provision also aims to carry through Japanese legal values with relations to the distribution of a succession.[78] On the other hand, the partial admission of *renvoi* may result in importing a scission of the succession into a system that rejected such an approach from the outset.[79] These mixed consequences can be illustrated by two examples relating to a Sino-Japanese succession.

If a Chinese citizen habitually resides in Japan where he or she owns real property, the admission of *renvoi* makes it possible to restore international harmony, since Japanese law applies to the whole estate, both from the Chinese point of view (the law of the habitual residence and the law of the location of real property) and from the Japanese perspective by means of the remission of the Chinese conflict rules to Japanese law.

On the other hand, if the same Chinese citizen residing in Japan owns real property in Switzerland, the partial admission of *renvoi* introduces a scission in the Japanese system.[80] This is because the Chinese conflict-of-law rules designate Japanese law for all movable assets and Swiss law as the *lex rei sitae* for real property. From the Japanese point of view, only the first *renvoi* is taken into account as a remission. Thus, the Japanese conflict-of-law rules will accept that movable assets are subject to Japanese law. In contrast, they will designate Chinese law as the *lex patriae* to be applied to real property in Switzerland. In this example, we can see that the 'imported scission', in addition to being completely foreign to the Japanese legal system, does not achieve international harmony, since the law applicable to the immovable property located in Switzerland differs between the two legal systems, which is highly detrimental in terms of legal certainty.

[76] The doctrine of *renvoi* does not apply to the formal validity of a will; art 43(2) AGRAL.
[77] Nishioka and Nishitani (n 56) 13.
[78] ibid 9; Kim (n 25) 37 ff.
[79] Kim (n 25) 34. For more details on this controversial issue, see Nishioka and Nishitani (n 56) 194; Hayashi (n 59) 445 and 451.
[80] For a similar Japanese court decision, see Judgment of the Supreme Court, 8 March 1994, *Shumin* 172, 1.

C. South Korea

i. From Imitation of Japanese Conflict-of-Law Rules to Innovations

After the development of an independent statute on private international law was interrupted during the Japanese occupation, the first Korean piece of legislation in this area of law was enacted in 1962 (hereinafter the '1962 PIL Act').[81] This statute was modelled after the Japanese *Hōrei* of 1898, itself heavily inspired, as we have seen, by early drafts of the German EGBGB of 1896. In these circumstances, this law was considered outdated from the moment of its promulgation.[82]

As a result, the first Korean conflict rules governing inheritance were a carbon copy of the Japanese provisions, which have remained virtually unchanged since the end of the nineteenth century, with the fundamental principles being the application of the nationality of the deceased and the unity of the succession (Articles 26 and 27 of the 1962 PIL Act).[83]

In 2001, Korea completely revised this law, moving away from Japanese influence and taking inspiration from the Hague Conference and several European jurisdictions.[84] This new law (국제사법/國際私法 *Gukjesabeop*, hereinafter the '2001 PIL Act') also included provisions on international jurisdiction, inspired by Switzerland's comprehensive PIL Act. It was at this stage that Korean inheritance rules, although still similar to their Japanese counterparts, were supplemented with innovations unparalleled in neighbouring legal systems.[85]

The main connecting factor used to determine the *lex hereditatis* remained the nationality of the deceased. The 2001 PIL Act specified – although there was no doubt about it – that nationality had to be assessed at the time of death (Article 49(1)). As regards the formal validity of a will or its revocation, the criterion was that of the nationality at the time when the will was made or revoked (Article 50(1) and (2)). Korea has not ratified the 1961 Hague Convention, but the relevant conflict rule provided for the same alternative connecting factors – with the exception of the criterion of the domicile – with a view to favouring the formal validity of a will (Article 50(3)).[86]

In addition to these relatively standard rules, the most remarkable innovation of the 2001 PIL Act is undoubtedly the admission of party autonomy (당사자자치/當事者自治 *dangsajajachi*) in cross-border succession matters (Article 49(2)).[87] This mechanism, which remains unique in East Asia to this day,[88] will be examined in the next section.

It should also be noted that the Korean PIL Act was revised in 2022 (hereinafter the '2022 PIL Act'), with the addition of more detailed rules on international jurisdiction,

[81] 섭외사법/涉外私法 *Seoboesabeop* of 15 January 1962.

[82] KH Suk, 'New Conflict of Laws Act of the Republic of Korea' (2001) *Journal of Korean Law* 197.

[83] K Aoki [青木 清], 'Kaisei Kankoku Kokusai Shihō' (2003) *Japanese Yearbook of Private International Law* 288, 305.

[84] Suk (n 82) 203.

[85] K-H Sohn, 'New Private International Law in Korea' (2001) *Japanese Yearbook of Private International Law* 267.

[86] Suk (n 82) 200. Article 27(3) of the 1962 PIL Act only took account of the *lex loci actus*; KB Pißler, 'Einführung in das neue Internationale Privatrecht der Republik Korea' (2006) *Rabels Zeitschrift für ausländisches und internationales Privatrecht* 279, 328 ff.

[87] Pißler (n 86) 289; Sohn (n 85) 267 and 289; Suk (n 82) 202.

[88] Although Japan considered including a form of *professio iuris* when revising the AGRAL in 2006, this solution was rejected from the final text; Hayashi (n 59) 446 ff.

including in matters of succession (Article 76). That being said, the provisions relating to the designation of the *lex successionis* have remained unchanged, apart from their numbering (Articles 77 and 78).[89] As a result, the above considerations relating to Japanese law, including regarding the partial admission of *renvoi* (Article 22),[90] can be applied, mutatis mutandis, to Korean law.

ii. Admission of the Professio Iuris

One of the most striking features of Korean law is that it allows the *de cuius* to set aside the objectively applicable *lex patriae* by choosing himself or herself, in his or her will, the law applicable to his or her succession. To this end, he or she may choose the law of his or her habitual residence at the time of the designation, provided that he or she maintains his or her habitual residence in that state until his or her death, or the law of the location of real property with respect to the inheritance of the said property (Article 77(2) of the 2022 PIL Act).[91]

Such a mechanism, commonly known as *professio iuris*,[92] has its origins in the intercantonal conflicts of laws that took place in Switzerland in the second half of the nineteenth century, at a time when each canton still had its own civil code. When the Swiss Parliament seemed to be at an impasse because no consensus was emerging on the appropriate connecting factor in matters of succession, the idea of enabling the *de cuius* himself or herself to choose the applicable law resurfaced as a *deus ex machina*, leading to the adoption of the first Swiss PIL Act in 1891.[93] The *professio iuris* gradually spread to several national legal systems, before being incorporated into the 1989 Hague Convention and then enshrined in the European Succession Regulation (Article 22(1)).

The *professio iuris* entrusts the person concerned with the task of determining for himself or herself, within the predefined framework of the law, the legal system that best corresponds to his or her conception of proximity and cultural identity. In so doing, this legal institution combines a more individualised application of the conflict-of-law rules with an improvement in legal certainty, since the testator himself or herself initiates the change in the connecting factor. It is thus a tool that accommodates both flexibility and legal certainty. In this sense, the *professio iuris* transcends, as a compromise, the age-old conundrum between nationality and domicile or habitual residence.[94]

Among other advantages, the *professio iuris* can help to achieve international harmony with all the states concerned by a cross-border estate. The resulting foreseeability of the applicable law is beneficial to both the *de cuius* and the presumptive heirs. The former can organise his or her estate planning with full knowledge of the mandatory rules with which

[89] For more details on the 2022 amendment, see JH Lee, ch 9 in this volume.

[90] Kim (n 25) 31 ff. However, the admission of remission is broader in Korean law: Sohn (n 85) 274; Suk (n 82) 200 ff.

[91] Y Kim, J Park and I Kim, *Gugje Saboeb*, 4th edn (Bobmunsa, 2022) 462 ff. Some authors are in favour of a wider range of eligible laws; see J Jang, 'Gugje Sangsogbeob-ui Ibbeoblon' (2021) *Korea Private International Law Journal* 337, 350 ff.

[92] For the origins of this Latin expression, see Gaillard (n 29) §§ 50 ff.

[93] For more details, see Gaillard (n 29) §§ 17 ff.

[94] Gaillard (n 23) 414.

he or she will have to comply. The latter can discuss the settlement of the succession without first having to consider in concrete terms the authorities that might be seised in the event of a dispute. Such 'dejudicialisation' undoubtedly creates a more suitable environment for peaceful family discussions. Furthermore, the issue of the 'race to the forum', which may unduly favour one heir who is the quickest or has the most financial means, is averted, since the different states concerned would apply the same law.[95]

Even if the Korean provision resembles, mutatis mutandis, a combination of the former German and Italian regulations,[96] the modalities of this *professio iuris* are distinctive. The eligible laws specifically enable effective coordination with the Chinese scissionist and territorialist system, thus avoiding the discrepancies we highlighted above in the case of a succession involving China and Japan.

Despite its merits, it should be borne in mind that the *professio iuris* is by no means free from drawbacks, which may be inherent in this legal institution or specific to the Korean version.

First, by granting a unilateral conflict-of-law prerogative to the *de cuius*, the *professio iuris* disturbs the balance struck, in each legal order involved, among the material interests relating to a succession, which are, by definition, opposed to each other. In this context, the protection of statutory shares and the implementation of limits to mitigate the undesirable substantive consequences of the *professio iuris* – notably with the intervention of the public policy clause[97] – have always been a bone of contention for the acceptance of this legal institution.[98] In this respect, we can note that the inclusion of special protection for heirs with a compulsory share, based on the model of the former Italian provision (Article 46(2) of the 1995 PIL Act), was discussed during the codification of the 2001 PIL Act, but was not incorporated into the final text.[99]

The *professio iuris* is also likely to add a complicating factor for the judge who has to interpret a will, especially in the case of an implicit choice of law. Korean law seeks to avoid such a situation by requiring the *professio juris* to be clear, if not explicit (명시적/明示的 *myeongsijeog*).[100]

It may also be noted that the requirement of Korean law relating to the continuity of the habitual residence in the same state from the time of the making of the will until death is not optimal in terms of foreseeability of the *lex successionis*, even if this requirement is intended to compensate for the instability of this connecting factor.[101] In this case, the applicable law is held in abeyance until the *de cuius*' death and the *professio juris* may lapse in the event of a change of habitual residence. The use of a connecting factor assessed solely at the time of the drafting of the will (*tempore designationis*) would be more effective in this respect, as is provided for in the European Succession Regulation (Article 21(1)) and the 2020 Swiss Draft of Private International Law (Article 91(1)).[102]

[95] Jang (n 91) 341 ff; Gaillard (n 23) 415 ff.
[96] Pißler (n 86) 2006, 327. For more details on these provisions, see Gaillard (n 29) §§ 234 ff.
[97] For a recent decision on that topic, see the German Supreme Court's Judgment of 29 June 2022 (IV ZR 110/21).
[98] For more details on this issue, which goes beyond the scope of this chapter, see Gaillard (n 29) §§ 1436 ff.
[99] Pißler (n 86) 327 ff.
[100] For a similar approach, see art 22(2) of the European Succession Regulation.
[101] Jang (n 91) 352 ff.
[102] See Gaillard (n 29) §§ 834 ff.

Finally, the onerous task of using the *professio iuris* wisely falls to the sole *de cuius*, who must be cautious not to disrupt a harmonious situation that would have been achieved with the objectively applicable law, as is the case in a succession involving South Korea and Japan.

III. Conclusion

The conflict-of-law rules in inheritance matters in China, Japan and South Korea have a few features in common. Even though they have not all ratified the 1961 Hague Convention, they seek to promote the formal validity of wills by providing for numerous alternative connecting factors. These jurisdictions also have a separate provision (*Sonderanknüpfung*) for the material validity of wills, even if its scope is not always free from controversy.

On the other hand, they have adopted diametrically different approaches to the determination of the law applicable to a cross-border succession.

In Japan, the predominance of the connecting factor of the nationality and the principle of the unity of the succession have remained unchanged for nearly 130 years. These elements are a direct result of the influence of Mancini's theories and former German law. Only the partial admission of *renvoi* departs from these fundamental principles, but only in favour of the application of Japanese law.

At the other end of the spectrum, the Chinese system is closely aligned with common law jurisdictions and their principle of the scission of the succession. The use of the connecting factor of the habitual residence also echoes recent developments in the Hague Conventions and in EU law.

Between these two extremes, the evolution of Korean law stands out as an exception. The first version of its Private International Law Act in 1962 was a true imitation of the Japanese law of the late nineteenth century and, indirectly, of old German law. However, a paradigm shift took place in the early 2000s, when the new PIL Act was enacted. Freed from the overwhelming influence of Japanese law, this new law was the cradle of many innovations without counterparts in East Asia. One of the most striking was the admission of the *professio iuris*, inspired in part by Swiss law and other European jurisdictions,[103] but with features specifically designed to ensure a smoother settlement of cross-border successions in the region.

In this sense, Korean law could rapidly become a source of inspiration for neighbouring jurisdictions, including those from which it had previously drawn inspiration, thus swapping its original position as a norm-taker for the role of exporter of innovative legal ideas and mechanisms.[104]

[103] C Shin, *Gugje Saboeb*, 5th edn (Sechang, 2022) 376.

[104] For other examples of South Korea's new role, see E-K Cho, 'Sur la contribution coréenne à l'unification du droit international privé: l'achèvement de la réforme de la LDIP coréenne' (2022) *Revue critique de droit international privé* 169; S Lee and HE Lee, 'Korea: From Norm Taker to Norm Maker in International Law' (2020) 26 *Asian Yearbook of International Law* 3.

15

Conclusions

OLIVIER GAILLARD

This volume includes a wide range of contributions, both in terms of the jurisdictions covered (China and Japan, but also South Korea, Taiwan and Hong Kong) and the areas of law addressed; while mainly focused on the rules of private international law, it also took up general principles of domestic and international law, commercial law, family law and inheritance law. This diversity made it possible to illustrate and explain, from several perspectives, a paradigm shift that is taking place in East Asian jurisdictions. Whereas these states were characterised by their propensity to adopt legal principles and concepts of Western systems, which were previously often regarded as the pinnacle of modernity, they have been progressively departing from their former models to propose innovative legal mechanisms, more closely suited to local or regional needs. We have seen that this trend has now reached a new stage, with several of the innovative approaches to private international law developed in these states now being adopted by other legal orders, thus shifting the locus of influence in this important area of law.

This phenomenon, which we have formalised by the imitation-innovation-exportation triptych, is far from being either a straightforward or a linear process. On the contrary, we could identify, throughout the chapters, significant disparities depending on the jurisdiction or the area of law under consideration. While some aspects of the conflict-of-law rules of these jurisdictions are remarkably innovative, other aspects still seem heavily permeated by past influences. In addition, in certain instances, historical or political considerations seem to act as a hindrance to fully benefiting from the spectacular development of private international law in these jurisdictions. The chapters of this book have provided conceptual tools to help decipher these different patterns and better understand their underlying rationale and their future implications, even if some questions remain as to their evolution and growing influence not only in the East Asian region but also more globally.

The first stage of *imitation* is certainly the best documented, since it flourished as early as the nineteenth century. However, the complexity of this process should not be underestimated, as it cannot be reduced to the mere transplantation of a legal concept of one state to another. Imitation could be a consequence of colonialism or a conscious and selective phenomenon with a view to modernising a legal system with the most advanced Western principles. Western influences may also have been indirect, as illustrated with the Taiwanese legal system, which imitated some Japanese ideas and concepts, themselves imitations of German provisions. Moreover, the 'imported' legal institution did not arrive on a 'blank page'. On the contrary, it had to be combined with and adapted to local customs, philosophical ideas, and religious or moral precepts, all of which are especially prevalent in East Asia. Adaptation to this indigenous substrate led to hybrid legal concepts, which were more or less distinct from their original counterparts. In this sense, imitation may undoubtedly be a first step towards innovation.

China offers a representative example of a system whose legal heritage is deeply rooted in numerous traditions. Confucianism – which is extremely prevalent in many other East Asian systems – or Taoism, among others, have shaped the entire Chinese legal system and continue to do so today. This historical heritage is interwoven with important political considerations that have a direct impact on substantive law. These factors result in a system with a complex and unique structure, into which all external elements must be able to fit.

The development of Japanese law is a good example of how complex the imitation stage can be. The influence of foreign legal systems can be divided into three distinct waves. Each of these periods has its own characteristics, which depend on the historical context and the state of development of Japanese law at the time. While the first selective importation of foreign legal concepts at the end of the nineteenth century sought to modernise – which at the time was a direct reference to European standards – the Japanese legal system with a view to setting aside the so-called 'unequal treaties' that Japan had been forced to conclude with Western powers, the following waves stemmed from American influence in the aftermath of the Second World War – the watchword at that time being 'democratisation', with the change of the Constitution – and after the financial crisis of the 1990s. Needless to say, the process of adopting and adapting foreign legal institutions varied considerably according to the circumstances, earning the Japanese system the reputation of being a 'legal potpourri'.[1]

The overwhelming influence of comparative law in Japan is also evident in its conflict-of-law rules. We have seen that the theories of Mancini and the influence of the old German Private International Law Act of 1896 have been significant, even up to the present day. This may be seen clearly in the provisions determining the applicable law to a cross-border succession, which have remained unchanged since 1898 – apart from a purely linguistic update – and appear to be relatively rudimentary compared with the modern standards. This is especially evidenced by the exclusive and uninterrupted use of the connecting factor of the nationality of the deceased, which contrasts starkly with the widespread trend to adopt the criterion of the habitual residence, as in many Hague Conventions, the European Succession Regulation and Chinese law.

This last example shows how legal transplants can, in some cases, act as a hindrance to the development of certain rules that seem to stagnate in a state that no longer corresponds to current reality.

Other provisions were qualified as outdated, vague or rudimentary. The Chinese rules on conflicts of jurisdiction were deemed too generic, as they do not provide specific provisions for family law disputes. It is worth noting that it is only recently that Japanese

[1] CR Stevens, 'Modern Japanese Law as an Instrument of Comparison' (1971) 19 *American Journal of Comparative Law* 665, 667. For similar expressions, see K Nishioka and Y Nishitani, *Japanese Private International Law* (Hart Publishing, 2021) 3 ('unique mixture of Western elements and East-Asian ethics and customs'); O Gaillard, 'Le droit des successions japonais' (2014) *Successio* 328; JO Haley, *The Spirit of Japanese Law* (University of Georgia Press, 2006) xvi ('self-selected reception of European law'); M Dean, *The Japanese Legal System: Text and Materials* (Cavendish Publishing, 1997) 2 ('laboratoire de droit comparé').

law has refined its provisions on conflicts of jurisdiction to take account of the specificities of this sensitive area of law.

Certain social developments are also ignored in the conflict-of-law rules. As highlighted in one chapter, this is the case in Japan with regard to surrogacy and same-sex marriage, even if it should be noted that a law relating to assisted reproduction technology was passed in 2020. The absence of specific rules – with the exception of Taiwan, where same-sex marriage was legitimised in 2019 – creates legal uncertainty as to how such situations should be dealt with. This is particularly detrimental in view of the interests involved, especially those of a child born of a surrogate mother.

As regards the recognition of foreign decisions in the absence of an international convention, the importance of the reciprocity requirement in China and Japan – a concept that had been imported from Germany – now seems outdated from a European perspective, where this requirement has largely been abandoned. It has been noted that this condition of reciprocity has had a negative impact on the circulation of judicial decisions precisely between the East Asian jurisdictions. To avoid this situation, Hong Kong and Mainland China have recently enacted ordinances to facilitate the reciprocal recognition and enforcement of their judgments in several areas of law.

It is widely acknowledged that there is a need for reform in these areas.

It should also be noted that the historical, political and diplomatic context in East Asia creates an additional layer of complexity that may hinder the development of private international law relationships and the circulation of judicial decisions within the region. For example, Japan's colonial past – particularly with regard to compensation for forced labour or 'comfort women' or the non-recognition of Taiwan – have given rise to delicate conflict-of-law issues that remain unresolved to this day and are frequently the subject of heated controversy between governments.

That being said, the chapters in this book have highlighted numerous examples where East Asian legal systems have managed to depart from their Western model to reshape and transform in order to suit their specific needs, legal mechanisms imported from Europe or the US, or to create new legal institutions *ex nihilo*. This is the second stage of our triptych – that of *innovation*, which already began a few decades ago, but which has recently seen exponential evolution, unfettered by foreign influences. As with the imitation stage, here too developments are not homogeneous, with some innovations being relatively minor while others are revolutionary.

As already mentioned, Japanese private international law refined its conflict-of-jurisdiction rules in 2011 for civil and commercial disputes, and in 2018 for status and family matters. These new laws aim to incorporate existing Japanese case law and in relation to several points depart from their counterparts in European law. For example, the provisions applicable to civil and commercial litigation include 'special jurisdiction' grounds that are more extensive and flexible than the fixed, restrictive grounds under the Brussels or Lugano systems. These rules also show a favourable attitude towards party autonomy with new provisions on choice-of-court agreements, which aim to strike a balance between the need for predictability in international transactions and the protection of weaker parties in consumer and labour contracts. Japan is also seeking to improve its alternative dispute resolution systems, with the adoption and amendments of a series of laws in 2023 with a view of attracting more cases, even if Singapore and Hong Kong remain the undisputed hubs in East Asia for arbitration and mediation.

The Chinese conflict-of-law rules in family matters feature several progressive elements, such as the adoption of 'result-selecting' provisions in favour of the protection of the weaker party in family relationships (*favor debilis*) or the admission of party autonomy in consensual divorces. This last point, which was also implemented, mutatis mutandis, in EU Regulation 1259/2010 almost concomitantly, differs starkly from the more conservative approach adopted in 2017 by the Swiss Private International Law Act, which provides for the exclusive application of Swiss law as *lex fori* to divorce cases, even consensual ones (Article 61). Chinese inheritance rules also include some original elements, such as specific provisions for the administration of the succession and the distribution of estates with no known heir (*bona vacantia*), even if a lack of clarity in these rules has been pointed out.

It is also worth mentioning the 2018 launch of the China International Commercial Court, which offers a 'one-stop' dispute resolution centre, including mediation, arbitration and litigation for international business disputes with a connection to China. This new court, established in the context of the Belt and Road Initiative, has attracted a lot of international attention.

All these innovative elements, and many more besides, are likely to inspire other jurisdictions – not only in Asia but also in other regions of the world – as they develop their own rules of private international law. This third stage therefore concerns the *exportation* of new ideas and new legal concepts.

In this context, the jurisdictions that have been discussed in this volume have seen their traditional role shift from that of 'imitators' to that of exporters of their own innovations. This change can already be perceived in comparative studies, where these legal orders, which had been regularly dismissed as 'followers' or a 'rerun' of a particular European system, can be considered legal orders in their own right.

The whole process we have described can be synthesised in a concrete example, namely the relationship between Japan and South Korea in the context of the designation of the law applicable to a cross-border estate. It has been shown that Japan has exerted considerable influence on the development of the Korean legal system, not only during the colonial era but also long afterwards. In substantive inheritance law, for example, the Korean Civil Code borrowed heavily from Japanese law when it introduced a compulsory share system. At the conflict-of-law level, Korean private international law had initially reproduced word for word a Japanese provision of 1898, which designated the national law of the deceased as the unique law applicable to his or her succession. However, gradually departing from its model, Korean law improved on the Japanese rule – this process is sometimes referred to as *Koreanisierung* of Japanese law – to create an innovative mechanism, allowing the deceased to choose the applicable law (*professio iuris*). This new legal institution, which is unprecedented in East Asia, has been specifically designed to ensure a smoother settlement of a succession that has contacts with several states in the region, especially with China. In this sense, Korean law has the potential to serve as a source of inspiration for other jurisdictions, including those from which it has previously drawn inspiration.[2] The roles would thus be

[2] This kind of 'reciprocal influence' is not unprecedented. The same phenomenon can be observed in the context of the current reform of the conflict-of-law rules governing inheritance in Switzerland. While the *professio iuris* was originally created in Switzerland at the end of the nineteenth century, this legal institution was subsequently introduced into the European Regulation on Successions (650/2012). The current reform now seeks to bring the Swiss rules closer to the European model that they themselves inspired. For more details, see O Gaillard, *La professio*

reversed – from being a norm-taker, Korea would become an exporter of innovative legal concepts.[3] The famous 'Korean wave' (*Hallyu* 한류/韓流) would then assume a whole new meaning!

We hope that the insightful and thought-provoking chapters in this volume have helped to capture the idiosyncratic evolution of private international law in East Asia and thus contribute to reducing the 'research gap' that still exists in this field, which is still difficult for the uninitiated to access. Future research could look at the influence that China, Japan or South Korea might have on so-called emerging Asian jurisdictions in developing their own conflict-of-law rules.

juris en droit international privé suisse – Contexte, fondements et limites de l'élection de la loi successorale (Schulthess, 2022) 47 ff.

[3] For more details on this approach to the role of Korean law, see E-K Cho, 'Sur la contribution coréenne à l'unification du droit international privé: l'achèvement de la réforme de la LDIP coréenne' (2022) *Revue critique de droit international privé* 169 ff; S Lee and HE Lee, 'Korea: From Norm Taker to Norm Maker in International Law' (2020) 26 *Asian Yearbook of International Law* 3.

INDEX

www.ingramcontent.com/pod-product-compliance
Ingram Content Group UK Ltd.
Pitfield, Milton Keynes, MK11 3LW, UK
UKHW050944290926
15470UKWH00005B/1628

9 781509 970100